HARPER FORUM BOOKS
MARTIN E. MARTY, *General Editor*

Phenomenology of Religion

Eight Modern Descriptions
of the Essence of Religion

HARPER FORUM BOOKS

Martin E. Marty, *General Editor*

Published:

Phenomenology of Religion

Eight Modern Descriptions of the Essence of Religion

edited by

Joseph Dabney Bettis

1817

HARPER & ROW, PUBLISHERS

NEW YORK AND EVANSTON

PHENOMENOLOGY OF RELIGION. Copyright © 1969 by Joseph Dabney
Bettis. Printed in the United States of America. All rights reserved. For
information address Harper & Row, Publishers, Incorporated, 49 East
33rd Street, New York, N. Y. 10016.

FIRST UNITED STATES EDITION

Published as a Harper Forum Book, 1969, by Harper & Row, Publishers,
Incorporated, New York and London.

LIBRARY OF CONGRESS CATALOG CARD NUMBER: 69-17005

CONTENTS

HARPER FORUM BOOKS

Often dismissed with a shrug or accepted with thoughtless piety in the past, religion today belongs in the forum of study and discussion. In our society, this is particularly evident in both public and private colleges and universities. Scholars are exploring the claims of theology, the religious roots of culture, and the relation between beliefs and the various areas or disciplines of life. Students have not until now had a series of books which could serve as reliable resources for class or private study in a time when inquiry into religion is undertaken with new freedom and a sense of urgency. *Harper Forum Books* are intended for these purposes. Eminent scholars have selected and introduced the readings. Respectful of the spirit of religion as they are, they do not shun controversy. With these books a new generation can confront religion through exposure to significant minds in theology and related humanistic fields.

MARTIN E. MARTY, GENERAL EDITOR
The Divinity School
The University of Chicago

INTRODUCTION

Joseph Dabney Bettis

"Phenomenology of religion" can mean at least three things. First, it can refer to the philosophical school or tradition which began with the German philosopher, Edmund Husserl (1859–1938), and includes, among others, Martin Heidegger, Jean-Paul Sartre, Maurice Merleau-Ponty, and Paul Ricoeur. The main themes of phenomenological philosophy are discussed below in Chapter 1. Understood in this way, phenomonology of religion would be that part of phenomenological philosophy devoted to the study of religion.

Second, "phenomenology of religion" can refer to a group of scholars who have applied broad phenomenological methods to the study of the history of religions. This group includes, among others, Mircea Eliade, Gerardus van der Leeuw, W. Brede Kristensen, and Joachim Wach. These men are primarily scholars in the field of religion rather than philosophers. They usually take data from primitive religions, and are usually concerned more with symbolic and ritualistic forms of religious expression than with theological and doctrinal expressions. In this sense "phenomenology of religion" would be that part of the study of religion which utilized phenomenological methods. Chapter 2 below illustrates this approach.

Third, "phenomenology of religion" can be understood in a much broader sense as the application of general phenomenological methods to the whole spectrum of religious ideas, activities, institutions, customs, and symbols. This entire volume illustrates this meaning of "phenomenology of religion" by bringing together diverse accounts from disparate orientations which have one thing in common: each has tried to describe the essence of religion. The latitude with which "phenomenology" is understood in this third way is indicated by the fact that some of the selections in this volume were published before Husserl was born.

"Phenomenology", Merleau-Ponty writes, "can be practiced and identified as a manner or style of thinking.... It existed as a movement before arriving at complete awareness of itself as a philosophy." There are disadvantages to using "phenomenology of religion" in such a general and non-technical way, but there are also advantages. By identifying the phenomenological element in a great variety of descriptions of religion, one calls attention to a common similarity among what might otherwise appear to be unrelated items. The following selections represent a variety of academic disciplines: philosophy, theology, sociology, psychology. By bringing them together through the identification of a common style of thought, the temptation to excuse their differences by assigning them to isolated spheres of enquiry is minimized. Fundamental problems are often avoided by an intellectual schizophrenia which accounts for conflicting observations by scholastic compartmentalization. But by identifying the phenomenological elements present in these diverse disciplines, the issues are joined. Each of the following selections attempts to describe the phenomenon of religion and each must, therefore, be evaluated in terms of its treatment of the data and not in terms of some abstract, *a priori* standards of academic disciplines. Phenomenological analysis involves a risk. It demands that its descriptions be evaluated not in the relative safety of already established methodological norms, but in light of the way the data present themselves to us. In Husserl's terms: "Back to the data!"

Phenomenology of religion is not philosophy of religion. Philosophy of religion emerged as an academic discipline during the early nineteenth century, growing from Hegel's idealistic philosophical system. Hegel attempted to organize all human activity into a system and to apply philosophical methods of study to each segment. He established the framework for the various philosophical areas: philosophy of art, philosophy of law, philosophy of religion, etc. The philosophy of religion concerns itself with the philosophical viability of religious doctrines and attempts to probe beneath the culturally conditioned forms of religious expression to their common presuppositions.

Phenomenology of religion differs from philosophy of religion in at least three important ways. First, it is not exclusively or even primarily concerned with religious ideas and doctrines. Rather it attempts to include all forms of religious expression – ritualistic, symbolic, mythic, and doctrinal – in its description. It is unwilling to reduce these forms of expression to their ideational content.

Second, the phenomenology of religion does not attempt to get beneath the cultural forms of expression to a common ground. When it seeks to describe the essence of religion the phenomenology of religion does not look for a common "natural" religion beneath the various culturally conditioned forms. It recognizes that culturally conditioned forms are the only forms of expression men have. What it seeks to do, however, is to raise to the level of conscious, reflective awareness what is actually taking place in religious activity.

Third, phenomenology of religion attempts to describe religious behavior rather than explain it.

The following selections represent some of the most important modern classical descriptions of religion. They were selected, however, not only on the basis of their historical importance but also because each represents a major option among the many ways of understanding religion. As the table of contents illustrates, the selections represent a typology of the major options, covering the spectrum of possibilities and showing something of their relationships.

The "ontological" descriptions (Chapters 3, 4, and 5) concentrate on the object toward which religious activity is directed: the god or gods, the holy or the mysterious, power, society, or however that object may be specified. Each of the three ontological descriptions locates the object in a different place and describes it in a different way. Van der Leeuw identifies the religious object as a part of the natural experienced environment. Maritain describes it as a part of the supernatural order rather than as a part of the natural. Feuerbach attempts to show that it is a projected object.

The "psychological" descriptions (Chapters 6, 7, and 8) attend not to the object of religious activity but to the activity itself. Here the interest is not in what religious men worship, but in religious behavior. Again, each describes this activity differently. Schleiermacher attempts to show that it is rooted in a unique mental faculty. Tillich describes it as any human activity in its deepest dimensions. Malinowski identifies it with a function of society.

The "dialectical" descriptions point to the unique relationship between subject and object in religious activity. Eliade emphasizes the significance of religious images and symbols in providing an archetypal framework for the way in which religious men experience their world. Buber singles out the unique encounter between subject and object in religious experience.

None of the following selections proves or disproves the claims of any particular religious tradition. That is not their intention. Religious traditions demand existential participation and not theoretical validation. But participation in religious symbols – either positively or negatively – does not require abandonment of the life of the mind. Phenomenology of religion is an effort to focus the perception of religious symbolic data to the degree of clarity demanded by the sharply focused questions of the inquiring modern intellect.

PART ONE: THE PHENOMENOLOGICAL METHOD AND THE STUDY OF RELIGION

I

AN INTRODUCTION TO PHENOMENOLOGY

Maurice Merleau-Ponty

Editor's Introduction

PHENOMENOLOGY IS A type of philosophy first explicitly formulated by the German philosopher, Edmund Husserl (1859–1938). Although many phenomenological elements can be found in earlier philosophy, Husserl was the first consciously to develop a phenomenological method. His successors have expanded phenomenology into an important element in continental European thought. Its impact has been less pronounced in England and America, although interest is growing in these countries.

Phenomenology is not a philosophical doctrine, but a philosophical method. The phenomenologist is identified neither by the particular objects with which he deals, as for example is the epistemologist who studies the way people learn and know, nor by a doctrine which he is concerned to elaborate, as for example is the humanist who attempts to organize all his data in terms of human value. Rather the phenomenologist is identified by the way in which he goes about his work of attempting to understand and describe his environment. The phenomenological method can be applied to a wide variety of studies, and it is now possible to find phenomenologies of science, ethics, language, society, and many other subjects.

The following essay by Maurice Merleau-Ponty provides a brief introduction to the phenomenological method by discussing five central concepts: description, reduction, essence, intentionality, and world.

1. *Description*

The phenomenological method is a way of describing rather than a way of explaining. The scientific method, as it has developed during the past two or three hundred years in Europe and America and which now dominates Western thought, is a way of explaining. It attempts to push behind the data of experience to the "laws of nature" which control the data. In more modern terms, it attempts to construct "models" that are increasingly more adequate organizational structures for the data.

Of course scientific explanation has its usefulness, but it often becomes so involved in explaining that it loses sight of the original data altogether. This results in scienticism or reductionism. Reductionism identifies the scientifically observable causes of an event with the meaning or significance of the event. In its extreme forms the scientific mentality becomes a criterion of what kind of data can be entertained rather than a method of approaching the data that present themselves. Reductionism assumes that the only important data are those that fit its pre-conceived criteria of significance – usually those of quantitative evaluation. It assumes that if one wants to find out, for example, what really happened in a complex event, he must reduce all the data to quantitative forms. Data which could not be quantified is dismissed as "subjective". For example, because the concept of cause and effect has become a scientific dogma, the scientific mentality refuses to admit the human and existential reality of free decision making, in spite of the immediately present awareness of constantly making decisions, e.g., shall I go home now or later; should I read this book or that; should I buy this car or that one. This scientific reductionism is a form of the generic fallacy in logic, which understands the truth of a proposition to be a function of its source, e.g., "that can't be true, since you read it in *Mad Magazine*". This is a fallacy because, just as the location of a proposition doesn't affect its truth, so the origin of an experience doesn't affect its meaning. I may decide to buy a Sting Ray rather than a Corvair because I have a deep psychic need for power, and on this basis a psychologist might have predicted which I would choose, but that doesn't in the least alter the existential reality of having to make that decision.

The scientific enterprise of explaining becomes especially dangerous when it leads to schizophrenic dishonesty. Dishonesty results when this reductionism produces a cleavage within a person between the meaning of an event for him and its scientific meaning. Then one says, for example when analyzing a religious phenomenon, "as a sociologist, I must say that we have here an example of social stratification, but as a religious person I must say that we have here evidence of the hand of God at work". He has removed himself from the data into a compartmentalized schizophrenia. What is needed is not a commentary on the data *from one perspective or another* which really only tells something about the perspective and nothing about the data, but a description of the data themselves. This becomes possible only when scientific reductionism is abandoned in favor of phenomenological description of what appears. Operating in this way, one does not speak "as a sociologist" or "as a religious person", but as a living individual observing an event in the world. The basis for honest humanity and honest communication resides in your telling me how you can see it and my telling you how I see it, and not in conforming the situation to pre-established criteria.

N. B.

Just as phenomenology rejects the empirical method of natural science because it leads to reductionism, it also rejects the deductive method of logic, or in Merleau-Ponty's phrase, "analytic reflection". The phenomenologist rejects the notion that philosophy consists in the logical development of basic ideas — propositions or truths. Phenomenology is not the development of a position, pushing out the implications as far as possible in every direction, as if one were to begin with a geometrical axiom and deduce theorems and corollaries. Rather, it is the description of elements within one's environment.

2. Reduction

In his task of describing the phenomenologist employs a method called "reduction". The operation of reduction is the "bracketing out" the question of existence in order to devote attention to the question of meaning. This operation has a variety of forms and becomes very complex at times, but the basic idea is quite simple. Phenomenological reduction is the method for overcoming the naturalistic prejudice of scientific reductionism. This phenomenological method is really the development of a way of thinking that everyone uses frequently. When we discuss a work of fiction, its significance does not depend on the historical factuality of its characters, but on the meaning they are able to convey. The question of "reality" or "truth" does not take into consideration at this point "existence", but "brackets out" that question in order to get at the question of meaning. The meaning of the great white whale in *Moby Dick*, for example, can and should be discussed quite apart from any consideration about whether Captain Ahab is an historically factual person. The character in the novel, the great white whale, and Captain Ahab all exist "for me" in that I can think about them. And they exist "for us" in that we can talk about them. Whether they exist "in themselves" or "out there" is bracketed out.

The phenomenologist also brackets out the question of truth as "actually being the case" to expose the question of truth as "meaning". If I should say, "I believe that the Bible is the Word of God", the phenomenologist might say in reply, "Let us bracket out for the moment the question of whether or not your statement is true and ask the question, "What do you mean by 'believe'? It is not self-evident what you mean. Describe what you mean." Or he might say, "I suppose we might concern ourselves with whether or not the Bible is really the word of God as you say, but before we do that, let us bracket out that question and ask what you mean by 'Word of God'. Only after you have described what you mean by that term will I be able to discuss with you the truth or falsity of the statement." ...

The phenomenologist grasps meaning through "intuition". This has led to the charge that phenomenology lacks precision and is based on hunches and opinions that are not open to discursive evaluation. But this is to misunderstand the meaning of phenomenological intuition. As a matter of fact, our most important kinds of knowledge are intuitive. For example, we have intuitive knowledge of the principles of logic: A is not non-A. No proposition can be both true and false in the same way at the same time. A is not both B and not-B. We also have intuitive knowledge of our own feelings. I know intuitively that I feel mad or happy or tired. And we have intuitive knowledge of other persons.

This intuitive knowledge is not deductive or inferential. No reasons can be given in support of it – only examples. On the other hand, it is not an experience or a perception. I do not perceive that A is not both B and not-B in the way that I would perceive that the typewriter before me is black. But while I cannot deductively prove nor empirically demonstrate intuitive knowledge, the result is not a relativism in which anyone's intuition is as good as another's. Phenomenology description is the beginning of discursive conversation and not a denial of its possibility.

3. *Essence*

Phenomenology is not a description of particular concrete things, but of essences. By essence, the phenomenologist means what one refers to when he uses a general term such as "chair" or "man" to refer not to a particular individual, but to a genus or type. Essence is what one is concerned with when he considers "mankind", or "humanness", or "chairness" rather than when he considers this particular chair or this particular man.

In medieval philosophy, the problem of essences was discussed as the problem of universals, and the major question was over the "reality" of these universal ideas. The medieval idealists claimed that we only experience particular things and that universal ideas are simply ideal abstractions built up from multiple particular experiences. Medieval realists, on the other hand, argued that we have an awareness of universals that goes beyond what could be abstracted from particular experiences. Therefore, the realist argued, the universals must possess some reality in themselves. This same argument has occupied a central position in modern philosophy, although the names for the positions have been reversed. A modern realist is an empiricist who holds that our general ideas are simply abstractions based on particular experiences. He argues that only things are real. A modern idealist holds that we have an immediate intuitive grasp of general ideas that carries more mental weight than could be provided by an accumulation of particular experiences. He argues that ideas are the basic reality.

Phenomenology seeks to move beyond these traditional problems by avoiding the question of the status of universals, or essences, altogether. While the status of essences, in terms of their reality or ideality, is open to debate, no one will deny that we do have universal ideas. We do think in terms of essences: e.g., "man", "mankind", "chair", "goodness", etc. The phenomenologist begins with the realization of this fact and asks for a description of the content of these essences. The goal of the phenomenologist is to describe the essence of a phenomenon, not to "locate" it. Essence is not to be found by referring to some pre-conceived notion of what is really real about an event, but is to be found through the method of reduction whereby the phenomenologist brackets out questions of origin or status so that the phenomenon may present itself. He is seeking the meaning or essence rather than cause or truth.

4. *Intentionality*

This is another term that has roots in medieval philosophy. Medieval philosophers identified "intentionality" as the unique dimension of psychical existence that distinguished it from physical existence. Psychical or mental existence was characterized by having intentionality: I intend something, or I intend to do something.

The phenomenologist expands on this meaning of intentionality. He uses the term to call attention to the fact that there is no such thing as mental activity apart from some object toward which it is directed. There is no such thing as thinking without thinking about something. There is no such thing as pure willing; it is willing to do something. There is no such thing as pure feeling; it is feeling about something. Thinking necessarily implies not only a thinker, but also something thought about. This primordial unity of subject and object, thinker and thought about, is characteristic of phenomenology.

Merleau-Ponty refers to a "broadened notion of intentionality". Here he means to refer to the fact that intentionality does not describe a reflective state of man, after he becomes aware of the world around him. Rather it refers to the fact that the only kind of existence we know is the existence of a man in the world. Existence is not isolated; to exist means to exist in a world – to be part of a world. This is the level of lived existence that is prior to and behind conscious awareness of existence. I am, in Wittgenstein's words, myself in motion. As a living, acting person, I am not conscious of myself but my consciousness is totally involved in the process of intending what I am engaged in. In reflection, I become aware of this primary state. Phenomenological description is the effort to open up this reflective state so that the primordial reality of lived existence discloses itself.

This insistence on the primacy of lived existence which is always in the world is the way in which the phenomenologist meets the charges of fabricating a world of his own imagination.

5. *World*

This is one of the most difficult and controversial phenomenological concepts, but at least two general observations are in order. First, the phenomenologist argues that the world is not something that exists prior to reflection. Prior to reflection there is lived existence, but this is an immediate and non-reflective spontaneity. "World" implies reflective organization – rationality – and that means that the notion of "world" emerges at the state of reflection. The "world", therefore, is something that we create and not the presupposition of our existence.

Second, the attitude of the phenomenologist is not one of

attempting to unlock the secrets of Nature, as did the philosophers and scientists of the seventeenth century and their heirs ever since. As Merleau-Ponty writes, the world is not problematical. The problem lies in our own inability to see what is there. The attitude of the phenomenologist, therefore, is not the attitude of the technician, with a bag of tools and methods, anxious to repair a poorly operating machine. Nor is it the attitude of the social planner, who has at his control the methods for straightening out the problems of social existence. Rather it is an attitude of wonder, of quiet inquisitive respect as one attempts to meet the world, to open a dialogue, to put himself in a position where the world will disclose itself to him in all its mystery and complexity.

Maurice Merleau-Ponty was one of the leading contemporary phenomenologists. He was born in 1908 and died at the height of his career in 1961. After teaching at the University of Lyons and at the Sorbonne he was called to the chair of philosophy at the College de France in 1952. This is one of the most prestigious positions in France and it was quite unusual for a man of his youth to be appointed to it. He was the editor of *Les Temps modernes*, a journal which he founded with Jean-Paul Sartre and Simone de Beauvoir. His major books which are available in English include *The Structure of Behavior* (1963), *Phenomenology of Perception* (1962), *Sense and Nonsense* (1964), *In Praise of Philosophy* (1963), *Signs* (1964), and *The Primacy of Perception* (1964). The following essay is the Preface to *Phenomenology of Perception*. A different translation appeared under the title of "What is Phenomenology?" in *Cross Currents*, Vol. VI, No. 1 (Winter, 1956), pp. 59–70.

What is Phenomenology?*

WHAT IS PHENOMENOLOGY? It may seem strange that this question has still to be asked half a century after the first works of Husserl. The fact remains that it has by no means been answered. Phenomenology is the study of essences; and according to it, all problems amount to finding definitions of essences: the essence of perception, or the essence of consciousness, for example. But phenomenology is also a philosophy which puts essences back into existence, and does not expect to arrive at an understanding of man and the world from any starting-point other than that of their "facticity". It is a transcendental philosophy which places in abeyance the assertions arising out of the natural attitude, the better to understand them; but it is also a philosophy for which the world is always "already there" before reflection begins – as an inalienable presence; and all its efforts are concentrated upon re-achieving a direct and primitive contact with the world, and endowing that contact with a philosophical status. It is the search for a philosophy which shall be a "rigorous science", but it also offers an account of space, time, and the world as we "live" them. It tries to give a direct description of our experience as it is, without taking account of its psychological origin and the causal explanations which the scientist, the historian, or the sociologist may be able to provide. Yet Husserl in his last works mentions a "genetic phenomenology", and even a "constructive phenomenology". One may try to do away with these contradictions by making a distinction between Husserl's and Heidegger's phenomenologies; yet the whole of *Sein und Zeit* springs from an indication given by Husserl and amounts to no more than an explicit account of the "natürlicher Weltbegriff" or the "Lebenswelt" which Husserl, toward the end of his life, identified as the central theme of phenomenology, with the result that the contradiction re-appears in Husserl's own philosophy.

* Maurice Merleau-Ponty, Preface to *Phenomenology of Perception*, tr. Colin Smith, Humanities Press, Inc., New York, and Routledge & Kegan Paul Ltd., London, 1962.

The reader pressed for time will be inclined to give up the idea of covering a doctrine which says everything, and will wonder whether a philosophy which cannot define its scope deserves all the discussion which has gone on around it, and whether he is not faced rather by a myth or a fashion.

Even if this were the case, there would still be a need to understand the prestige of the myth and the origin of the fashion, and the opinion of the responsible philosopher must be that *phenomenology can be practiced and identified as a manner or style of thinking, that it existed as a movement before arriving at complete awareness of itself as a philosophy*. It has been long on the way, and its adherents have discovered it in every quarter, certainly in Hegel and Kierkegaard, but equally in Marx, Nietzsche, and Freud. A purely linguistic examination of the texts in question would yield no proof; we find in texts only what we put into them, and if ever any kind of history has suggested the interpretations which should be put on it, it is the history of philosophy. We shall find in ourselves, and nowhere else, the unity and true meaning of phenomenology. It is less a question of counting up quotations than of determining and expressing in concrete form this *phenomenology for ourselves* which has given a number of present-day readers the impression, on reading Husserl or Heidegger, not so much of encountering a new philosophy as of recognizing what they had been waiting for. Phenomenology is accessible only through a phenomenological method. Let us, therefore, try systematically to bring together the celebrated phenomenological themes as they have grown spontaneously together in life. Perhaps we shall then understand why phenomenology has for so long remained at an initial stage, as a problem to be solved and a hope to be realized.

It is a matter of describing, not of explaining or analyzing. Husserl's first directive to phenomenology, in its early stages, to be a "descriptive psychology", or to return to the "things themselves", is from the start a rejection of science. I am not the outcome or the meeting-point of numerous causal agencies which determine my bodily or psychological make-up. I cannot conceive myself as nothing but a bit of the world, a mere object of biological, psychological, or sociological investigation. I cannot shut myself up within the realm of science. All my knowledge of the world, even my scientific knowledge, is gained from my own particular point of view, or from some experience of the world without which the symbols of science would be meaningless. The whole universe of science is built upon the world as directly experienced, and if we want to subject science itself to rigorous scrutiny and arrive at a precise assessment of its meaning and scope, we must begin by reawakening the basic experience of the world of which science is the second-order expression. Science has not and never will have, by its nature, the same significance *qua* form of being as the world which we perceive, for the simple reason that it is a rationale or explanation of that world. I am, not a "living creature" nor even a "man", nor again even "a consciousness" endowed with all the characteristics which zoology, social anatomy, or inductive psychology recognize in these various products of the natural or historical process – I am the absolute source, my existence does not stem from my antecedents, from my physical and social environment; instead it moves out toward them and sustains them, for I alone bring into being for myself (and therefore into being in the only sense that the word can have for me) the tradition which I elect to carry on, or the horizon whose distance from me would be abolished – since that distance is not one of its properties – if I were not there to scan it with my gaze. Scientific points of view, according to which my existence is a moment of the world's, are always both naïve and at the same time dishonest because they take for granted, without explicitly mentioning it, the other point of view, namely that of consciousness, through which from the outset a world forms itself round me and begins to exist for me. To return to things themselves is to return to that world which precedes knowledge, of which knowledge always *speaks*, and in relation to which every scientific schematization is an abstract and derivative sign-language, as is geography in relation to the countryside in which we have learnt beforehand what a forest, a prairie, or a river is.

This move is absolutely distinct from the idealist return to consciousness, and the demand for a pure description excludes equally the procedure of analytical reflection on the one hand, and that of scientific explanation on the other. Descartes and particularly Kant *detached* the subject, or consciousness, by showing that I could not possibly apprehend anything as existing unless I first of all experienced myself as existing in the act of apprehending it. They presented consciousness, the absolute certainty of my existence for myself, as the condition of there being anything at all; and the act of relating as the basis of relatedness. It is true that the act of relating is nothing if divorced from the spectacle of the world in which relations are found; the unity of consciousness in Kant is achieved simultaneously with that of the world. And in Descartes methodical doubt does not deprive us of anything, since the whole world, at least in so far as we experience it, is reinstated in the *Cogito*, enjoying equal certainty, and simply labelled "thought about ...". But the relations between subject and world are not strictly bilateral: if they were, the certainty of the world would, in Descartes, be immediately given with that of the *Cogito*, and Kant would not have talked about his "Copernican revolution". Analytical reflection starts from our experience of the world and goes back to the subject as to a condition of possibility distinct from that experience, revealing the all-embracing synthesis as that without which there would be no world. To this extent it ceases to remain part of our experience and offers, in place of an account, a reconstruction. It is understandable, in view of this, that Husserl, having accused Kant of adopting a "faculty psychologism", should have urged, in place of a noetic analysis which bases the world on the synthesizing activity of the subject, his own *"noematic reflection"* which remains within the object and, instead of begetting it, brings to light its fundamental unity.

The world is there before any possible analysis of mine, and it would be artificial to make it the outcome of a series of syntheses which link in the first place sensations, then aspects of the object corresponding to different perspectives, when both are nothing but products of analysis, with no sort of prior reality. Analytical reflection believes that it can trace back the course followed by a prior constituting act and arrive, in the "inner man" – to use St. Augustine's expression – at a constituting power which has always been identical with that inner self. Thus reflection itself is carried away and transplanted in an impregnable subjectivity, as yet untouched by being and time. But this is very ingenuous, or at least it is an incomplete form of reflection which loses sight of its own beginning. When I begin to reflect my reflection bears upon an unreflective experience; moreover, my reflection cannot be unaware of itself as an event, and so it appears to itself in the light of a truly creative act, of a changed structure of consciousness, and yet it has to recognize, as having priority over its own operations, the world which is given to the subject, because the subject is given to himself. The real has to be described, not constructed or formed. Which means that I cannot put perception into the same category as the syntheses represented by judgments, acts, or predications. My field of perception is constantly filled with a play of colors, noises, and fleeting tactile sensations which I cannot relate precisely to the context of my clearly perceived world, yet which I nevertheless immediately "place" in the world, without ever confusing them with my daydreams. Equally constantly I weave dreams round things. I imagine people and things whose presence is not incompatible with the context, yet who are not in fact involved in it: they are ahead of reality, in the realm of the imaginary. If the reality of my perception were based solely on the intrinsic coherence of "representations", it ought to be for ever hesitant and, being wrapped up in my conjectures on probabilities, I ought to be ceaselessly taking apart misleading syntheses, and reinstating in reality stray phenomena which I had excluded in the first place. But this does not happen. The real is a closely woven fabric. It does not await our judgment before incorporating the most surprising phenomena, or before rejecting the most plausible figments of our imagination. Perception is not a science of the world, it is not even an act, a deliberate taking up of a position; it is the background from which all acts stand out, and is presupposed by them. The world is not an object such that I have in my possession the law of its making; it is the natural setting of, and field for, all my thoughts and all my explicit perceptions. Truth does not "inhabit" only "the inner man", or more accurately, there is no inner man, man is in the world, and only in the world does he know himself. When I return to myself from an excursion into the realm of dogmatic common sense or of science, I find, not a source of intrinsic truth, but a subject destined to be in the world.

All of which reveals the true meaning of the famous phenomenological reduction. There is probably no question over which Husserl has spent more time – or to which he has more often returned, since the "problematic of reduction" occupies an important place in his unpublished work. For a long time, and even in recent texts, the reduction is presented as the return to a transcendental consciousness before which the world is spread out and completely transparent, quickened through and through by a series of apperceptions which it is the philosopher's task to reconstitute on the basis of their outcome. Thus my sensation of redness is *perceived as* the manifestation of a certain redness experienced, this in turn as the manifestation of a red surface, which is the manifestation of a piece of red cardboard, and this finally is the manifestation or outline of a red thing, namely this book. We are to understand, then, that it is the apprehension of a certain *hylè*, as indicating a phenomenon of a higher degree, the *Sinngebung*, or active meaning-giving operation which may be said to define consciousness, so that the world is nothing but "world-as-meaning", and the phenomenological reduction is idealistic, in the sense that there is here a transcendental idealism which treats the world as an indivisible unity of value shared by Peter and Paul, in which their perspectives blend. "Peter's consciousness" and "Paul's consciousness" are in communication, the perception of the world "by Peter" is not Peter's doing any more than its perception "by Paul" is Paul's doing; in each case it is the doing of pre-personal forms of consciousness, whose communication raises no problem, since it is demanded by the very definition of consciousness, meaning, or truth. In so far as I am a consciousness, that is, in so far as something has meaning for me, I am neither here nor there, neither Peter nor Paul; I am in no way distinguishable from an "other" consciousness, since we are immediately in touch with the world and since the world is, by definition, unique, being the system in which all truths cohere. A logically consistent transcendental idealism rids the world of its opacity and its transcendence. The world is precisely that thing of which we form a representation, not as men or as empirical subjects, but in so far as we are all one light and participate in the One without destroying its unity. Analytical reflection knows nothing of the problem of other minds, or of that of the world, because it insists that with the first glimmer of consciousness there appears in me theoretically the power of reaching some universal truth, and that the other person, being equally without thisness, location or body, the Alter and the Ego are one and the same in the true world which is the unifier of minds. There is no difficulty in understanding how *I* can conceive the Other, because the I and consequently the Other are not conceived as part of the woven stuff of phenomena; they have validity rather than existence. There is nothing hidden behind these faces and gestures, no domain to which I have no access, merely a little shadow which owes its very existence to the light. For Husserl, on the contrary, it is well known that there is a problem of other people, and the *alter ego* is a paradox. If the other is truly for himself alone, beyond his being for me, and if we are for each other and not both for God, we must necessarily have some appearance for each other. He must and I must have an outer appearance, and there must be, besides the perspective of the For Oneself – my view of myself and the other's of himself – a perspective of For Others – my view of others and theirs of me. Of course, these two perspectives, in each one of us, cannot be simply juxtaposed, *for in that case it is not I that the other would see, nor he that I should see.* I must be the exterior that I present to others, and the body of the other must be the other himself. This paradox and the dialectic of the Ego and the Alter Ego are possible only provided that the Ego and the Alter Ego are defined by their situation and are not freed from all inherence; that is, provided that philosophy does not culminate in a return to the self, and that I discover by reflection not only my presence to myself, but also the possibility of an "outside spectator"; that is, again, provided that at the very moment when I experience my existence – at the ultimate extremity of reflection – I fall short of the ultimate density which would place me outside time, and that I discover within myself a kind of internal weakness standing in the way of my being totally individualized: a weakness which exposes me to the gaze of others as a man among men or at least as a consciousness among consciousnesses. Hitherto the *Cogito* depreciated the perception of others, teaching me as it did that the I is accessible only to itself, since it defined *me* as the thought which I have of myself, and which clearly I am alone in having, at least in this ultimate sense. For the "other" to be more than an empty word, it is necessary that my existence should never be reduced to my bare awareness of existing, but that it should take in also the awareness that *one* may have of it, and thus include my incarnation in some nature and the possibility, at least, of a historical situation. The *Cogito* must reveal me in a situation, and it is on this condition alone that transcendental subjectivity can, as Husserl puts it, *be* an intersubjectivity. As a mediating Ego, I can clearly distinguish from myself the world and things, since I certainly do not exist in the way in which things exist. I must even set aside from myself my body understood as a thing among things, as a collection of physico-chemical processes. But even if the *cogitatio*, which I thus discover, is without location in objective time and space, it is not without place in the phenomenological world. The world, which I distinguished from myself as the totality of things or of processes linked by causal relationships, I rediscover "in me" as the permanent horizon of all my *cogitationes* and as a dimension in relation to which I am constantly situating myself. The true *Cogito* does not define the subject's existence in terms of the thought he has of existing, and furthermore does not convert the indubitability of the world into the indubitability of thought about the world, nor finally does it replace the world itself by the world as meaning. On the contrary it recognizes my thought itself as an inalienable fact, and does away with any kind of idealism in revealing me as "being-in-the-world".

It is because we are through and through compounded of relationships with the world that for us the only way to become aware of the fact is to suspend the resultant activity, to refuse it our complicity (to look at it *ohne mitzumachen*, as Husserl often says), or yet again, to put it "out of play". Not because we reject the certainties of common sense and a natural attitude to things – they are, on the contrary, the constant theme of philosophy – but because, being the presupposed basis of any thought, they are taken for granted, and go unnoticed, and because in order to arouse them and bring them to view, we have to suspend for a moment our recognition of them. The best formulation of the reduction is probably that given by Eugen Fink, Husserl's assistant, when he spoke of "wonder" in the face of the world. Reflection does not withdraw from the world toward the unity of consciousness as the world's basis; it steps back to watch the forms of transcendence fly up like sparks from a fire; it slackens the intentional threads which attach us to the world and thus brings them to our notice; it alone is consciousness of the world because it reveals that world as strange and paradoxical. Husserl's transcendental is not Kant's and Husserl accuses Kant's philosophy of being "worldly", because it *makes use* of our relation to the world, which is the motive force of the transcendental deduction, and makes the world immanent in the subject, instead of *being filled with wonder* at it and conceiving the subject as a process of transcendence toward the world. All the misunderstandings with his interpreters, with the existentialist "dissidents" and finally with himself, have arisen from the fact that in order to see the world and grasp it as paradoxical, we must break with our familiar acceptance of it and, also, from the fact that from this break we can learn nothing but the unmotivated upsurge of the world. The most important lesson which the reduction teaches us is the impossibility of a complete reduction. This is why Husserl is constantly re-examining the possibility of the reduction. If we were absolute mind, the reduction would present no problem. But since, on the contrary, we are in the world, since indeed our reflections are carried out in the temporal flux on to which we are trying to seize (since they *sich einströmen*, as Husserl says), there is no thought which embraces all our thought. The philosopher, as the unpublished works declare, is a perpetual beginner, which means that he takes for granted nothing that men, learned or otherwise, believe they know. It means also that philosophy itself must not take itself for granted, in so far as it may have managed to say something true; that it is an ever-renewed experiment in making its own beginning; that it consists wholly in the description of this beginning and, finally, that radical reflection amounts to a consciousness of its own dependence on an unreflective life which is its initial situation, unchanging, given once and for all. Far from being, as has been thought, a procedure of idealistic philosophy, phenomenological reduction belongs to existential philosophy: Heidegger's "being-in-the-world" appears only against the background of the phenomenological reduction.

A misunderstanding of a similar kind confuses the notion of the "essences" in Husserl. Every reduction, says Husserl, as well as being transcendental is necessarily eidetic. This means that we cannot subject our perception of the world to philosophical scrutiny without ceasing to be identified with that act of positing the world, with that interest in it which delimits us, without drawing back from our commitment which is itself thus made to appear as a spectacle, without passing from the *fact* of our existence to its *nature*, from the Dasein to the Wesen. But it is clear that the essence is here not the end, but a means, that our effective involvement in the world is precisely what has to be understood and made amenable to conceptualization, for it is what polarizes all our conceptual particularizations. The need to proceed by way of essences does not mean that philosophy takes them as its object, but, on the contrary, that our existence is too tightly held in the world to be able to know itself as such at the moment of its involvement, and that it requires the field of ideality in order to become acquainted with and to prevail over its facticity. The Vienna Circle, as is well known, lays it down categorically that we can enter into relations only with meanings. For example, "consciousness" is not for the Vienna Circle identifiable with what we are. It is a complex meaning which has developed late in time, which should be handled with care, and only after the many meanings which have contributed, throughout the world's semantic development, to the formation of its present one, have been made explicit. Logical positivism of this kind is the antithesis of Husserl's thought. Whatever the subtle changes of meaning which have ultimately brought us, as a linguistic acquisition, the word and concept of consciousness, we enjoy direct access to what it designates. For we have the experience of ourselves, of that consciousness which we are, and it is on the basis of this experience that all linguistic connotations are assessed, and precisely through it that language comes to have any meaning at all for us. "It is that as yet dumb experience ... which we are concerned to lead to the pure expression of its own meaning." Husserl's essences are destined to bring back all the living relationships of experience, as the fisherman's net draws up from the depths of the ocean quivering fish and seaweed. Jean Wahl is therefore wrong in saying that "Husserl separates essences from existence". The separated essences are those of language. It is the office of language to cause essences to exist in a state of separation which is in fact merely apparent, since through language they still rest upon the ante-predicative life of consciousness. In the silence of primary consciousness can be seen appearing not only what words mean, but also what things mean: the core of primary meaning round which the acts of naming and expression take shape.

Seeking the essence of consciousness will therefore not consist in developing the *Wortbedeutung* of consciousness and escaping from existence into the universe of things said; it will consist in rediscovering my actual presence to myself, the fact of my consciousness which is in the last resort what the word and the concept of consciousness mean. Looking for the world's essence is not looking for what it is as an idea once it has been reduced to a theme of discourse; it is looking for what it is as a fact for us, before any thematization. Sensationalism "reduces" the world by noticing that after all we never experience anything but states of ourselves. Transcendental idealism, too, "reduces" the world since, in so far as it guarantees the world, it does so by regarding it as thought or consciousness of the world, and as the mere correlative of our knowledge, with the result that it becomes immanent in consciousness and the aseity of things is thereby done away with. The eidetic reduction is, on the other hand, the determination to bring the world to light as it is before any falling back on ourselves has occurred, it is the ambition to make reflection emulate the unreflective life of consciousness. I aim at and perceive a world. If I said, as do the sensationalists, that we have here only "states of consciousness", and if I tried to distinguish my perceptions from my dreams with the aid of "criteria", I should overlook the phenomenon of the world. For if I am able to talk about "dreams" and "reality", to bother my head about the distinction between imaginary and real, and cast doubt upon the "real", it is because this distinction is already made by me before any analysis; it is because I have an experience of the real as of the imaginary, and the problem then becomes one not of asking how critical thought can provide for itself secondary equivalents of this distinction, but of making explicit our primordial knowledge of the "real", of describing our perception of the world as that upon which our idea of truth is for ever based. We must not, therefore, wonder whether we really perceive a world, we must instead say: the world is what we perceive. In more general terms, we must not wonder whether our self-evident truths are real truths, or whether, through some perversity inherent in our minds, that which is self-evident for us might not be illusory in relation to some truth in itself. For in so far as we talk about illusion, it is because we have identified illusions, and done so solely in the light of some perception which at the same time gave assurance of its own truth. It follows that doubt, or the fear of being mistaken, testifies as soon as it arises to our power of unmasking error, and that it could never finally tear us away from truth. We are in the realm of truth and it is "the experience of truth" which is self-evident. To seek the essence of perception is to declare that perception is not presumed true, but defined as access to truth. So, if I now wanted, according to idealistic principles, to base this *de facto* self-evident truth, this irresistible belief, on some absolute self-evident truth, that is, on the absolute clarity which my thoughts have for me; if I tried to find in myself a creative thought which bodied forth the framework of the world or illumined it through and through, I should once more prove unfaithful to my experience of the world, and should be looking for what makes that experience possible instead of looking for what it is. The self-evidence of perception is not adequate thought or apodeictic self-evidence. The world is not what I think, but what I live through. I am open to the world, I have no doubt that I am in communication with it, but I do not possess it; it is inexhaustible. "There is a world", or rather: "There is the world"; I can never completely account for this ever-reiterated assertion in my life. This facticity of the world is what constitutes the *Weltlichkeit der Welt*, what causes the world to be the world; just as the facticity of the *cogito* is not an imperfection in itself, but rather what assures me of my existence. The eidetic method is the method of a phenomenological positivism which bases the possible on the real.

We can now consider the notion of intentionality, too often cited as the main discovery of phenomenology, whereas it is understandable only through the reduction. "All consciousness is consciousness of something"; there is nothing new in that. Kant showed, in the *Refutation of Idealism*, that inner perception is impossible without outer perception, that the world, as a collection of connected phenomena, is anticipated in the consciousness of my unity, and is the means whereby I come into being as a consciousness. What distinguishes intentionality from the Kantian relation to a possible object is that the unity of the world, before being posited by knowledge in a specific act of identification, is "lived" as ready-made or already there. Kant himself shows in the *Critique of Judgment* that there exists a unity of the imagination and the understanding and a unity of subjects *before the object*, and that, in experiencing the beautiful, for example, I am aware of a harmony between sensation and concept, between myself and others, which is itself without any concept. Here the subject is no longer the universal thinker of a system of objects rigorously interrelated, the positing power who subjects the manifold to the law of the understanding, in so far as he is to be able to put together a world – he discovers and enjoys his own nature as spontaneously in harmony with the law of the understanding. But if the subject has a nature, then the hidden art of the imagination must condition the categorical activity. It is no longer merely the aesthetic judgment, but knowledge too which rests upon this art, an art which forms the basis of the unity of consciousness and of consciousnesses.

Husserl takes up again the *Critique of Judgment* when he talks about a teleology of consciousness. It is not a matter of duplicating human consciousness with some absolute thought which, from outside, is imagined as assigning to it its aims. It is a question of recognizing consciousness itself as a project of the world, meant for a world which it neither embraces nor possesses, but toward which it is perpetually directed – and the world as this pre-objective individual whose imperious unity decrees what knowledge shall take as its goal. This is why Husserl distinguishes between intentionality of act, which is that of our judgments and of those occasions when we voluntarily take up a position – the only intentionality discussed in the *Critique of Pure Reason* – and operative intentionality (*fungierende Intentionalität*), or that which produces the natural and antepredicative unity of the world and of our life, being apparent in our desires, our evaluations and in the landscape we see, more clearly than in objective knowledge, and furnishing the text which our knowledge tries to translate into precise language. Our relationship to the world, as it is untiringly enunciated within us, is not a thing which can be any further clarified by analysis; philosophy can only place it once more before our eyes and present it for our ratification.

Through this broadened notion of intentionality, phenomenological "comprehension" is distinguished from traditional "intellection", which is confined to "true and immutable natures", and so phenomenology can become a phenomenology of origins. Whether we are concerned with a thing perceived, a historical event, or a doctrine, to "understand" is to take in the total intention – not only what these things are for representation (the "properties" of the thing perceived, the mass of "historical facts", the "ideas" introduced by the doctrine) – but the unique mode of existing expressed in the properties of the pebble, the glass, or the piece of wax, in all the events of a revolution, in all the thoughts of a philosopher. It is a matter, in the case of each civilization, of finding the Idea in the Hegelian sense, that is, not a law of the physico-mathematical type, discoverable by objective thought, but that formula which sums up some unique manner of behavior toward others, toward Nature, time, and death: a certain way of patterning the world which the historian should be capable of seizing upon and making his own. These are the *dimensions* of history. In this context there is not a human word, not a gesture, even one which is the outcome of habit or absent-mindedness, which has not some meaning. For example, I may have been under the impression that I lapsed into silence through weariness, or some minister may have thought he had uttered merely an appropriate platitude, yet my silence or his words immediately take on a significance, because my fatigue or his falling back upon a ready-made formula are not accidental, for they express a certain lack of interest, and hence some degree of adoption of a definite position in relation to the situation.

When an event is considered at close quarters, at the moment when it is lived through, everything seems subject to chance: one man's ambition, some lucky encounter, some local circumstance or other appears to have been decisive. But chance happenings offset each other, and facts in their multiplicity coalesce and show up a certain way of taking a stand in relation to the human situation, reveal in fact an *event* which has its definite outline and about which we can talk. Should the starting-point for the understanding of history be ideology, or politics, or religion, or economics? Should we try to understand a doctrine from its overt content, or from the psychological make-up and the biography of its author? We must seek an understanding from all these angles simultaneously, everything has meaning, and we shall find this same structure of being underlying all relationships. All these views are true provided that they are not isolated, that we delve deeply into history and reach the unique core of existential meaning which emerges in each perspective. It is true, as Marx says, that history does not walk on its head, but it is also true that it does not think with its feet. Or one should say rather that it is neither its "head" nor its "feet" that we have to worry about, but its body. All economic and psychological explanations of a doctrine are true, since the thinker never thinks from any starting-point but the one constituted by what he is. Reflection even on a doctrine will be complete only if it succeeds in linking up with the doctrine's history and the extraneous explanations of it, and in putting back the causes and meaning of the doctrine in an existential structure. There is, as Husserl says, a "genesis of meaning" (*Sinngenesis*), which alone, in the last resort, teaches us what the doctrine "means". Like understanding, criticism must be pursued at all levels and, naturally, it will be insufficient, for the refutation of a doctrine, to relate it to some accidental event in the author's life: its significance goes beyond, and there is no pure accident in existence or in coexistence, since both absorb random events and transmute them into the rational.

Finally, as it is indivisible in the present, history is equally so in its sequences. Considered in the light of its fundamental dimensions, all periods of history appear as manifestations of a single existence, or as episodes in a single drama – without our knowing whether it has an ending. Because we are in the world, we are *condemned to meaning*, and we cannot do or say anything without its acquiring a name in history.

Probably the chief gain from phenomenology is to have united extreme subjectivism and extreme objectivism in its notion of the world or of rationality. Rationality is precisely measured by the experiences in which it is disclosed. To say that there exists rationality is to say that perspectives blend, perceptions confirm each other, a meaning emerges. But it should not be set in a realm apart, transposed into absolute Spirit, or into a world in the realist sense. The phenomenological world is not pure being, but the sense which is revealed where the paths of my various experiences intersect, and also where my own and other people's intersect and engage each other like gears. It is thus inseparable from subjectivity and intersubjectivity, which find their unity when I either take up my past experiences in those of the present, or other people's in my own. For the first time the philosopher's thinking is sufficiently conscious not to anticipate itself and endow its own results with reified form in the world. The philosopher tries to conceive the world, others and himself and their interrelations. But the meditating Ego, the "impartial spectator" (*uninteressierter Zuschauer*) do not rediscover an already given rationality, they "establish themselves", and establish it, by an act of initiative which has no guarantee in being, its justification resting entirely on the effective power which it confers on us of taking our own history upon ourselves.

The phenomenological world is not the bringing to explicit expression of a pre-existing being, but the laying down of being. Philosophy is not the reflection of a pre-existing truth, but, like art, the act of bringing truth into being. One may well ask how this creation is *possible*, and if it does not recapture in things a preexisting Reason. The answer is that the only pre-existent Logos is the world itself, and the philosophy which brings it into visible existence does not begin by being *possible*; it is actual or real like the world of which it is a part, and no explanatory hypothesis is clearer than the act whereby we take up this unfinished world in an effort to complete and conceive it. Rationality is not a *problem*. There is behind it no unknown quantity which has to be determined by deduction, or, beginning with it, demonstrated inductively. We witness every minute the miracles of related experiences, and yet nobody knows better than we do how this miracle is worked, for we are ourselves this network of relationships. The world and reason are not problematical. We may say, if we wish, that they are mysterious, but their mystery defines them: there can be no question of dispelling it by some "solution", it is on the hither side of all solutions. True philosophy consists in relearning to look at the world, and in this sense a historical account can give meaning to the world quite as "deeply" as a philosophical treatise. We take our fate in our hands, we become responsible for our history through reflection, but equally by a decision on which we stake our life, and in both cases what is involved is a violent act which is validated by being performed.

Phenomenology, as a disclosure of the world, rests on itself, or rather provides its own foundation. All knowledge is sustained by a "ground" of postulates and finally by our communication with the world as primary embodiment of rationality. Philosophy, as radical reflection, dispenses in principle with this resource. As, however, it too is in history, it too exploits the world and constituted reason. It must therefore put to itself the question which it puts to all branches of knowledge, and so duplicate itself infinitely, being, as Husserl says, a dialogue or infinite meditation, and, in so far as it remains faithful to its intention, never knowing where it is going. The unfinished nature of phenomenology and the inchoative atmosphere which has surrounded it are not to be taken as a sign of failure, they were inevitable because phenomenology's task was to reveal the mystery of the world and of reason. If phenomenology was a movement before becoming a doctrine or a philosophical system, this was attributable neither to accident, nor to fraudulent intent. It is as painstaking as the works of Balzac, Proust, Valéry, or Cézanne – by reason of the same kind of attentiveness and wonder, the same demand for awareness, the same will to seize the meaning of the world or of history as that meaning comes into being. In this way it merges into the general effort of modern thought.

2

THE PHENOMENOLOGY OF RELIGION

W. Brede Kristensen

Editor's Introduction

W. BREDE KRISTENSEN uses the phenomenological method to organize data in the study of religion. This is only one of several methods or organization. For example, it is possible to organize religious data historically. Then one would study the historical development of a particular tradition, e.g., Christianity. One would begin with the pre-Christian foundations of Christianity in ancient near eastern religions and follow its development through Greece, Rome, Medieval Europe, into the present. Or, the data of religion can be organized geographically. In that case, one might study religion in America. One would begin with the early settlers, and watch the changes in religious ideas and forms of expression as the patterns of the old world met the frontier and as new waves of immigrants came into contact with the earlier settlers. Or the data of religion can be organized phenomenologically. In this study one seeks the essence of religious phenomena. One attempts to describe the meaning of common themes among religions, regardless of their historical tradition or geographic location. One would, for example, study the similarities between various initiatory ceremonies, or common forms of priesthood among a variety of religions.

The purpose of phenomenological study is not to show the superiority or inferiority of one religion over others. Neither is it to show that all religions are basically similar. The effort to discover the essence of religious phenomena must be clearly distinguished from the effort to find a common religion lying beneath the many historically conditioned forms of religious expression. During the nineteenth and early twentieth centuries it was fashionable to say that basically all religions were similar and that their differences were due merely to cultural modifications of fundamental ethical and metaphysical positions. To strip religion of the historically conditioned formulations was to expose "natural religion" as opposed to the "positive religions" such as Christianity, Judaism, Buddhism, etc.

There are three problems with this approach. First, it overlooks the fact that men in the twentieth century are as historically conditioned as any other men. It is no more possible for me to throw off the particular and finite forms of religious expression than it is for me to throw off the particular English language that I use to express my thoughts. I am an historical being and can only understand my world and express myself in historically conditioned terms. When the seekers of "natural religion" in the late nineteenth and early twentieth century thought they had found the "natural religion" they had really found only the nineteenth century ideal of religion.

Second, the search for a common denominator overlooks the fact that there are as many differences among religions as there are similarities. In *Introduction to Religion* (Harper & Row, 1954 and 1968) Winston King illustrates this point:

The ancient Aztec sacrificed human beings on occasion, cutting out at the climax of the act of worship the pulsing heart of the victim bound on the altar, while the Jain of India will not knowingly harm even a louse, mosquito, or the living root of a plant. The Egyptians tried to immortalize the human body by mummification, that it might serve as a familiar point of reference for the occasional return of the departed spirit; the Christian (not quite so successfully) seeks to preserve his dead by concrete vaults and metal caskets for less obvious reasons; most Hindus burn their dead on funeral pyres floating on a river; and the Parsee places the bodies of the faithful dead in "towers of silence", open to the sky, for vultures to consume.

To extend the table of differences a little further: the ancient

Greeks worshipped some of their gods through alcoholic intoxication, being thereby taken out of themselves and filled with the power of the god. Sexual intercourse with the temple priestess was often viewed in the same light. On the other hand Buddhist and Christian have set a high value on sexual purity; perpetual celibacy for both men and women has been accorded a saintly quality, while drunkenness is condemned out-of-hand. Early Buddhism taught that the world was evil, or at least illusory, and was to be escaped; the Christian divides his energies by trying to make this world into the Kingdom of God and simultaneously achieve heaven in the next life; Psychiana, a home-grown American sect, believes that true religion brings the God-power to us in health and prosperity here and now. The Mohammedan prays five times daily toward Mecca, and abhors images and saints; Roman and Greek Orthodox Catholics worship by elaborate, colorful pageantry in the sacrament of the Mass, adorn their churches with images, icons, and pictures, and venerate the saints; the Protestant, who avoids imagery as strenuously as the Moslem, considers himself a better Christian than the Catholic, more truly religious than the Moslem, yet worships a Triune God, which the latter regards as idolatrous. (pp. 7–8)

Third, the search for "natural religion" overlooks one of the most critical elements of any religion: the believers take the particular "positive" elements of the religion to be essential to their life and faith. It is exactly the "positive" elements that give religion its significance.

This absolute character of religious ideas and symbols provides some of the most difficult methodological problems in the study of religion. How is it possible to study religion "objectively" when the essential religious element is the revelatory impact it makes on its adherents – an impact that is missing for the outside observer? What is the relation between the phenomenological search for meaning in religious phenomena and the meaning found in various religions by their adherents? Two apparently contradictory axioms must be preserved. First, knowledge about religion does not necessarily make anyone a more religious person. The saints and holy men of many religious traditions are more often than not uneducated and quite lacking in formal knowledge. This is not to say that they are not wise – on the contrary, they are often extremely wise. But they often lack the kind of knowledge that is the goal of the university and of studies such as the phenomenology of religion. A corollary of this axiom is that religious traditions have nothing to fear from rigorous academic study. The atavistic supposition that intellectual enquiry into religion is somehow irreverent or liable to "destroy a person's faith" simply misunderstands the distinction between the pursuit of knowledge and the wisdom that is associated with religious conviction.

The other side of the coin is equally important. Failure to enquire as deeply as possible into religion can be a religiously dangerous failing. While knowledge cannot take the place of religious commitment, religious commitment that is uncritical is often superficial. There is no one so pathetic as the person who is well-educated politically, socially, scientifically, and historically, but who is theologically and religiously illiterate. Religious and theological literacy must keep pace with a person's general level of knowledge if some strange schizophrenic tendencies are not to be manifest.

Religious knowledge is participating knowledge. It is immediate and existential and is communicated through symbols. Its goal is immediate participation in and commitment to the fundamental images which orient individual and corporate existence. Mircea Eliade writes that "Religious man's desire to live in the sacred is in fact equivalent to his desire to take up his abode in objective reality, not to let himself be paralyzed by the never-ceasing relativity of purely subjective experiences, to live in a real and effective world, and not in an illusion." "Objective" historical or philosophical knowledge, on the other hand, is discursive or descriptive rather than participating. It seeks to question critically the patterns of existence with which a culture articulates its experience. This reflective knowledge cannot replace, or even promote, immediate participation.

An analogous relationship exists between the artist and the art critic. The artist is concerned to evoke immediate participation in his image. The critic is concerned to clarify this participation. These functions cannot be absolutely distinguished. There is something of the critic in every artist; this is reflected in his work. And criticism often reaches the level of artistic creativity. But the modes of operation are fundamentally different. Criticism cannot take the place of the work of art. The critic attempts to cut away the encrustations of limited perceptual patterns that obscure the immediacy of the art-work. But the immediate participation must always rely on the art-work itself. I may "understand" a poem through criticism, but that will never take the place of re-reading the poem itself.

Within the area of "objective" study, Kristensen distinguishes three types of study: historical, phenomenological, and philosophical. In contrast to the naïve assumption that one begins with the collection of historical data and moves through the phenomenological organization of that data to the philosophical interpretation of its meaning, he points out the reciprocal relationship among these three areas of study. One does not begin without philosophical presuppositions; these help formulate the questions that shape the search for the data.

Kristensen limits phenomenology to the organization of data and leaves interpretation to "philosophy". He wants to distinguish phenomenological studies from the kind of philosophy that seeks explanations and theories rather than descriptions. But when he locates the description of "essences" within the philosophical rather than phenomenological disciplines, he deviates from the main tradition of phenomenology.

W. Brede Kristensen (1867–1953) was a Norwegian phenomenologist of religion who, although an outstanding scholar, has not been widely known outside Scandinavia and the low countries. Between 1884 and 1896 he studied at various European universities, devoting special attention to the mastery of a number of esoteric languages needed for his studies in ancient religions. After teaching at the University of Oslo he went to the University of Leyden in 1901 where he stayed until his retirement in 1953. In 1913 he became a Dutch citizen. Few of Kristensen's many publications have appeared in English. The outstanding exception is *The Meaning of Religion*. The following essay is taken from the introduction to that book.

The Meaning of Religion*

PHENOMENOLOGY OF RELIGION is the systematic treatment of History of Religion. That is to say, its task is to classify and group the numerous and widely divergent data in such a way that an over-all view can be obtained of their religious content and the religious values they contain. This general view is not a condensed History of Religion, but a systematic survey of the data. The different religions present a rich variety of facts. The ritual acts and doctrinal tenets within each separate religion do indeed exhibit a certain similarity; they bear the stamp of that particular religion, but the religions differ in character from one another. The correspondences are only partial. History of Religion leads only to consideration of the particular; the over-all view that it gives, which we call general History of Religion, is not systematic or comparative. It is this systematic view that Phenomenology of Religion attempts to provide.

Instead of "Phenomenology of Religion", we could use the older and more familiar name, "Comparative Religion", if usage had not given to the latter term a meaning which is scarcely suitable for the scientific pursuit of this discipline. The term "Comparative Religion", which has been in use since about 1880, has always signified a comparison of religions for the purpose of determining their value. During the nineteenth century, many religions about which there was previously little knowledge became much better known through the discovery and study of the original documents. This was especially the case with the ancient religions, such as the Avesta religion, and the ancient Indian, Egyptian, and Babylonian religions, but it was also true of the so-called primitive religions, which do not possess any written documents. When an over-all picture was thus obtained, a picture taking in a large and varied terrain of mankind's religious life, the first question arousing general interest was this: what is the relative value of these religions? By comparing them with one an-

* W. Brede Kristensen, from the Introduction to *The Meaning of Religion*, tr. John B. Carmen, Martinus Nijhoff, The Hague, 1960.

other, it should be possible to determine the degree of each religion's development, to determine which religions were lower and which were higher. And most important, could not the comparative approach clearly demonstrate the superiority of Christianity? Thus the most important task of the comparison was to give a general view of the different degrees of religious development and to indicate the place of each religion in this line of development. In the minds of most people, "Comparative Religion" still continues to have this meaning. I shall have more to say about this later, but I should now like to proceed immediately to mention in addition to this first type of comparison a second one, completely different from the first and better characterized by the name "phenomenology". It is this second method of comparison which we shall apply in our study.

Phenomenology does not try to compare the religions with one another as large units, but it takes out of their historical setting the similar facts and phenomena which it encounters in different religions, brings them together, and studies them in groups. The corresponding data, which are sometimes nearly identical, bring us almost automatically to comparative study. The purpose of such study is to become acquainted with the religious thought, idea, or need which underlies the group of corresponding data. Its purpose is not to determine their greater or lesser religious value. Certainly, it tries to determine their religious value, but this is the value that they have had for the believers themselves, and this has never been relative, but is always absolute. The comparative consideration of corresponding data often gives a deeper and more accurate insight than the consideration of each datum by itself, for considered as a group, the data shed light upon one another. Phenomenology tries to gain an over-all view of the ideas and motives which are of decisive importance in all of History of Religion.

The corresponding data in different religions are very numerous. Completely unique phenomena hardly ever occur. Here is an example. Sacrifices take place in almost all religions, although in different forms. This cannot be accidental. How is this fact to be explained? The sacrificial acts evidently issue from a religious need of a very universal nature. How are we to become acquainted with this need? In any given religion perhaps only one particular conception of sacrifice is expressed. We wish to know more: what religious need has caused men, in all times and places, to present offerings to the gods? To learn this, we must study the category "sacrifices" in the various religions; we must pay attention to that which in the actions and conceptions of the various peoples is common to the basic idea of sacrifice. Now to determine what is common is not so simple. It is certainly not to be sought in the outward traits which are held in common, in how the priests are clad and how the rites are divided among them. It is the common meaning of the sacrificial acts that is important, and that we must try to understand.

How do we come to see what the religious significance of a sacrifice is? Of the innumerable data, not all give equally clear indications. Sometimes the religious idea is indicated quite precisely by the accompanying texts or by other particulars which make its religious meaning clear. To such data we have to give special attention. It is not important in which religion we find them. We must then try to see whether they do not clarify other cases where the religious meaning comes less clearly to light. Thus data from one religion can shed light on data from another because the meaning of the former happens to be clearer than that of the latter. Current opinion holds that we must conceive of sacrifices as gifts to the gods similar to gifts offered to princes as evidence of respect and homage, gifts which sometimes meet real needs. But is that conception right? I think not. It is difficult to give an answer on the basis of data from one particular religion. We must have a general view based on observations gathered from as many religions as possible in order that we may achieve certainty. Therefore we must compare them with one another, and that is the research undertaken in Phenomenology; to consider the phenomena, not only in their historical context, but also in their idea connection. We call this kind of study "phenomenological", because it is concerned with the systematic treatment of phenomena. Phenomenology is a systematic science, not just an historical discipline which considers the Greek, Roman, or Egyptian religion by itself. The problem is to determine what sacrifice itself is, not just what Greek, Roman, or Hebrew sacrifice is. It is clear that Phenomenology in this way makes an important contribution toward a better and deeper understanding of the separate historical data.

Take for example such a characteristic religious phenomenon as prayer. In every religion it has a different form and a different character, but there is no single religion that informs us completely about the religious need which has led to the practice of prayer. We are acquainted with "magic prayer", often connected with sacred rites (sacrifices, for example) which are intended to ensure the effectiveness of prayer or at least to strengthen the compelling power of prayer. But besides this first type there is "spiritual prayer" that signifies surrender to God's will and from this surrender draws spiritual power. But in both cases we speak of "prayer". Now it is the task of Phenomenology of Religion to answer the question of what we should understand by the concept "prayer" and what is common to its various forms.

Here is another example. "Ritual purification" is a practice which occurs in most religions. What is its religious significance? Only on the basis of comparative study of corresponding data is it possible to ascertain whether the purification has the positive effect of strengthening the one purified, or whether it has the negative aim of washing off spiritual stains.

Another instance is that of the oracle. What religious significance has been ascribed to the oracle? One particular case, such as that of the Delphic Oracle, does not give us sufficient information. The significance was self-evident to the believers, but just for that reason they often do not dwell upon it and thus leave us uncertain. They could suffice with hints, immediately comprehensible to them, but not sufficiently clear to us. We have to take great pains in order to try to understand that which was self-evident to them, for from our own religious experience we are either not acquainted with oracles, sacrifices, purifications and sacraments at all, or only incompletely. Our principal aid in learning to understand them is the comparative method of study. "Sacrifice", "purification", and the like are universal terms common to all religions; it is on the basis of a fairly complete knowledge of their application that they are to be understood.

Still another instance is the Greek and Roman concept of kingship. It is clear from certain ritual acts that in these nations not only was the king the high priest, but he was also conceived as a divine personage. What did that mean? What capacities were ascribed to him? What position did this god-man occupy among them? It has been thought that *dios*, "divine", should not be taken literally. Homer uses the term, not only for gods and princes, but also for other eminent men. The use of the term is thought to have arisen simply from an extravagantly great respect for the head of the people. Or the term is explained as survival from earlier primitive circumstances before the dawn of history.

It is, indeed, impossible to probe much more deeply into this question on the basis of the vague and meager literary materials of the Greeks and Romans: it is difficult to find a religious explanation. The notion strikes us as strange and "primitive"; that is to say, we don't understand it. Yet among other nations of Antiquity the notion of the divinity of the king is not only a fact, but a fact about which we are well informed. We cannot remain in doubt about the religious significance of this notion among some of the Semitic peoples, especially the Babylonians. God appears on earth as man (the king) to lead the people on the way of life, abiding life. He stands at the head of their social and political institutions, which are the divinely determined structures of the nation's life. Wars are the wars of the god with his enemies; treaties with other people are divine agreements, concluded not in the perceptible, finite world, but in the infinite, other world embodied in the organic order of the cosmos, in the divine order of the universe. The king who leads the people actualizes the abiding life of his people; that is, the continually repeated resurrection of that life. It is he who realizes for the people victory over death, who is responsible for the fertility of the soil and for triumphing over outside enemies who threaten destruction. Therefore he is repeatedly identified with the god of death and resurrection; and thus he represents among the Greeks and Romans Dionysus, Jupiter or Janus. The comparative approach enables us to understand the sacredness of kingship among the Greeks and Romans. The meager data, which by themselves are not readily understandable, gain a meaning, indeed a very deep meaning. Greek and Roman society, too, were based upon that same religious foundation which is clearly distinguishable among other peoples. Indubitable certitude or clarity cannot be obtained and, indeed, can never be reached when we are seeking understanding, but we can come to the greatest attainable probability.

The divine world order is another subject about which there is a group of related data; how has it been conceived in the various religions? It has become clear that certain definite forms of nature worship appear in a large number of religions, though always in different forms. The worship of the earth (as god or goddess) occurs in a great many religions. What religious idea is the basis of this and what religious values does it represent? Furthermore, just what did the sacredness of fire, water, etc. mean for the adherents of so many religions? And what particular elaboration of the idea do we find in the particular cases of fire worship or water worship? The answer is not precisely the same in all religions, and no answer is complete. Only after comparative analysis are we able to penetrate to the thoughts which lie deeper, and more or less exactly to determine the religious significance or value of each separate form of worship.

Comparative study is in numerous instances a quite necessary aid to the understanding of alien religious ideas, but it is certainly not an ideal means. Every religion ought to be understood from its own standpoint, for that is how it is understood by its own adherents. The result of comparative research, and of every kind of historical research, is likewise less than ideal; only approximate knowledge is possible. Let us be completely aware of the limited validity of historical research. This limitation is imposed by the subject itself; namely, the absolute character of all faith. Every believer looks upon his own religion as a unique, autonomous, and absolute reality. It is of absolute value and thus incomparable. This is true not only for the Christian, but just as surely for the adherent of a non-Christian religion. And it is true not only for every religion conceived as a whole, but also for every part and every particular of religious belief. Not only "Christianity" or any other particular religion is unique, autonomous, and incomparable; so too is every belief and each sacred rite. The belief that Hades is the giver of all life and the sacred act by means of which that belief is actualized in the ritual of the mystery religion are absolute truths for the believers. But the historian cannot understand the absolute character of the religious data in the same way that the believer understands them. The historian's standpoint is a different one. There is a distance between him and the object of the research, he cannot identify himself with it as the believer does. We cannot become Mohammedans when we try to understand Islam, and if we could, our study would be at an end: we should ourselves then directly experience the reality. The historian seeks to understand, and he is able to do that in an approximate way, approximate, but no more. By means of empathy he tries to relive in his own experience that which is "alien", and that, too, he can only approximate. This imaginative re-experiencing of a situation strange to us is a form of representation, and not reality itself, for that always asserts itself with sovereign authority. We can even assume such an outside position in respect to our own spiritual inheritance: we can form a more or less clear picture of our own national character, and we often do so. But then we always feel the shortcomings of our own formulation; the representation is always something else than the reality. The "existential" nature of the religious datum is never disclosed by research. That cannot be defined. Here we see the limit to the validity of historical research. But recognizing a limit of validity is not to deny the value of this research.

In order to understand particular (historical) data, we must frequently (and perhaps always) make use of the generalizations which are the results of comparative research. The sacredness of the Greek and Roman kings must be seen in the light of the ancient concept of kingship; particular sacrifices in the light of the religious essence of sacrifice. Now it is true the Ancient conception

of kingship or the religious essence of sacrifice is a concept and
not historcal reality (only the particular applications are reality),
but we cannot dispense with those concepts. In historical research
they are virtually considered as realities: to an important extent
they give the research direction and lead to the satisfying result of
understanding the data. The limit of validity of scientific results,
which is the consequence of using such fictitious realities, is not
a phenomenon unique to historical science. Such fictitious realities
and general formulations are assumed in all science, even in the
natural science, where they are formulated as "natural laws". Research always anticipates the essence of the phenomena, which
essence is nevertheless the goal of all scientific endeavor.

The relationship between history and phenomenology thus becomes clear. The one assumes the presence of the other, and *vice
versa*. Phenomenology's way of working (the grouping of characteristic data) and its task (the illustration of man's religious disposition) make it a systematic discipline. But if we must group
the phenomena according to characteristics which correspond as
far as possible to the essential and typical elements of religion, how
do we then determine which data typically illustrate men's
religious disposition, and how do we determine what are the
essential elements of religion? This question cannot be answered
on the basis of the phenomena themselves, although this has indeed been tried. There is a popular notion that that which all
religions have in common must be religion's core. If we but set
aside all that is peculiar to a particular religion, what we have
left are the common ideas, feelings, and practices, and they express what is essentially religious. This is a method which seems
so simple as to be almost mechanical, but it is impracticable.
There are a great many elements which appear in all religions.
Inessential and unimportant elements also occur in large num-
bers. On the other hand, none of all the facts which have been
observed occurs in all religions. We do not even find the well-
known trio of "God, soul, and immortality" everywhere. When we
consider the idea, "God", even ignoring the fact that this is absent
in Buddhism, we must conclude that there is no particular idea of
deity which is everywhere applicable. And if we relinquish the

given forms of particular ideas of deity in order to find that which is common behind them, we are then left with empty concepts. The common element that we find in this way is so vague and fleeting that it gives no guidance in the research of Phenomenology. It can be said just as truly that all religious data, seen more deeply, are held in common. If we but pay attention to their religious significance, they prove not to be alien to us, and certainly not to other believers. Consider, for instance, the many nature gods, such as Osiris, Demeter, and Athene. As soon as we learn to understand their essence, the alien element disappears, and they correspond to feelings and insights which are echoed in ourselves. Just for this reason we can understand that which is alien. This is the case with all religious ideas and practices as soon as we comprehend them in their true significance. Seen more deeply, therefore, everything is held in common. Nothing and everything. It is clear that by following this path we do not learn to know the essence of religion.

That which is really essential is shown by philosophical investigation. Essence is a philosophical concept, and it is the chief task of Philosophy of Religion to formulate that essence. The principal ideas in Phenomenology are borrowed from Philosophy of Religion. Philosophy must furnish the guiding principle in the research of Phenomenology. In other words, a mutual relation exists between the two. Yes, Philosophy presupposes personal religious experience; the theory of religion presumes the practice of religion. Whoever seeks to know the essence of religion must possess a general picture of the different types of religious thinking and action, of ideas of deity and cultic acts; this is the material for his research. This material is precisely what Phenomenology provides.

Phenomenology of Religion and History of Religion also stand in this same mutual relation. Naturally History provides the material for the research of Phenomenology, but the reverse is also true.

Thus we see that anticipated concepts and principles are used in all the provinces of the general science of religion: history, typology, and philosophy. We are continually anticipating the results of later research. That typifies the character and the "authority" of each of the three subdivisions of the science of religion. None of the three is independent; the value and the accuracy of the results of one of them depend on the value and accuracy of the results of the other two. The place which the research of Phenomenology occupies between history and philosophy makes it extraordinarily interesting and important. The particular and the universal interpenetrate again and again; Phenomenology is at once systematic History of Religion and applied Philosophy of Religion.

It is evident that in the philosophical determination of the essence of religion, we make use of data which lie outside the territory of philosophy, outside our knowledge. We make use of our own religious experience in order to understand the experience of others. We should never be able to describe the essence of religion if we did not know from our own experience what religion is (not: what the essence of religion is!). This experience forces itself upon us even in purely historical research. That has already been demonstrated by the mutual relation of the three areas of study. A rational and systematic structure in the science of religion is impossible. Again and again a certain amount of intuition is indispensable. We are certainly not confronted with a comparative science of religion (history-phenomenology-philosophy) systematically built up as a logical unity. The purely logical and rational does not indicate which way we must follow because in Phenomenology we are constantly working with presumptions and anticipations. But that is just what makes our labor important. This study does not take place outside our personality. And the reverse will also prove to be the case: the study exerts an influence on our personality. This gives a personal character and value to the research in the areas we have mentioned. An appeal is made to our feeling for the subjects which we want to understand, a feeling which gives us a sureness to our "touch". There is an appeal made to the indefinable sympathy we must have for religious data which sometimes appear so alien to us. But this sympathy is unthinkable without an intimate acquaintance with the historical facts – thus again an interaction, this time between feeling and factual knowledge. It is true that our study is a theoretical activity with which our practical life is not concerned. There is simply no doubt that we grow during our scientific work; when religion is the subject of our work, we grow religiously. In saying this, we have indicated the highest significance of our scientific task. We believe that we work objectively and scientifically, but the fruitful labor, without any doubt, takes place by the illumination of a Spirit who extends above and beyond our spirit. Let us simply call it intuition – then at least no one will contradict us!

Now we must make a few remarks about the method which Phenomenology applies. Phenomenology has as its object to come as far as possible into contact with and to understand the extremely varied and divergent religious data, making use of comparative methods. Let me now contrast with this object the popular conception of the task of "Comparative Religion" to which I alluded in the beginning. According to that conception, it must determine the relative value of the data; it must provide us with the standard by means of which we can distinguish between the lower and the higher forms in the religious life of mankind. This comparison is worked out systematically in an evolutionary interpretation of the history of religion. This interpretation was held in high regard about the end of the last century, both in scholarly circles and elsewhere. At present, however, it has practically disappeared among scholars, but it still persists among large sections of the historically and religiously interested public. It is really popular, and therefore we cannot leave it outside our consideration. We shall be well advised to consider it carefully both in its strengths and in its weaknesses. The basic conviction is this, that the history of mankind has had just ourselves as its goal, and after frightfully great pains it has generated our civilization, as the result of all that which had preceded it. History has a meaning: it follows a continuous line from the primitive through the developed up to the highest. In religion as well as in the rest of our culture we stand on the apex of the historical pyramid. This is clearly shown, according to the evolutionary view, by comparative analysis of the historical types of religion. Such analysis leads to an evolutionary interpretation of the history of religion.

Evolutionary theory is of two types: historical and idealist. According to historical evolutionism, the results achieved in each historical period are handed down to the following generation by them and further developed. The values never disappear; they are always taken over by the succeeding generations. There is a historical contact between all periods of culture. That was the theory of Tiele, and many agreed with him. According to idealistic evolutionism, the idea of humanity and of the essence of religion has an existence of its own. It realizes itself by means of historical phenomena, even by those beyond observable historical relations. It detaches itself more and more from the undeveloped reality which is clothed in primitive forms and comes to light in full clarity in the highest civilization and the highest religions. The idealistic evolutionism includes (among other views) the Hegelian conception of development; the history of religion is understood as the dialectical self-development of the Idea of religion.

From a philosophical standpoint it must be recognized that a case can be made for this evolutionary type of comparative research. It is the task of Philosophy of Religion to describe the essence of religion by determining the relation of religion to other spiritual realities – the intellectual, moral, and aesthetic factors in our spiritual life – and thus to arrive at a definition of religion's distinctive nature. Of course, when the essence is described, the unessential element in the religious phenomena has also a right to be shown. This is the indisputable right of Philosophy of Religion. Some religious forms, some formulations of belief and some sacred rites then prove to express this essential element better than others. Higher and lower forms are thus distinguished and pointed out in history. And religion is seen to be in its essence a living force, which maintains itself even when confronted with ignoble tendencies and obstructive circumstances. Such a conception of religion leads automatically to the notion of growth, a development of religion in the course of history. On philosophical grounds historical and idealistic evolutionism can both be defended. The philosophical method is deductive; by discerning how the phenomena develop from the essence, the historical data are understood.

It must be recognized, furthermore, that the essence of religion is a concept which not only the philosopher, but also the historian and the student of Phenomenology cannot neglect. The scholar must be able to separate the essentially religious from the unessential in all the given historical phenomena which are the object of his research. In order to reach the right conclusions he must have a feeling for religion, an awareness of what religion is, and this awareness is precisely what Philosophy of Religion attempts to formulate. Many historians are gravely lacking in this "feeling". But the reverse is just as true: the philosopher who wants to describe the essential element must work with historical data. He does not conjure them up by pure deduction. He cannot decide that particular data must have existed. History and philosophy must work together; that is to say, the one may not lay down the law to the other. Each is equally autonomous in its own territory.

But the autonomy is denied if a particular pattern of development, the evolutionary pattern, is forced on history. History of Religion and Phenomenology do not have as their object the formulation of our conception of the essence of religious data. This is the task of the philosopher. They must, on the contrary, investigate what religious value the believers (Greeks, Babylonians, Egyptians, etc.) attached to their faith, what religion meant for them. It is *their* religion that we want to understand, and not our own, and we are therefore not concerned here with the essence of religion, for this is necessarily expressed for us in our own religion.

All evolutionary views and theories therefore mislead us from the start, if we let them set the pattern for our historical research. Believers have never conceived of their own religion as a link in a chain of development. Perhaps they have thought of it sometimes as the goal, but never as an intermediate link; yet in the evolutionary view, this is an indispensable concept. No believer considers his own faith to be somewhat primitive, and the moment we begin so to think of it, we have actually lost touch with it. We are then dealing only with our own ideas of religion, and we must not delude ourselves that we have also learned to know the ideas of others. The historian and the student of Phenomenology must therefore be able to forget themselves, to be able to surrender themselves to others. Only after that will they discover that others surrender themselves to them. If they bring their own ideas with them, others shut themselves off from them. No justice is then done to the values which are alien to us, because they are not allowed to speak in their own language. If the historian tries to understand the religious data from a different viewpoint than that of the believers, he negates the religious reality. For there is no religious reality other than the faith of the believers.

The concepts, "primitive" and "highly developed" forms of religion, are therefore fatal for historical research. Religious ideas and sacred rites are degraded to a series of relative values, whereas in reality they have functioned as absolute values. We must understand the others as autonomous and spiritual individuals; we must not let our appraisal be determined by the degree of agreement or difference between them and ourselves. For the historian only one evaluation is possible: "the believers were completely right". Only after we have grasped this can we understand these people and their religion.

That does not imply, of course, that every passing religious tendency to be found in history can lay claim to such an evaluation. Of course, insignificant or superficial points of view appear again and again which are of such slight value that they scarcely merit our attention or respect. How can the one be separated from the other? That is no great problem. That which is insignificant always proves to have no lasting existence in history. Because of their slight value, these phenomena have only a brief existence. As far as the Ancient religions are concerned, most of the data of this sort have disappeared without leaving us any trace, or at least they are no longer visible because of their distance from us. The religious phenomena which primarily engage the attention of the historian and the phenomenologist, however, are the formulations of belief and cultic practices which have endured for centuries and sometimes for thousands of years. They have proved themselves able to bear the life of numerous generations, because they have accurately expressed the religious consciousness of an entire people. This is true of the very ancient forms of worship of nature and of spiritual beings (the two cannot be sharply separated) which have survived, even into our own time. It is also the case with the mythical images in which faith is formulated and with the sacred practices and usages, such as the numerous forms of sacrifices, divinations, etc. The enduring existence of all these religious data proves their religious value: they have been felt to be as essential values of life, and they have indeed been just that. The impressive civilizations of the Ancient peoples were founded upon them. That cannot be said of the passing movements and temporary phenomena. Just as insignificant individuals cannot command the same attention as outstanding personalities, so transient ideas cannot claim the same interest as convictions which have proved their inner power. In studying the Ancient religions, the great distance in time (between them and ourselves) offers this advantage: numerous passing fluctuations have undoubtedly disappeared from sight, and the principal lines indicating what is enduring and valuable come much more clearly into focus. That which has been carefully weighed and approved by generations and has been able to serve as the basis of life has proved its inner value. And we can understand that only in the same sense in which the believers have understood it – that this value is the absolute value of life.

The evolutionary point of view is therefore an unhistorical viewpoint. It is extraordinarily popular because a feeling for history is so extraordinarily rare. For most people it is a difficult task to do justice to the viewpoint of others when the spiritual issues of life are at stake. In historical research, we confront religious data as observers; most people find this attitude difficult to achieve, and so place themselves directly in the stream of life and adopt only those ideas which fit the realities of practical life. When this has been done, a condemnation of the other point of view on the basis of our own is inevitable. From a practical point of view these people are right, for in practice we show our disapproval of that which is alien by not adopting it ourselves. From a theoretical point of view, however, they are wrong.

PART TWO: THE OBJECT OF RELIGION: ONTOLOGICAL DESCRIPTIONS

3

A NATURALISTIC DESCRIPTION

Gerardus van der Leeuw

Editor's Introduction

IN THE FOLLOWING essay, Gerardus van der Leeuw attempts to show how religion is the response of men to elements within their empirical environment. There is nothing at all supernatural or mystical about this. Difficulties in understanding religion have arisen because people have from time to time become insensitive to this empirical object. Van der Leeuw identifies the object as "power". His essay is an effort to describe power in such a way that those who have lost sensitivity to it will be able to experience it again.

Van der Leeuw's essay, therefore, might be considered an essay in the phenomenology of power. He cannot prove that there is such a thing. He can only seek to call our attention to it. Many modern men, with an insured and secure existence, protected by technology on every side, have lost the sensitivity to power in their environment. There does not appear to be anything powerful out there. But it might be possible, through a phenomenological description, to re-kindle the primordial awareness of power. Van der Leeuw employs a device often used by phenomenologists: appeal to data from primitive societies on the grounds that in the primitive context the primary experience of the phenomenon has not been overly distorted by interpretation and explanation.

Primitive people, van der Leeuw argues, experience power in a variety of ways. At the most fundamental level, there is no reflection on what distinguishes powerful, exceptional, or especially successful things from ordinary, everyday occurrences. There is simply an awareness of a quality of existence that distinguishes the unusual or extraordinary from the usual and ordinary.

Van der Leeuw makes a sharp distinction between the primordial experience of power and the constant reflection on power. Theories about power have undergone a gradual development, but the primordial experience remains the same. Reflection arose when primitive men asked the question of universality: "Is there some common basis for the power that is seen in a variety of unusual things and events?" The theoretical answer is the postulation of a unified power, of which various experiences are merely expressions.

The notion of unified power beyond the immediately given implies a sub-structure for the world of appearances. This leads to the idea of a world order and to the ideal of achieving harmony with the world order as a means of obtaining power. Men achieve their true destiny when they conform to "fate" or the world order and not when they struggle against it. This identification of the human soul with world order leads to the positing of a world soul. "Thus the primitive and intensely empirical idea of Power developed into religious Monism." This development contrasts with the common evolutionary and usually chauvinistic interpretation of monotheism as the highest form of religion because it has evolved out of pantheism through polytheism. While there may be an historical development, it is merely the development of theories about a primordial experience which itself remains constant.

Preoccupation with this theoretical development can result in a loss of the original experience. This is what has happened to many modern men who have so identified the original experience with the theory of the world soul, that they are no longer capable of the actual experience of concrete power. However, there are particular places and things which continue to be unique locations for power, and these become *fetishes*. The *Playboy* "bunny" is such a *fetish* for modern Americans. As an advertising symbol, it has tremendous power.

Because sexual symbols have this extraordinary power, they are potentially dangerous and therefore *tabu*. Although sex holds a tremendous fascination for many modern people, it is not a suitable subject for conversation in most circumstances. Because it is dangerous, it must be closely guarded and discussed in carefully prepared contexts. Van der Leeuw tells of the Kurnai boy who died after breaking a ritual dietary tabu. That may seem strange to us, but it is no more strange than the adolescent who commits suicide after violating the sexual tabus of modern society. William Faulkner's *The Sound and the Fury* and William Styron's *Lie Down in Darkness* portray the tragedy that befalls anyone who violates the tabu.

To call attention to these tabu dimensions of life is to suggest that the experience of modern men still does contain an experience of "power". Most of our contacts with objects, people, and events is routine; we relate to them in one way or another, but within a common framework. They interest us or they bore us, we use them to our ends or are used by them. At other times, we are engaged by events, objects, or people in quite a different way. Like the haunted house which each of us has known as a child, or the object of romantic love, these events, although apparently like other events, have a strange effect on us. We are both attracted and repelled by them. They are laden with potency, with unspecified power. We do not relate to them as we do to other objects, but become involved with them. We encounter them in a context of risk and expectation. In this distinction between the usual and common on one side and the mysterious and dangerous on the other, modern men can become aware of the primordial experience of power.

Gerardus van der Leeuw was born in The Netherlands in 1890. After studying anthropology, philosophy, and theology at a number of European universities, he taught at the University of

Groningen from 1918 to 1950. His interests were broad. He studied music, painting, literature, and poetry in addition to religion, theology, phenomenology, philosophy, and related disciplines. During 1945–46 he served as Minister of Education, Art, and Science for The Netherlands. Van der Leeuw wrote several books and numerous articles. His two most important books have been translated into English as *Sacred and Profane Beauty: The Holy in Art*, and *Religion in Essence and Manifestation*. The following selection comprises the first four chapters from the latter.

Religion in Essence and Manifestation*

POWER

1. THAT WHICH THOSE sciences concerned with Religion regard as the *Object* of Religion is, for Religion itself, the active and primary Agent in the situation or, in this sense of the term, the *Subject*. In other words, the religious man perceives that with which his religion deals as primal, as originative or causal; and only to reflective thought does this become the Object of the experience that is contemplated. For Religion, then, God is the active Agent in relation to man, while the sciences in question can concern themselves only with the activity of man in his relation to God; of the acts of God Himself they can give no account whatever.

2. But when we say that God is the Object of religious experience, we must realize that "God" is frequently an extremely indefinite concept which does not completely coincide with what we ourselves usually understand by it. Religious experience, in other terms, is concerned with a "Somewhat". But this assertion often means no more than that this "Somewhat" is merely a vague "something"; and in order that man may be able to make more significant statements about this "Somewhat", it must force

* G. van der Leeuw, Ch. 1–4 from *Religion in Essence and Manifestation*, tr. J. E. Turner, Allen & Unwin Ltd., London, 1938.

itself upon him, must oppose itself to him as being Something *Other*. Thus the first affirmation we can make about the Object of Religion is that it is a *highly exceptional* and *extremely impressive "Other"*. Subjectively, again, the initial state of man's *mind* is amazement; and as Söderblom has remarked, this is true not only for philosophy but equally for religion. As yet, it must further be observed, we are in no way concerned with the supernatural or the transcendent: we can speak of "God" in a merely figurative sense; but there arises and persists an experience which connects or unites itself to the "Other" that thus obtrudes. Theory, and even the slightest degree of generalization, are still far remote; man remains quite content with the purely practical recognition that this Object is a departure from all that is usual and familiar; and this again is the consequence of the *Power* it generates. The most primitive belief, then, is absolutely empirical; as regards primitive religious experience, therefore, and even a large proportion of that of antiquity, we must in this respect accustom ourselves to interpret the supernatural element in the conception of God by the simple notion of an "Other", of something foreign and highly unusual, and at the same time the consciousness of absolute dependence, so well known to ourselves, by an indefinite and generalized feeling of remoteness.

3. In a letter written by the missionary R. H. Codrington, and published by Max Müller in 1878, the idea of *mana* was referred to for the first time, and naturally in the style of those days, as a "Melanesian name for the Infinite", this description of course being due to Müller; while Codrington himself gave, both in his letter and his own book of 1891, a much more characteristic definition: "It is a power or influence, not physical, and in a way supernatural; but it shows itself in physical force, or in any kind of power or excellence which a man possesses. This *mana* is not fixed in anything. and can be conveyed in almost anything; but spirits ... have it and can impart it.... All Melanesian religion consists, in fact, in getting this *mana* for one's self, or getting it used for one's benefit." Taken generally, this description has completely justified itself. In the South Sea Islands *mana* always means a Power; but the islanders include in this term, together

with its derivatives and compounds, such various substantival, adjectival, and verbal ideas as Influence, Strength, Fame, Majesty, Intelligence, Authority, Deity, Capability, extraordinary Power: whatever is successful, strong, plenteous: to reverence, be capable, to adore, and to prophesy. It is quite obvious, however, that the supernatural, in our sense of this term, cannot here be intended; Lehmann even reproached Codrington for referring to the supernatural at all, and proposed to retain the simple meaning of "successful, capable". Now *mana* actually has this significance; the warrior's *mana*, for instance, is demonstrated by his continuous success in combat, while repeated defeat shows that his *mana* has deserted him. But Lehmann, on his part, sets up a false antithesis between the ideas of "the super-normal" and "the amazing" on the one hand, and on the other the primitive ideas of "the powerful" and "the mighty" in general. It is precisely a characteristic of the earliest thinking that it does not exactly distinguish the magical, and all that borders on the supernatural, from the powerful; to the primitive mind, in fact, all marked "efficiency" is *per se* magical, and "sorcery" *eo ipso* mighty; and Codrington's own phrase, "in a way super-natural", appears to have expressed the accurate implication. Here we must certainly clearly distinguish such ideas from what we ourselves regard as supernatural. Power is authenticated (or verified) empirically: in all cases, whenever anything unusual or great, effective or successful is manifested, people speak of *mana*. There is, at the same time, a complete absence of theoretical interest. What is "natural" in the sense of what may ordinarily be expected never arouses the recognition of *mana*; "a thing is *mana* when it is strikingly effective; it is not *mana* unless it is so", asserts a Hocart Islander. It is just as unmistakably authenticated by a dexterous plunge into the sea as by the conduct of the tribal chieftain. It indicates equally good luck (veine) as potency, and there is no antithesis whatever between secular acts and sacred, every extraordinary action generates the experience of Power, and the belief in Power is in the fullest sense practical: "originally, therefore, the conception of magical power and that of capacity in general are most probably identical". Power may be employed in magic, while the magical character pertains to every unusual action; yet it would be quite erroneous to designate potency in general as magical power, and Dynamism as the theory of magic. Magic is certainly manifested by power; to employ power, however, is not in itself to act magically, although every extraordinary action of primitive man possesses a tinge of the magical. The creation of the earth is the effect of the divine *mana*, but so is all capacity; the chief's power, the happiness of the country, depend on *mana*; similarly the beam of the latrine has its own mode, probably because excreta, like all parts of the body, function as receptacles of power. That any reference to magic in the technical sense is superfluous is clear from the statement that "the foreigners were after all victorious, and now the Maori are completely subjected to the *mana* of the English". Yet to the primitive mind the alien authority is no such perfectly reasonable a power as it is to ourselves; again Codrington has described the situation correctly by his "in a way supernatural". Characteristic also is the manner in which the indigenes explain the power of the Christian mass: "If you go to the priest and ask him to pray so that I may die, and he consents, then he celebrates mass, so that I shall die. I die suddenly, and the people say that the priest's mass is *mana*, because a youth has perished."

It is inevitable, still further, that since Power is in no degree systematically understood, it is never homogeneous nor uniform. One may possess either great or limited *mana*; two magicians may attack each other by employing two sorts of *mana*. Power enjoys no moral value whatever. *Mana* resides alike in the poisoned arrow and in European remedies, while with the Iroquois *orenda* one both blesses and curses. It is simply a matter of Power, alike for good or evil.

4. Codrington's discovery was followed by others in the most diverse parts of the world. The *orenda* of the Iroquois has just been referred to; "it appears that they interpreted the activities of Nature as the ceaseless strife between one *orenda* and another". The Sioux Indians, again, believe in *wakanda*, at one time a god of the type of an originator, at another an impersonal Power which acquires empirical verification whenever something extra-

ordinary is manifested. Sun and moon, a horse (*a wakanda-dog!*), cult implements, places with striking features: all alike are regarded as *wakan* or *wakanda*, and once again its significance must be expressed by widely different terms: powerful, holy, ancient, great, etc. In this instance also the theoretical problem of the universality of *wakanda* is not raised; the mind still remains at the standpoint of empirically substantiating the manifestation of Power.

In contrast with *mana*, however, and together with some other ideas of Power, *wakanda* represents one specific type, since it is capable of transformation into the conception of a more or less personal god. This is also the case with the *manitu* of the Algonquins of North-West America, which is a power that confers their capacity on either harmful or beneficent objects, and gives to European missionaries their superiority over native medicine-men. Animals are *manido* whenever they possess supernatural power; but *manitu* is also employed in a personal sense for spirit, and *kitshi manitu* is the Great Spirit, the Originator. The Dyaks of Borneo, similarly, recognize the power of *petara*, which is something, but also someone, while in Madagascar the *hasina*-power confers upon the king, on foreigners and whites their striking and supernormal qualities.

Among the ancient Germans, too, the idea of Power was dominant. The power of life, luck (*hamingja*), was a quantitative potency. Men fought by inciting their luck against somebody (Old Nordic: *etia hamingju*), and were defeated because they possessed too little "luck". The Swedish peasant senses "power" in bread, in the horse, while in Nordic folklore the woman whose child has been stolen by a troll is unable to pursue her because she "has been robbed of her power".

Finally, Power may be assigned to some definite bearer or possessor from whom it emanates. Such a power is the Arabian *baraka*, which is regarded as an emanation from holy men and closely connected with their graves; it is acquired by pilgrimage, and to be cured of some disease a king's wife seeks the *baraka* of a saint. This beneficent power is confined to specific localities; thus the place in which to study is not indifferent so far as its

results are concerned, and in Mecca "the attainment of knowledge is facilitated by the *baraka* of the spot".

5. But even when Power is not expressly assigned a name the
idea of Power often forms the basis of religion, as we shall be
able to observe almost continually in the sequel. Among extensive divisions of primitive peoples, as also those of antiquity, the
Power in the Universe was almost invariably an impersonal
Power. Thus we may speak of Dynamism – of the interpretation
of the Universe in terms of Power: I prefer this expression to
both Animatism and Pre-Animism: – to the former because
"Universal Animation" smacks too much of theory. The primitive
mind never halts before the distinction between inorganic, and
organic, Nature; what it is always concerned with is not Life,
which appears to explain itself, but Power, authenticated purely
empirically by one occurrence after another; thus the Winnebago
(Sioux) offers tobacco to any unusual object because it is *wakan*.
From the term "Pre-Animism", however, it would be inferred that,
chronologically, priority is due to the idea of Power as contrasted
with other conceptions such as the animistic. But here there can
be no question whatever as to earlier or later stages in development, but quite simply of the texture or constitution of the religious spirit, as this predominated in other and earlier cultures
than our own, but also as it lives and flourishes even in our own
day.

6. To recapitulate: I have dealt with the idea of Power which
empirically, and within some form of experience, becomes
authenticated in things and persons, and by virtue of which
these are influential and effective. This potency is of different
types: it is attributed to what we regard as sublime, such as
Creation, exactly as it is to pure capacity or "luck". It remains
merely dynamic, and not in the slightest degree ethical or
"spiritual". Nor can we speak of any "primitive Monism", since
to do so presupposes theory that does not as yet exist. Power is
thought of only when it manifests itself in some very striking way;
with what confers efficiency on objects and persons in ordinary
circumstances, on the other hand, man does not concern himself.
At the same time it is quite true that the idea of Power, as soon as

it becomes incorporated within other cultural conditions, expands
and deepens into the concept of a Universal Power.

To this Power, in conclusion, man's reaction is amazement
(*Scheu*), and in extreme cases fear. Marett employs the fine term
"awe"; and this attitude is characterized by Power being regarded, not indeed as supernatural, but as extraordinary, of some
markedly unusual type, while objects and persons endowed with
this potency have that essential nature of their own which we
call "sacred".

THEORIZING ABOUT POWER

1. An Esthonian peasant remains poor, while his neighbor
grows steadily richer. One night he meets this neighbor's "luck"
engaged in sowing rye in the fields. Thereupon he wakes his own
"luck", who is sleeping beside a large stone; but it refuses to
sow for him, because it is not a farmer's "luck" at all, but a
merchant's; so he himself becomes a merchant and gains wealth.

In this story Power has become a specific power; and this transition occurs very early. The power, the effects of which can be
quite readily substantiated, becomes power in particular instances
– royal authority, that of some craft, etc. In India this led to the
stratification into ruling castes each of which possesses an appropriate power: – *Brahman* pertaining to brahmins, *kshatra* to
kshatriyas. In this way, too, a special magical power occasionally
becomes differentiated from others, as in the case of the Egyptian
sa, a kind of fluid transmitted by the laying on of hands and other
manipulations; while the advance from empirically authenticated
and undefined power to theoretically specified potency is also
noteworthy in the idea of Hindu *tapas*. Similarly in Australia, as
elsewhere, "replete with power", "warm" and "hot" are closely
related conceptions. Power develops heat, the primitive mind believes, with an almost modern scientific accuracy of observation;
in Ceram a house afflicted with smallpox (in which power consequently appears) is regarded as a "warm house". Similarly
tapas is heat, that is the heat of the specific energy of chastening,
its power.

But there is another aspect of this systematic differentiation of potency; for the problem of the universality of Power becomes expressly postulated and affirmed. A certain Monism already constantly present, but concealed by practically oriented primitive thought, now rises unmistakably into view; and what has hitherto been erroneously maintained about the actual idea of Power becomes quite correct – namely that "this interesting sketch of a unified apprehension of Nature and of the Universe reminds us, in virtue of its principle of unity, of Monotheism, and in the light of its realism, of dynamic Monism": more indubitably, it is true, of the latter than of the former. For Power is never personal. It becomes a universal Energy, whether in the psychological sense and in direct application to humanity, or on the other hand as cosmological. In the first instance Power becomes Soul, but a super-personal Soul closely akin to Power; in the second it assumes the form of a divine agency immanently activating the Universe. "Pantheists and monists are the heirs of a very ancient tradition; they sustain among ourselves a conception whose original founders, primitive or savage peoples, deserve more respect and sympathy than they usually receive."

2. Such theoretical considerations, generally foreign to the primitive world, attain steadily increasing influence under the conditions of so-called intermediate or partially developed culture. The changes and processes of the Universe are then no longer accidental and arbitrary effects of distinct powers that emerge at each event and disappear again; they are rather the manifestations of a unitary World-Order, appearing in conformity to rules, and indeed to laws. Many ancient peoples were familiar with the idea of a World-course, which however is not passively followed but rather itself moves spontaneously, and is no mere abstract conformity to Law such as are our Laws of Nature, but on the contrary a living Power operating within the Universe. *Tao* in China, *Rta* in India, *Asha* in Iran, *Ma'at* among the ancient Egyptians, *Dike* in Greece: these are such ordered systems which theoretically, indeed, constitute the all-inclusive calculus of the Universe, but which nevertheless, as living and impersonal powers, possess *mana*-like character.

Tao, then, is the path which the Universe follows, and in a narrower sense the regularly recurring revolutions of the seasons. The "two shores" of warmth and heat which define this cycle together constitute *Tao*; there is no place for a God "applying outward force" (to quote Goethe). Creation is the annual renewal of Nature. This regulated cycle, still further, is completely impartial and just; and man should strive to conform to *Tao*. But in so doing he need not excite himself: *Tao* demands a calm, indeed an almost quietist mood. To good deeds it is hostile: "Great *Tao* was deserted; then 'humanity' and 'justice' came into existence, cleverness and sagacity arose, and hypocrisy flourished." Man should do right in conformity to *Tao*, which is "eternal without acting (*wu wei*), and yet there is nothing that it does not effect". Thus from this belief in a primal Power there arises a type of quietist mysticism. In itself it is self-sufficient, needing neither gods nor men: "the Norm of men is the earth, that of the earth is heaven, of heaven Tao, but the Norm of Tao is ... its very self". Again, "Tao generates and nourishes all beings, completes and ripens them, cares for and protects them". But just as little as *mana* is it exhaustively manifested in the empirical: the essential nature of *Tao* is inscrutable. "In so far as it is nameless it is the primal ground of heaven and earth; when it has a name it is the mother of a myriad of beings. For lack of a better term, call it 'the Great'." Here the old *mana* significance returns once more; but its content has now been "transposed", and is no longer empirical but speculatively mystical.

The Vedic *Rta*, again, is the Law of the Universe, identical with moral law; it is regarded as the Law of certain gods, Varuna and Mitra, and the World-Process is merely the apparent form behind which the actual *Rta* is concealed: "The gods are thus addressed: Your *Rta* (Law), which is hidden behind the *Rta* (the course of the Universe), stands eternally constant, there, where the sun's chargers are unharnessed." Thus it becomes the ultimate court of appeal, the ground of the Universe, its concealed and motivating Power. Just as with Asha in the religion of Zarathustra, *Rta* is good disposition, correct belief, the Law of the gods and World-Power simultaneously. The dominating faith is that the ground of the world may be trusted, and thus the chaotic empiricism of primitive conditions has been superseded by a firm conviction of Order.

3. When gods exist they become either elevated above the World-Order, or subjected thereto. Both the Israelites and the Greeks were conscious of the flaming power of divine energy, of the *orge* which strikes with demonic force – for there can be no question of punishment here; but in contrast to the Israelites, the Greeks were unable to bring this demonic power into relation with the gods. They were intensely aware of the antithesis between the arbitrary rule of potencies in this world and the idea of a just order in the Universe: *Moira* or *Aisa*, originally the lot apportioned to each man by the gods – it is διόθεν, "sent from Zeus" – becomes in the brooding mind of an Aeschylus a Power more than divine which, if so it must be, against even the gods guarantees a morally satisfactory control of the world. From the incalculable dominance of gods, whom the poets had transformed into persons, man sought escape in Destiny, as a universal ground and territory over which the gods enjoyed only limited freedom of action.

In the course of natural processes, then, man discovered a secure and, if not sympathetic, at least an impartial foundation even for human life. If for many peoples, even the most primitive, the course of the sun served as a rule of their own lives, still religious theory perceived no inexorable Fate in this necessity of Nature, but rather a guarantee of World-Order. This attitude, therefore, is not fatalism because the living Power, despite all theorizing, perpetually maintains its central position. Conformity to Law implies no blind Necessity, but a vital Energy realizing a purpose. It was called *Dike*, as in India *Rta*; but its path is the cycle of natural process: "the sun will not exceed his measures", said Heracleitus; "if he does, the Erinyes, the avenging handmaids of Justice, will find him out". To Law, similarly, Sophocles dedicates pious resignation:

My lot be still to lead
        The life of innocence and fly
Irreverence in word or deed,
To follow still those laws ordained on high
Whose birthplace is the bright ethereal sky.
        No mortal birth they own,
        Olympus their progenitor alone:
Ne'er shall they slumber in oblivion cold,
The god in them is strong and grows not old.

And the late-born of the tragedians, Euripides, the advocate
of every doubt and the friend of all unrest, places in the mouth
of his Hecuba this marvellously calm and heartfelt prayer:

Thou deep Base of the World, and thou high Throne
Above the World, whoe'er thou art, unknown
And hard of surmise, Chain of Things that be,
Or Reason of our Reason; God, to thee
I lift my praise, seeing the silent road
That bringeth justice ere the end be trod
To all that breathes and dies.

Thus early Greek speculation, which set out to discover an
arche, a primal unity and primal Power in one, ultimately discerned an impersonal, divinely living, cosmic Law; the divine,
τὸ θεῖον, more and more superseded the gods. The Stoics then
drew the final conclusion: *Heimarmene*, that is, what is allotted,
or Destiny, is the *Logos*, the Reason of the comos, in accord
with which all proceeds; Cleanthes prays to *Pepromene*, the pre-
destined. But even this view of the idea of Fate was just as little
an abstraction as was the Necessity of the tragedians and the
pre-Socratics. Still the essence of the Universe is always Power,
but now an immanent Power, a World-Soul: or better, a "Fluid"
dwelling within the Universe, "the personality and the nature of
the divinities pervading the substance of the several elements".
To the contemporary of Julian the Apostate, finally, divine
Power and the creative Necessity of Nature were absolutely one:
"To say that God turns away from the evil is like saying that the
sun hides himself from the blind."

4. The theoretic treatment of Power thus far presented bears a
prominently cosmological character; but it may also possess

psychological significance. The power that operates within man then becomes regarded not as his "soul", in the sense familiar to ourselves, but as a particular power subsisting in a peculiar relation to its possessor. It is his own power, though nevertheless it is superior to him.

Before *Moira* became the Power of Destiny it was already the personal lot of man, and this it still remains even today among modern Greeks as *Mira*. The Germanic *hamingja*, again, was not the soul, but the power ruling in and over a man. Soul is in no way a primitive concept, and even when primitive mentality began to theorize it had generally not grasped the idea of Soul. We ourselves speak of our psychical qualities, and can "verify" these whenever we wish to do so. But to primitive mind, on the other hand, what we regard as purely personal and pertaining to the "soul" appears as actually inherent in man but still superior to him, and in any case as distinguished from him. The Red Indian, according to his own and our ideas, may be very brave; but that avails him naught if he has no war-medicine, that is, no accumulated power for the purpose of war. Power can be bound up with all sorts of material or corporeal objects; it is this state of affairs that has led to the designation of "soul-stuff". From the soul as such, however, all these ideas were distinguished by the power being impersonal, while one might have a greater or smaller quantity of it, and could either lose it or acquire it; in other terms, it was independent of man and superior to him.

In the Greek-Christian world we find the ideas of Power transformed, theoretically, into that of the single Power by means of the concept of *pneuma*. The Stoics had already placed the individual soul, the *hegemonikon*, which from the heart as center governs the whole body, in the same category as the World-Soul, the *pneuma*, which, as Power, overflows into all things: the human *pneuma* is of the same type as the *pneuma* of the Universe. Thus the primitive idea of power, together with the equally primitive concept of soul-breath, or rather of the breath-stuff of the soul, were united in a single theory.

In Gnosticism, and also for St. Paul, the *pneuma* is the life principle of man together with the *psyche* and divine power, which penetrates man from without and transforms him into a "pneumatized" or "spiritual" man. By St. Paul himself, however, the idea of the impersonal divine "fluid" becomes slightly changed and circumscribed through the union with Christ: "the Lord is that Spirit". On the other hand, for Philo the *pneuma* emanating from the Godhead remains impersonal, though for him as for the late Stoics the *pneuma*, when contrasted with the *psyche* and the flesh, is a power superior to man.

But in spite of the identification of the spiritual and the immaterial, originating in Plato's philosophy, in the eyes of the heathen the *pneuma* was just as little purely spiritual – in our own sense – as in those of Christians. Its designation as soul-stuff was always much more than a mere name. In the New Testament, for example, the *pneuma* becomes transmitted like some sort of fluid, as are the other psychological powers *charis*, *dynamis*, and *doxa*. They flow from God to man, and the Divine *charis* is imparted by formulas of benediction. We translate this as the Grace of God, although it should not be understood as friendly disposition or mercy, but as Power that is poured out and absorbed. It enables man to perform miracles: Stephen, full of *charis* and *dynamis*, "of faith and power, did great wonders among the people". *Charis* effects *charismata*, Gifts of Grace; these however are no gifts of divine generosity, as we might rationalistically interpret them, but the consequences of divine Power. Ancient Christian terminology perpetuates these ideas: in the Eucharist Christ appears with His powers, His *pneuma*, His *doxa* or *dynamis*. The "glorification" in St. John's Gospel again, is a transformation of man which takes place through the infusion of divine Power; and as Wetter affirms quite correctly: "when classical writers refer, e.g., to religious gnosis, *charis*, or *doxa*, who does not feel that these primitive tones (of the idea of Power) frequently re-echo from them?"

Not merely the "psychic" powers but also the deeds, thoughts, and principles of men frequently become represented as a store of power, largely independent of the bearer. I refer here to the idea of *thesaurus*, in consequence of which cumulative deeds constitute a potency that is effective in favor of the doer, but eventually of another person also; thus, the treasury of grace accumulated through the merit of Christ and the saints, is a living power "operating" in favor of the Church. Certainly the connection between Power and the historic Christ has long become illusory here; it has been forgotten that the Lord is the Spirit, and the Power of Christ dispensed among believers.

In India the *thesaurus* concept is absolutely impersonal; *karma* is Power, Law, and *thesaurus* simultaneously: "not in the heavens nor in the midst of the sea, not if he hides in the clefts of the mountains, will man escape the power of *karma*". Thus action has become an impersonal mechanism; and human worth is then appraised as a sum of favorable or unfavorable *karma*, a sort of financial value, that can be transferred to others.

5. In India, then, there has been completed the great equalization that is the final word in the theory of Power, the unification of human and cosmic Power, the identification of psychology and cosmology. The substance of the self and the substance of the ALL are one and the same, their separation being merely provisional and, ultimately, no more than misunderstanding. The *ātman*, originally as soul-breath the most primitive soul-stuff, became in the theory of the *Upanishads* a silently operating and immanent Power conforming to Law: "If the slayer thinks he slays and the slain that he is slain, they both fail to understand; the one slays not and the other is not slain. The *ātman* reposes, subtler than the subtle and greater than the great, in the hearts of creatures. He who is free from desires and without care sees the greatness of the *ātman* by the grace of the creator. Seated, he wanders far away; reclining, he travels everywhere; apart from me, who can recognize this god who is in a state of changing ecstasy?" On the other hand *Brahman*, originally the power of the word, as it reveals itself to the brahmins in the sacrificial utterances and their reciters, became the designation of cosmic Power. *Ātman* and *Brahman*, however, in the last resort are one: here is there, there is here; he who understands *tat tvam asi*, "that art thou", knows of only *one* all comprehending Power. And thus the primitive and intensely empirical idea of Power developed into religious Monism.

THINGS AND POWER

1. We moderns have accustomed ourselves to regard things as mere objects with which we deal exactly as we please. Only a poet could vindicate things:

> Gladly do I hearken to the Things singing.
> Touch them – How stiff and mute they are!
> You kill all my Things. (*Rilke*)

Here once again a philosopher is sensitive to the potency of things, which possess a life of their own despite that "loss of power that has befallen them since the days of the Greeks"; for the prevailing emphasis on the spiritual and internal, as contrasted with the merely institutional – Spiritualismus – the cult of personality, and finally modern machinery, have transformed the living, "self-activated" things into merely dead material.

To the primitive mind, on the contrary, the thing is the bearer of a power; it can effect something, it has its own life which reveals itself, and once again wholly practically. During an important expedition, for example, an African Negro steps on a stone and cries out: "Ha! are you there?" and takes it with him to bring him luck. The stone, as it were, gives a hint that it is powerful. Again: an Ewe tribesman in West Africa enters the bush and finds a lump of iron there; returning home, he falls ill, and the priests explain that a *tro* (a divine being) is manifesting its potency in the iron, which in future should be worshipped. Thus every thing may be a power bearer, and even if it itself provides no evidence of its influence, it suffices if someone tells it that it is powerful. What Rilke, in one of his *Stories of God*, makes the children do – they agree among themselves that the thimble shall be God: "anything may be God. You have only to tell it to be" – this is the frame of mind behind so-called Fetishism.

2. Every thing then, to repeat, can be a power bearer. Objects existing in intimate relation to soul-stuff possess indisputable potency; it is for this reason that the Maori, as has already been remarked, regard the latrine as replete with *mana*: the sick bite its beams in order to be cured. This systematic reckoning with

the power subsisting in things we call Fetishism, a term coined in the scientific sense by de Brosses in 1760, and originally used by the Portuguese with reference to Negro beliefs and customs. But it was applied only to potent things made by man himself, and therefore not to natural objects. Gradually, however, it attained a more comprehensive meaning, sometimes so extensive that even the worship of Nature could be included, so that the concept then became formless. But if it is really desired to indicate the structure of a spiritual viewpoint by the term usually employed, then it would be advisable to apply it only to those objects that we call "things", but with no distinction between natural and artificial, because primitive man venerates what he has himself made, provided this is "effective", just as much as what Nature gives him when this manifests power. In this latter respect, any peculiarity that differentiates the object from environing Nature is essentially significant: the striking shape of a crooked branch, of a round stone, etc., becomes the "pointer" to the existence of power. It is necessary, further, that the object be not too large, so that one may take it away, or as it were pocket it. Although mountains and trees are regarded as sacred, like the fetish, because of their potency, still they should not be called fetishes; it is just this feeling of being able to carry the sacred power with one that is characteristic of Fetishism. "Let us fetch the ark of the covenant of the Lord out of Shiloh unto us, that when it cometh among us, it may save us out of the hand of our enemies," said the Israelites when the Philistines beset them.

A good example of a fetish is the Australian *churinga*, a peculiarly shaped piece of wood on which an outline sketch of a totem emblem is scratched. The word itself means "the private secret", and the object must be kept secret from the women and children. It is the bearer of a power connected on the one hand with the individual, and on the other with his totem; here again subsists the power superior to, yet nevertheless overflowing into, humanity. The *churinga* are most carefully concealed in a kind of place of refuge.

Earlier research assumed that the potency of a fetish is a spirit permanently residing within it, but today the contrasted hypothesis is in favor. At the same time it is probable that the way in which this power is represented is of secondary significance for the constitution of Fetishism as such. Thus the power of the ark of the covenant sprang from Jahveh, a god, that of the *churinga* from a totem; and the potent influence of the fetish, naturally, is very often simply presupposed quite apart from any kind of attitude to spirits or gods being implied – purely dynamically therefore. Actually, Fetishism is always dynamic; and regarded as an ideal type, it was so originally also, because its essence lies in the idea that power resides within a thing and emanates from it. Whence the power arises is, however, a question in itself.

In view of these considerations we can understand the transition from fetish to idol. In many parts of the world piles of stones were erected, each traveller adding his stone to those already thrown there; such stone heaps being found in South Africa just as in ancient Israel. In later times these cairns were looked upon as monuments or burial mounds; originally, however, it was the potency of the accumulated stones that men thus assured for themselves. In Greece these stone heaps were called *hermae* and were the origin of a divinity – "he of the stone heaps": *Hermes.* But before Hermes received his marvellous human form from the hands of Praxiteles he had to stand by the wayside, as the phallic stone or *herm*, for many years. The august form of Pallas, again, was evolved from the fetish of the double thundershield or *palladion*. Of her, just as of Demeter, there were effigies which were half stone fetish and half woman, exactly as Aphrodite was originally a cone. The power of things, in fact, faded only very gradually before that of gods and even of animals. In ancient Egypt fetishes persisted together with animal and human forms of power, and in Greece people loved the *xoana*, the rough wooden blocks, more than Pheidias' marvellous statues; his "Attic Pallas and Rharian Ceres, which stand unsculptured in the shape of a rude and unformed log" (Tertullian), were dearer to him than the Lemnian Athene or the Cnidian Demeter. Forms contrasted with the human actually indicate a diviner remoteness, and yet at the same time a more intimate contact, than does anthropomorphic Power. And this extremely primitive association between transcendence and immanence is essentially characteristic of Fetishism. The time-honored, time-blackened, blocks of wood, which pious faith takes to have descended from heaven, were precious to the people's hearts; they remain so today in Catholic regions. For it is not before great art creations, nor forms that arouse his sympathy, that man prays most spontaneously and fervently and to which he makes pilgrimages, but the "black Madonnas". It is these that work miracles; and before the fetish numinous awe unites with the intimacy and the consciousness of dominance aroused by things.

The intensity of the attractive power enjoyed, even today, by Fetishism, is plainly evident from the use of so-called mascots in modern sport: dolls and animal figures still display themselves as potent, and this not as incarnations of gods in whom trust is no longer placed, but purely and simply as "things". At the missionary exhibition in Nice in 1925, for example, many fetishes were to be seen, and countless visitors wished to buy these at high prices. As this was naturally declined, the directors of the exhibition found themselves compelled to have these objects carefully guarded because attempts were made to steal them.

3. Among potent things *tools* assume a prominent place. To primitive man, indeed, work is the very antithesis of technical occupation – it is creative. The primitive craftsman experiences the power, in virtue of which he completes his task, not as his own; capacity, moreover, is here something far more than modern efficiency. The early hand-worker, therefore, particularly the smith, wields a power which he certainly understands how to employ, but of which nevertheless he is not the master; and thus we can realize why the smith's work is regarded as sacred in many parts of Africa and Indonesia. In Loango, again, whoever has cohabited the previous night may not watch the labor lest his impurity should ruin the work; for whatever comes into existence under human hands owes its being to a power superior to man. In the grips and blows of the tools, then, there dwells not only the strength of arms or legs, but also a specific power residing within the implements themselves; and this explains why tools are always made after the same model, since the slightest deviation would

injure the potency. Moreover, not only are the working parts of the implements essential, but their ornamentation also. The Toba-Batak of Sumatra sacrifices to his forge, hammer, and anvil, to his canoe, rifle, and furniture; the West African Ewe to his bush knife, axe, saw, etc.; and the gipsy, though decried as irreligious, swears his oath on the anvil.

Among implements, again, it is *weapons* that are especially potent; indeed, many weapons are nothing more than tools – the axe and hammer. The veneration of the Cretan double axe is universally familiar. The staff also was originally a weapon, which subsequently became the receptacle of royal power. In Egypt, not only was the staff worshipped, but the word denoting it, *shm*, also became an expression for "power" in general, for "to be potent", and at a later stage for a divine force which, together with other *mana*-like influences, rendered the dead king a ruler in the hereafter. Thus we find here three stages: the sceptre – its power – and finally power in general. When king Tuthmosis III sent his general against Joppa he gave him his sceptre which, like the staffs of even private individuals in Egypt, bore a special name – "adorned with beauty". At Chaeronea, again, the Greeks worshipped Agamemnon's sceptre with sacrifices, while the Romans regarded the spear as the fetish of the god Mars. Whoever undertook a war invoked the sacred lance: *Mars Vigila* – "Mars, Awake!" And like the *hasta*, the *ancile* or shield also, which was believed to have fallen from heaven in the days of Numa, was held to be holy.

4. The last instance leads from the mere brute potency of the thing to its significance as the hoard of a communal essence. For the presence of the *ancile* guaranteed that of the supreme government. Similarly, the *palladium*, originally a stone or double shield, and subsequently the *xoanon* or wooden image of the goddess Athene, was the hoard, the power-object of Troy. Were this lost, the town would perish. In ancient Israel the same rôle was filled by the ark of the covenant. The Fox Indians, too, possessed a "sacred bundle", consisting of an owl, a tobacco pipe, two turtles, a firestone, and a flute, which assured the tribal power. The Amandebele of South Africa had their *Mamchali*, a small basket

without an opening containing "holy" things, a genuine palladium; if it fell into hostile hands it proved itself invulnerable. On Taliabo (Sula Island) there is a sacred spot where a number of dishes, shells, etc., are preserved in the soil; only one man knows where this is, and in case of plague he brings water to the *kampong* or native village in one of the shells. The Indonesians, still further, provide very many instructive examples of this belief in a tribal or communal hoard. The Macassars and Bugis ascribe special significance to the state insignia; whoever possesses these has the country also in his power, for in them the "rulership of the land is as it were concentrated"; during a riot in Luwu the Dutch commanding officer required only to seize the insignia of state to break down opposition immediately. Such objects are of different kinds; old spears, daggers, a Koran, stones, etc. – these must usually have been handed down from the tribal ancestors. The imperial insignia of the Holy Roman Empire possessed a similarly concentrated potency even in the Middle Ages. They were regarded as sacred objects, to be approached in procession, and days when they were exhibited to the people were treated as great festival occasions. To a newly elected emperor, therefore, the possession of the insignia was extremely important; like the weapons of Mars in Rome, they were *pignora imperii* – pledges of the realm.

Not the power of the tribe or realm only, but similarly that of the family was associated with venerable objects. In Indonesia each family has its so-called *pusaka*, objects frequently of very slight value, which are, however, regarded as sacred and bequeathed from father to son. The ancient Germans, too, looked upon clothes, weapons, and jewels as luck-bearers, the family welfare being often intimately connected with so potent an object. The power of the hero's sword, again, which rendered its wielder invincible, became the permanent *motif* of saga, myth and fairy tale.

5. From fetishes amulets are distinguished; these also are certainly containers of power, only as it were in pocket size. Representations of sacred objects, crosses, suns, etc., but also knots intended to hold power together, stones and almost every imagin-

able thing were carried on the body as amulets to ward off danger and attract blessings. Like fetishes, these too can acquire their influence from some holy person or situation; but then they are preferably called relics.

POTENCY AWE TABU

1. The experience of the potency of things or persons may occur at any time; it is by no means confined to specific seasons and occasions. Powerfulness always reveals itself in some wholly unexpected manner; and life is therefore a dangerous affair, full of critical moments. If then one examines them more closely, even the most ordinary events, the customary associations with one's neighbors, or similarly one's long familiar tasks, prove to be replete with "mystic" interconnections. We may say indeed (as, e.g., Marett maintains) that the explanation of any fact, however natural it may appear, is ultimately always "mystic". But we should probably express ourselves in more primitive fashion if we completely ignored our own scheme of explanation in terms of single causes, and in place of this interpreted life as a broad current of mighty powers whose existence we do not specifically observe, but which occasionally makes itself conspicuous by either the damming or the flooding of its waters. If, for instance, one of the Toradja tribes in Celebes is preparing for an expedition and an earthen pot is broken, then they remain at home, saying that it is *measa*. This may be translated as "a sign": only not in any rationalistic sense as indicating some future misfortune, but that the current of life has been interrupted: if then one thing has been broken, why not more? Similarly, when an Ewe tribesman finds refuge from his enemies on a white ant-hill he ascribes his escape to the power residing there. Thus the place, the action, the person in which the power reveals itself receive a specific character. Bearers of *mana,* for example, are sharply distinguished from the rest of the world: they are self-sufficient. By the Greeks, similarly, a body struck by lightning was regarded as holy, ἱερός, because powerfulness was manifested in it.

Objects, person, times, places, or actions charged with Power are called *tabu* (*tapu*), a word from the same cultural domain as *mana*. It indicates "what is expressly named", "exceptional", while the verb *tapui* means "to make holy". *Tabu* is thus a sort of warning: "Danger! High voltage!" Power has been stored up, and we must be on our guard. The *tabu* is the expressly authenticated condition of being replete with power, and man's reaction to it should rest on a clear recognition of this potent fullness, should maintain the proper distance and secure protection.

The *tabu* is observed in different ways and with regard to highly contrasted objects. To the Greek the king and the *foreigner* or *stranger* appeared as objects of *aidos,* of awe, to be duly respected by keeping one's distance. Almost everywhere the king is looked upon as powerful, so that he should be approached only with the greatest caution, while the foreigner, bearer of a power unknown and therefore to be doubly feared, stands on an equal footing with an enemy; *hostis* is both stranger or foreigner, and enemy. One may either kill the alien, if one is in a position so to do, or bid him welcome; but in no case are his coming and going to be regarded with indifference. *Greeting* is therefore a religious act, intended to intercept the first onset of the power, and into which the name of God is introduced or to which an appeasing influence is attached (e.g. the Semitic peace greeting: *adieu*: *Grüssgott*). *Hospitality*, therefore, as well as *war*, is a religious act, intended either to repel the alien power or to neutralize it. *Sex life* is also full of potency, *woman* being distinguished from man by mysterious peculiarities; thus the *veil* served as a defence even before it became a symbol of bashfulness. Everything concerned with the sexual is "exceptional": when one is sexually impure one must be careful, and not, e.g., undertake any important matter such as war. Nor should one approach a menstruating woman, who is often excluded from a cult for this very reason: her potent influence would antagonize the power to be acquired by means of the cult; hence the formula: *hostis vinctus mulier virgo exesto* – "Let every stranger, bound person, woman or virgin stand aside" – associated with certain Roman sacrifices. Similarly as regards Cato's warning in connection with the "vow for the cattle: a woman may not take part in this offering nor see how it is performed". Some one day, again, or series of days, is regarded as being more potent than others. Sabbath, Sunday, Christmas Day and their primitive and heathen equivalents are sacred: no work is done, or at least no important affairs undertaken. Thus the battle of Thermopylae was lost because the "holy days" (ἱερομηνίνα) imposed on the Spartans a cessation of hostilities; and for the same reason they arrived at Marathon too late. On very sacred days even the slightest labor was forbidden; for critical times must never be allowed to pass unnoticed but must be met by some relevant exceptional behavior on man's own part, such as fasting. *Tabu*, then, is the avoidance of deed and of word, springing from awe in the presence of Power. Words concerning critical affairs like hunting, war, sex intercourse, should not be uttered, but rather be replaced by a specially elaborated *tabu* language, remnants of which we still retain in our sportsmen's slang and thieves' jargon. Even a peculiar women's terminology occurs side by side with the men's.

But the mere avoidance, as such, of potency cannot suffice. Among the Kaian of Central Borneo, for example, neither man nor woman may touch slaughtered fowl during the woman's pregnancy, nor may the man pound the soil, etc.; to our minds the connection and the purpose here are obscure. The *tabu*, however, is anything but a measure of utility: Power has revealed itself, either as cessation or as superfluity. It is therefore not only a question of avoiding it, but also of thinking of some defence against it. Sometimes the mode of protection is intelligible to us, as with the veil or some sort of ritual or discipline such as fasting; often, however, we cannot fathom it at all. Associations then appear which we moderns quite fail to understand, and feelings to which we are wholly insusceptible. But even when we do succeed, what we regard as a causative connection does not emerge, just as little as there arises an emotional reaction in the sense of our reverence or devotion, though both these may be incorporated in the primitive attitude. The *tabu*, further, may be decreed; some power-bearer, a king or priest, can endow an object with his own power and proclaim a season of potency; in Polynesia the king's messenger thus announces the *tabu*:

Tabu – no one may leave his house!
Tabu – no dog may bark!
Tabu – no cock may crow!
Tabu – no pig may grunt!
Sleep – sleep, till the *tabu* is past!

In Manipur, in Assam, the village priest ordains a similar communal *tabu* called *genna*; the gates of the village are closed; the friend outside must stay there, and the stranger who may chance to be within remains; the men cook their own food and eat it without the women. All the food *tabus* are carefully observed; trading and catching fish, hunting, mowing grass, and felling trees are forbidden. Thus an intentionally evoked interruption of life occurs: the moment is critical, one holds one's breath! At particularly sacred times, in fact, holiday-making still retains a ritual air even in some European rural districts. In Dutch Gelderland on Christmas Eve fifty years ago, for example, everything indoors was carefully arranged; neither plow nor harrow might be left outside, all implements being brought into the barns and the gates leading to the fields closed. Everything must be locked up and under cover in its right place, "otherwise *'Derk met den beer'* (the wild huntsmen) would take it with them".

Violation of the *tabu* brought in its train not punishment, but an automatic reaction of Power; it was quite unnecessary to inflict any penalties when Power assailed one spontaneously. With the best intentions, for instance, Uzzah wished to support the ark of the covenant; the touch of the sacred object, however, entailed death. But it was no divine arbitrariness, and still less divine justice, that struck him down: it was the purely dynamic anger of the Lord, אף־יהוה. Even a comic sidelight is instructive here: In Thuringia every form of work was most strictly prohibited on "Golden (Trinity) Sunday"; and a lad who, in spite of this, had sewn a button on the trousers on the holy day could only with the utmost difficulty save himself from death by a lightning stroke the next day, by sacrificing the garment concerned and allowing it to slip into the water, when it was promptly carried off by Nemesis. From our viewpoint, of course, only the lad was guilty and not his trousers! But Power questions not as to guilt or innocence; it reacts, exactly as the electric current shocks anyone who carelessly touches the wire. In Central Celebes death is the penalty for incest, not, however, as a punishment, but merely as a means of limiting the evil results of the outrage to the delinquents; that the latter should die was regarded as a matter of course. Death by being cast from the *Saxum Tarpeium*, which the Romans inflicted upon traitors, was likewise not punishment but a reaction of the Power; the *tribuni plebis*, who were sacrosanct, that is, the bearers of a most formidable potency, appear as the executioners, while whoever fell, without dying as a result, saved his life; "it is a matter less of an execution than of an intentional accident".

Naturally the effectiveness of the *tabu* was believed in without any reservations whatever. A Maori would die of hunger rather than light a fire with the lighting utensils of a chief, and Howitt heard of a Kurnai boy who had stolen some opossum meat and eaten this before the food *tabus* permitted. The tribal elders persuaded him that he would never be a man; he lay down, and in three weeks was dead. Similar examples might be multiplied indefinitely.

2. We characterize the distance between the potent and the relatively powerless as the relationship between *sacred* and *profane*, or secular. The "sacred" is what has been placed within boundaries, the exceptional (Latin *sanctus*); its powerfulness creates for it a place of its own. "Sacred" therefore means neither completely moral nor, without further qualification, even desirable or praiseworthy. On the contrary, sacredness and even impurity may be identical: in any event the potent is dangerous. The Roman *tribunus plebis*, just referred to, was so sacred, *sacrosanctus*, that merely to meet him on the street made one impure. Among the Maori also *tabu* means "polluted" just as much as "holy"; but in any case it carries a prohibition with it, and therefore prescribes keeping one's proper distance. It is, then, scarcely correct to regard the contrast between sacred and secular as developing out of the distinction between threatening danger and what is not perilous. Power has its own specific quality which forcibly impresses men as dangerous. Yet the perilous is

not sacred, but rather the sacred dangerous. In a quite classical way Söderblom has presented the contrast between holy and profane as the primal and governing antithesis in all religion, and has shown how the old viewpoint, that Wonder, θαυμάζειν, is the beginning of Philosophy, can be applied with yet greater justice to Religion. For whoever is confronted with potency clearly realizes that he is in the presence of some quality with which in his previous experience he was never familiar, and which cannot be evoked from something else but which, *sui generis* and *sui juris*, can be designated only by religious terms such as "sacred" and "numinous". All these terms have a common relationship in that they indicate a firm conviction, but at the same time no definite conception, of the completely different, the absolutely distinct. The first impulse aroused by all this is avoidance, but also seeking: man should avoid Power, but he should also seek it. No longer can there be a "why" or "wherefore" here; and Söderblom is undeniably correct when, in this connection, he defines the essence of all religion by saying that it is mystery. Of that aspect there was already a deep subjective assurance even when no god was invoked. For to religion "god" is a late comer.

3. In the human soul, then, Power awakens a profound feeling of awe which manifests itself both as fear and as being attracted. There is no religion whatever without terror, but equally none without love, or that *nuance* of being attracted which corresponds to the prevailing ethical level. For the simplest form of religious feeling Marett has suggested the fine word Awe, and Otto the term *Scheu*, which is somewhat less comprehensive; the Greek *aidōs* too is most pertinent. The expression adopted must be a very general one, since it is a question of establishing an attitude which includes the whole personality at all its levels and in countless *nuances*. Physical shuddering, ghostly horror, fear, sudden terror, reverence, humility, adoration, profound apprehension, enthusiasm – all these lie *in nuce* within the awe experienced in the presence of Power. And because these attitudes show two main tendencies, one away from Power and the other toward it, we speak of the *ambivalent* nature of awe.

Of course *tabu* means a prohibition, and Power reveals itself first of all always as something to be avoided. Everywhere, too, the prohibition announces itself earlier than the command; but Freud has very ably shown how the former always implies the latter. Man is fully conscious only of the prohibition, while the command usually remains unrecognized. What we hate we love, and what we truly love we could at the same time hate. "For each man kills the thing he loves", said Oscar Wilde, and this is far more than a brilliant phrase. In the presence of the something different which we recognize as "Wholly Other", our conduct is always ambivalent. Love may be described as an attempt to force oneself into the place of the other; hate, as the fear of love.

But whether the sacred releases feelings of hate and fear, or those of love and reverence, it always confronts man with some absolute task. The *tabu* has therefore, and not without justification, been described as the oldest form of the categorical imperative. Of course we must not think of Kant's argument in this connection. Nevertheless, *tabu* and categorical imperative have in common the character of complete irrationality as well as absoluteness. "Thou shalt" – what one should do is a secondary issue; why one should do it is not a question at all. Confronted with Power, which he experiences as being of completely contrasted nature, man apprehends its absolute demand. An irruption occurs in his life, and he is drawn in two directions: he is seized with dread, and yet he loves his dread.

4. Having once established itself, awe develops into *observance*; and we can trace this advance in the Roman concept *religio*, which originally signified nothing more than *tabu*. In the description of an eerie place, in Virgil, the primal awe still glimmers: the sacred grove of the Capitol has a "dread awe" (*religio dira.*) But the ancient shudder lives also in custom: a sudden death is a *portentum* – a sign of potency that enters *in religionem populi*, or as we should say, "renders the people impure". It was, then, preferable to put up with a ceremonial repetition of the consular election, rather than permit a *tabu* to remain in force over the people. Again, an illness is thus exorcised: *hanc religionem evoco educo excanto de istis membris* ... "I call out, I draw out, I sing out, this pollution from these limbs". Thus we can com-

prehend the definition given by Masurius Sabinus: *"religiosum* is that which because of some sacred quality is removed and withdrawn from us". This is, precisely, the sacred; and constant regard to it is the chief element in the relationship between man and all that is extraordinary. The most probable derivation of the word is from *relegere* – to observe or pay attention; *homo religiosus*, therefore, is the antithesis to *homo negligens.*

We can now understand, still further, how it is that awe, in the long run, must become pure observance, and intense dread mere formalism. In this respect Freud's conclusions are wholly justified: primeval prohibitions "descend, like a hereditary disease". Nevertheless, Freud has forgotten that no matter how much man's practical religious conduct may thus be governed by transmissible *tabus*, still profound awe and "aweful" potency must have subsisted to begin with. Observance, then, is just benumbed awe which, at any moment, can be revived. Even in our own country people's "ancient custom", in Indonesian *adat* and in court and university ceremonial, there still lives something of the awe of contact with Power. At the court of Philip IV of Spain, who died in 1665, an officer who freed the queen from the stirrup of her runaway horse had to go into exile; an incident in which it is obvious how the touch *tabu* had developed into court etiquette.

Even when vivid awe has been lost, observance continues to serve highly practical purposes. In Indonesia and Polynesia, for instance, the *tabu* is a means of asserting unquestionable right of possession to a piece of ground; some sign indicates the prohibition of stealing it or trespassing on it. We should none the less be quite mistaken in concluding that the *tabu* came into being by virtue of these purely utilitarian considerations, or even that it was invented by the great ones of the earth for their own profit and benefit. Frequently it may certainly be mere routine practice, but it always has intense awe as its presupposition. The "sign" again resembles our warning notices so closely that it may readily be confused with them; but the punishment threatened by the police is omitted, although it will doubtless appear of its own accord: on Amboina the trespasser is smitten with leprosy; and further, the prohibition itself is not rationally grounded; on the same island a rough sketch of a female sex organ – that is, something particularly "potent" – replaces the legal notification. "Property" in its primitive sense, then, is something quite different from what it is with us – it is a "mystical" relation between owner and owned; the possessor is not the *beatus possidens*, but the depository of a power that is superior to himself.

Once the belief in tabu has completely become mere observance, an empty shell, then man breaks his fetters. In the Euripidean *Herakles* neither Nature nor pure humanity can be defiled by the *tabu* of death; Herakles need only take off the veil and show his head to the light:

> Eternal is the element:
> Mortal, thou canst not pollute the heavens.

Again:

> No haunting curse can pass from friend to friend.

This is essentially the "modern" feeling, which opposes power in nature and personality.

4

A SUPERNATURALISTIC DESCRIPTION

Jacques Maritain

Editor's Introduction

VAN DER LEEUW'S description of power emphasizes the continuity between the sacred and the profane. Although it is true that these are two spheres, they are, nevertheless, two dimensions of the human environment. In the following essay, Jacques Maritain emphasizes the discontinuity between the natural order, or the human environment, and the supernatural order, or the realm of the true object of religion.

Maritain chooses to structure his description around the five "ways" to the knowledge of God, or "proofs" for the existence of God, that were advanced by the medieval theologian and philosopher, St. Thomas Aquinas (c. 1225–1274). Before discussing the five "ways" specifically, however, Maritain describes the natural knowledge of God. This knowledge is natural in the sense that it does not require some kind of special revelation but is simply human knowledge, like knowledge about trees or chairs. Moreover, it is pre-philosophic; it does not result from highly sophisticated reflection but is an awareness that is a basic part of the everyday, normal knowing of any human being. This distinction between the pre-philosophic and the more technical, philosophic knowledge is parallel to van der Leeuw's distinction between the first immediate awareness of power and the secondary reflection on that awareness. In the first part of his essay,

Maritain, like van der Leeuw, is attempting to call our attention to an element common to all our perceiving and knowing, but an element that we often overlook.

Maritain calls this common element "the primordial intuition of being". He is referring to the experience of wonder and amazement that comes to us at times when we suddenly become excitingly aware of the fact that there is something and not nothing. This acknowledgment of the basic fact of being is on the one hand more than a recognition of something, as, for example, when I recognize that an object coming within my vision is a car. It is an awareness of the fact that the car is a real thing – that it participates in being. In *Existence and the Existent*, Maritain writes: "What counts is to have seen that existence is not a simple empirical fact but a primitive datum for the mind itself, opening to the mind an infinite supra-observable field – in a word, the primary and super-intelligible source of intelligibility."

This intuition of being does not occur apart from perception of things (beings), but it is not identical with that perception. Just as we can perceive a person without knowing who it is, we can perceive things without being aware of the fact that they exist. Then, suddenly, something is added to our perception. We recognize who the other person is. We haven't perceived anything new, but we have recognized them. Similarly, we do not perceive being, but we recognize that a thing *is there*, that it exists in its own right apart from us.

Maritain elaborates this immediate recognition or intuition by describing three simultaneous components. First, there is the awareness of the existence of something "out there". Second, there is the awareness that the something out there implies my own existence as perceiver, but an existence conditioned by the object. This self-awareness is a self-awareness of a self defined by its context. (The existence of the object is also conditioned by my own presence – it is defined as an object-for-me.) Third, there is the intuition of unconditioned existence, the recognition that awareness of being conditioned carries with it a vague hunch about unconditioned existence. My own being is being-with-nothingness, pure being, prior to and beyond the contamination of contingency. But since my own being is a mixture of being and non-being and I am a part of the world, the world is also contaminated by non-being. This means that the pure being implied by my own contaminated being cannot be the world as a whole, but is somehow outside the world.

Modern men have difficulty in grasping the primordial intuition of being because science has produced a *maya*, an ignorance, which blinds them to the original perception. They have become so obsessed with scientific explanations that they have become insensitive to the primary experiences which their science is an effort to explain. They must overcome scientific learning in order to be able to perceive. Science arose as a window into Nature. Modern men have become enamored with the window rather than with what is visible through it.

Maritain locates the origin of religion in the awareness of being whereas van der Leeuw locates it in the awareness of power, but the mental process of immediate recognition is identical. And in each case the process of recognition and the object perceived are described phenomenologically. After this phenomenological description of the primordial intuition of being, Maritain turns to a description of the mental activity that occurs immediately following this initial recognition, just as van der Leeuw turned to "theorizing about power". For Maritain, this reflection can best be grasped in terms of the arguments for the existence of God.

Three points must be kept in mind if one is to approach Maritain's arguments appropriately.

1. When Maritain discusses the existence of God, he does not mean to imply that God belongs to that class of objects which have existence as a characteristic. That would make God into a member of a class – granted the largest class we know about, but nevertheless, one of a common genus. The proofs are sometimes understood in this way. Then they are analogous to the following syllogism: Fido is a dog; dogs are canine; therefore, Fido is canine. This, however, is not Maritain's intention. He contends that God exists in a *way* that is quite different from the way in which other things exist. While he is not willing to go as far as to say that existence is an inappropriate predicate for God, he does

insist that the argument is based on a recognition of the fact that God's existence is *sui generis*.

As a matter of fact, rather than showing God belongs to the class of objects that exist, the purpose of the arguments in the classical and traditional form is closer to exactly the opposite: to argue that God is not like anything in the world. What do things in the world have in common? Some things have life, some a particular color, some color itself, some materiality or spatiality. But all have existence in common. All objects in the world exist in one way or another, some as ideas, some as extended objects, some as feelings, etc. The arguments for the existence of God, traditionally, have attempted to say that God is not one of these things. They all may or may not exist. Their existence is contingent. God must exist; his existence is necessary.

2. The purpose of the proofs, according to Maritain, is not to provide knowledge at the end that we did not possess at the beginning, nor is it to establish the certitude of a proposition that was previously in doubt. They are elaborations of the primordial intuition of being that one already has. "... The philosophical proofs of the existence of God are like a decisive unfolding or development, on the level of 'scientific' or 'perfect' rational knowledge, of the natural pre-philosophic knowledge implied in the primitive intuition of the act of being; and because, on a level much more profound than that of the confused and inchoate 'philosophy' of common sense, this root knowledge, even when it is not yet explicitly awakened, is still present in us in a state of unconscious tension and virtuality."

The proofs are "a development and an unfolding" of the natural, primordial knowledge, or intuition of God. That is, they expand the immediate intuition into discursive and manageable chunks. They, in a sense, replay the complex primordial intuition in slow motion so that all its contents and implications can be examined more easily.

In investigating this primordial intuition one is not investigating merely some dimension of the mind nor some part of the experienced world. He is investigating a part of reality itself. The laws of being, Maritain says, "have as broad an extension as being itself". This important paragraph is a direct challenge to psychologism on the one hand (which seeks to explain logical maxims as probabilities based on a number of similar empirical observations) and to idealism on the other (which seeks to explain the laws of logic and nature as products of the way the mind works). These logical maxims refer to beings in themselves.

It is possible to understand this attack on psychologism and idealism of Maritain's as simply the assertion of a rather old-fashioned metaphysical dogmatism that does not take full cognizance of the recent investigations of psychology, to say nothing of recent empirical philosophy. On the other hand, it can be understood as arising out of a quite different orientation. Maritain asserts that, as they appear to us and as we use them, the laws of being are neither empirical probabilities nor mental constructs. They are for us, as we use them, characteristics of being itself. It is impossible for us to think of them in any other way. To explain them as empirical probabilities or as mental constructs does not take away from or add to this use-appearance they have for us. The situation is analogous to the attempt to psychologize one's emotions. To suggest to a person who is in love that his emotion is merely a result of enzyme and hormone activity in various segments of his brain bears absolutely no relationship whatsoever to his experiences of being in love. He experiences love for the beloved, not enzymes in motion. The psychologizing of the fears of the patient, therefore, has no bearing on the mental contents of the patient. Mental attitudes cannot be reduced to physical properties. The mental reality of the logical rules and intuitive knowledge Maritain discusses, therefore, is that they are laws of being.

3. Maritain's distinction between horizontal and vertical regression is absolutely crucial if his arguments are to be understood. The cosmological arguments for the existence of God have suffered a grave injustice at the hands of people who have distorted them into a naïve theory of the impossibility of an infinite regress. This naïve argument says that it may be possible to account for present realities in terms of past realities, but if one goes back far enough he must arrive at a first cause and that first

cause is God. On the contrary, Maritain argues that the notion of an infinite regress is implied in and demanded by the notion of cause and effect. By definition and by the laws of logic, the regress into the past in terms of cause and effect is infinite. Any cause by definition is also the effect of a prior cause. In this chain there can be no final termination. The first cause Maritain discusses is not the last cause in a horizontal regression. It is a reality outside the chain of horizontal regression and is necessarily implied by the infinitude of the horizontal regressive chain. This distinction is unfortunately not evident in the first argument Maritain presents, although it is made explicit in the second argument and especially in the commentary marked 8A(*a*) to the second argument.

The modern perversion of the cosmological argument really says that at some point the cause–effect sequence must be broken or come to an end. At this break or end one finds a first cause substituted for the expected secondary cause. Maritain and St. Thomas, on the other hand, emphasize the difference between the first cause and all secondary causes. God, the first cause, is not to be found in the world of secondary causes. The first cause is always outside the natural order.

Section 10A(*a*) illuminates the difference between horizontal and vertical regression. Maritain argues that the criterion of valuation is of a different order from the items it evaluates. If I judge A to be better than B, the criterion by which I make that selection is neither A nor B. At this point it is immaterial to ask where the criterion comes from or to question its validity. It may be an abstraction deduced from a random selection of varying elements and have no inherent being of its own, but the important thing is that the criterion is of a different order from the things it is used to evaluate.

Following St. Thomas, Maritain calls the knowledge we have of God *indirect knowledge*. For the modern mentality, there is no such thing as indirect knowledge. Either we have direct, experiential knowledge, or we have a blind faith that is based on authority and can make no claim to be actual knowledge. Maritain suggests that there is another kind of knowledge, indirect knowledge, in which we do not have the object of our knowledge before our eyes, but nevertheless do know something about it. This indirect knowledge is not deductive, in the sense that we might deduce something about an electron from observing the path it makes in a cloud chamber, but is immediate and intuitive. This is not the magic-like intuition of extra-sensory perception, but is merely a common form of knowing that we tend to overlook. It is the knowledge of essences that the phenomenologist refers to. When we know something about triangles, we know something about more than the particular triangle we have before us; we know something about triangles as a type or whole, even though all we have before our eyes is one particular triangle.

The proofs for the existence of God do not provide direct knowledge of God. They simply suggest that things in the world are effects; that they are not self-explanatory. Things in the world need a cause beyond. The proofs show that the world is a sign of something beyond. They speak of that something indirectly.

Maritain and St. Thomas at this point stand in the Augustinian tradition. St. Augustine insisted that men cannot see God, they can only see the world in the light of God's presence. It is as if we were in a room looking at objects illuminated by a colored light behind us. We cannot see the light but can know it by the fact that we can see the objects before us. Similarly, the knowledge of God is indirect. All men can ever see is the world. But they can know of its essential incompleteness. God does not, however, fill in the gaps in the incompleteness. The gaps remain. The mistake of the naïve interpretation of the cosmological arguments was to plug God into the gaps in Nature. But the real intention of the arguments is to say that the gaps cannot be filled. The world we see is essentially incomplete.

Jacques Maritain is one of the foremost contemporary interpreters of St. Thomas as well as an outstanding philosopher in his own right. He was born in Paris in 1882. He was converted to Roman Catholicism from Protestantism in 1906 and in 1914 was called to the chair of modern philosophy at the Institut catholique de Paris. From 1945 to 1948 he was French ambassador to the

Vatican. Afterwards he taught at Princeton University until his retirement in 1956. He has published over fifty philosophical works as well as numerous articles. Among them are *Existence and the Existent, The Range of Reason,* and *Approaches to God.* The following selections are taken from Chapters 1 and 2 of the latter.

Approaches to God*

THE PRIMORDIAL WAY OF APPROACH

Natural or Prephilosophic Knowledge of God

1. FROM PLATO AND Aristotle to St. Anselm and St. Thomas Aquinas, to Descartes and Leibniz, philosophers have proposed proofs or demonstrations of the existence of God, or, as Thomas Aquinas more modestly puts it, *ways* through which the intellect is led to the certitude of His existence. All are highly conceptualized and rationalized proofs, specifically philosophic ways of approach. Kant rightly criticized the proof advanced by Descartes (what is called "the ontological argument"), but wrongly claimed to reduce all the ways of demonstration to this particular proof. That was a great error; for the five ways indicated by Thomas Aquinas are completely independent of the ontological argument, and stand firm in spite of all criticism.

However, it is not these highly conceptualized, rationalized, and specifically philosophical ways of approach which I should like to consider at present. When St. Paul affirmed that:

that which is known of God is manifest in them. For God hath manifested it unto them. For the invisible things of Him, from the creation of the world, are clearly seen, being understood by the things that are made; His eternal power also, and divinity ...

he was thinking not only of scientifically elaborated or specific-

* Jacques Maritain, from Ch. 1 and 2 of *Approaches to God*, tr. Peter O'Reilly, Harper & Row, New York, 1954, and Allen & Unwin Ltd., London, 1956. Copyright by Jacques Maritain, 1954.

ally philosophical ways of establishing the existence of God. He had in mind also and above all the natural knowledge of the existence of God to which the vision of created things leads the reason of every man, philosopher or not. It is this doubly *natural* knowledge of God I wish to take up here. It is natural not only in the sense that it belongs to the rational order rather than to the supernatural order of faith, but also in the sense that it is *prephilosophic* and proceeds by the natural or, so to speak, instinctive manner proper to the first apperceptions of the intellect prior to every philosophical or scientifically rationalized elaboration.

Before entering into the sphere of completely formed and articulated knowledge, in particular the sphere of metaphysical knowledge, the human mind is indeed capable of a prephilosophical knowledge which is *virtually metaphysical*. Therein is found the first, the primordial way of approach through which men become aware of the existence of God.

2. Here everything depends on the natural intuition of being – on the intuition of that act of existing which is the act of every act and the perfection of every perfection, in which all the intelligible structures of reality have their definitive actuation, and which overflows in activity in every being and in the intercommunication of all beings.

Let us rouse ourselves, let us drop living in dreams or in the magic of images and formulas, of words, or signs and practical symbols. Once a man has been awakened to the reality of existence and of his own existence, when he has really perceived that formidable, sometimes elating, sometimes sickening or maddening fact *I exist*, he is henceforth possessed by the intuition of being and the implications it bears with it.

Precisely speaking, this primordial intuition is both the intuition of *my* existence and of the existence *of things*, but first and foremost of the existence of things. When it takes place, I suddenly realize that a given entity – man, mountain, or tree – exists and exercises this sovereign activity *to be* in its own way, in an independence of *me* which is total, totally self-assertive and totally implacable. And at the same time I realize that *I* also exist, but as thrown back into my loneliness and frailty by this other existence by which things assert themselves and in which I have positively no part, to which I am exactly as naught. And no doubt, in face of my existence, others have the same feeling of being frail and threatened. As for me, confronted with others, it is my own existence that I feel to be fragile and menaced, exposed to destruction and death. Thus the primordial intuition of being is the intuition of the solidity and inexorability of existence; and, second, of the death and nothingness to which *my* existence is liable. And third, in the same flash of intuition, which is but my becoming aware of the intelligible value of being, I realize that this solid and inexorable existence, perceived in anything whatsoever, implies – I do not yet know in what form, perhaps in the things themselves, perhaps separately from them – some absolute, irrefragable existence, completely free from nothingness and death. These three leaps – by which the intellect moves first to actual existence as asserting itself independently of me; and then from this sheer objective existence to my own threatened existence; and finally from my existence spoiled with nothingness to absolute existence – are achieved within the same unique intuition, which philosophers would explain as the intuitive perception of the essentially analogical content of the first concept, the concept of Being.

Next – this is the second stage – a prompt, spontaneous reasoning, as natural as this intuition (and as a matter of fact more or less involved in it), immediately springs forth as the necessary fruit of such a primordial apperception, and as enforced by and under its light. It is a reasoning without words, which cannot be expressed in articulate fashion without sacrificing its vital concentration and the rapidity with which it takes place. I see first that my being is liable to death; and second, that it is dependent on the totality of Nature, on the universal whole of which I am a part. I see that Being-with-nothingness, such as my own being, implies, in order that it should be, Being-without-nothingness – that absolute existence which I confusedly perceived from the beginning as involved in my primordial intuition of existence. But then the universal whole of which I am a part is itself Being-with-nothingness, by the very fact that I am part of it. And from this it follows finally that since this universal whole does not exist by virtue of itself, it must be that Being-without-nothingness exists apart from it. There is another Whole – a separate one – another Being, transcendent and self-sufficient and unknown in itself and activating all beings, which is Being-without-nothingness, that is, self-subsisting Being, Being existing through itself.

Thus the internal dynamism of the intuition of existence, or of the intelligible value of Being, causes me to see that absolute existence or Being-without-nothingness transcends the totality of Nature. And there I am, confronted with the existence of God.

3. This is not a new approach to God; it is human reason's eternal way of approaching God. What is new is the manner in which the modern mind has become aware of the simplicity and liberating power, of the natural and in some way intuitive character, of this eternal approach. The science of the ancients was steeped in philosophy. Their scientific imagery was a pseudo-ontological imagery. Consequently, there was a kind of continuum between their knowledge of the physical world and their knowledge of God. This latter knowledge was seen as the summit of the former, a summit which had to be scaled by the multiple paths of the causal connections at work in the sublunar world and the celestial spheres. And the sense of Being, which everywhere and always ruled their thought, was for them an atmosphere too habitual to be regarded as a surprising gift. At the same time, the natural intuition of existence was so strong in them that their proofs of God could take the form of the most conceptualized and the most rationalized scientific demonstrations, and be offered as a skilful unfolding of logical necessities, without losing the inner energy of that intuition. This logical machinery was surreptitiously enlivened by the deep-seated intuition of Being.

We are in quite a different position now. In order to reach physical reality in its own enigmatic way and to conquer the world of phenomena, our science has become a kind of *Maya* – a Maya which succeeds and makes us masters of Nature. But the sense of Being is absent from it. Thus when we come to experience the impact of Being upon our mind, it appears to us as a kind of intellectual revelation, and we become keenly aware both of its awakening and liberating power, and of the fact that it involves a knowledge separate from the sphere of knowledge peculiar to our science. At the same time we realize that the knowledge of God, before being developed in logical and perfectly conceptualized demonstrations, is first and foremost a natural fruit of the intuition of existence, and that it imposes itself upon our mind through the imperative force of this intuition.

In other words, we have become aware of the fact that in its primordial vitality the movement of the human reason in its approach to God is neither a pure intuition (which would be supra-human), nor the kind of philosophical reasoning of a technical type through which it will be expressed in its achieved form, and which at each of its stages is pregnant with conflicts and with problems to clarify. In its primordial vitality the movement of the human reason in its approach to God is a *natural* reasoning, that is, intuitive-like or irresistibly maintained in, and vitalized by, the intellectual flash of the intuition of existence. In this natural reasoning it is just this intuition of existence which, seizing in some existing reality Being-with-nothingness, by the same stroke makes the mind grasp the necessity of Being-without-nothingness. And nowhere is there any problem involved, because the illumining power of this intuition takes possession of the mind and obliges it to see, in such a way that the mind proceeds naturally, within a primordial intuitive flash, and from imperative certainty to imperative certainty. I believe that from Descartes to Kierkegaard the effort of modern thought – to the extent that it has not completely repudiated metaphysics and if it is cleansed of the irrationalism which has gradually corrupted it – tends to such an awareness of the specific *naturalness* of man's knowledge of God, definitely more profound than any scientifically developed logical process, and an awareness of the primordial and simple intuitiveness in which this knowledge originates.

4. I have just tried to describe the manner in which this natural prephilosophic knowledge spontaneously proceeds. It involves a reasoning, but a reasoning after the fashion of an intuitive grasp, bathed in the primordial intuition of existence. Let us say that this natural knowledge is a kind of *innocent* knowledge, a knowledge free of all dialectic. Such a knowledge is rich in certitude, a certitude that is indeed compelling, although it exists in an imperfect logical state. It has not yet crossed the threshold of *scientific* demonstration, whose certitude is critical and implies that the difficulties inherent in the question have been surmounted through a scrutiny of the rational connections and necessities involved. Such natural knowledge is still in happy ignorance of these difficulties and of all the *videtur quod non's*: because scientific certitude and the objections to be met – and the replies to the objections – all come into the world together.

It appears, therefore, that the philosophic proofs of the existence of God, let us say the five ways of Thomas Aquinas, are a development and an unfolding of this natural knowledge, raised to the level of scientific discussion and scientific certitude. And they normally presuppose this natural knowledge, not with regard to the logical structure of the demonstration, but with regard to the existential condition of the thinking subject. If the preceding observations are true, it would be necessary, before proposing the philosophic proofs, to be assured in so far as possible (by trying, where need be, to aid in such an awakening) that the minds to which one addresses oneself are alive to the primordial intuition of existence, and conscious of the natural knowledge of God involved in this intuition.

One more remark seems to be called for here. I have just used the expression "the philosophic proofs of the existence of God", and I noted above that St. Thomas Aquinas preferred to use the word *ways*. He had his reasons for this. These ways are proofs, but the words "proof" or "demonstration" may be misunderstood. To prove or to demonstrate is, in everyday usage, to render evident that which of itself was not evident. Now, on the other hand, God is not *rendered evident* by us. He does not receive from us and from our arguments an evidence which He would have lacked. For the existence of God, which is not immediately evident *for us*, is immediately evident *in itself* – more evident in itself than the principle of identity, since it is infinitely more than a predicate contained in the notion of a subject. It is the subject, the divine essence itself (but to know this from immediate evidence, it would be necessary to see God). On the other hand, what our arguments render evident for us is not God Himself, but the testimony of Him contained in his vestiges, His signs or His "mirrors" here below. Our arguments do not give us evidence of the divine existence itself or of the act of existing which is in God and which is God Himself – as if one could have the evidence of His existence without having that of His essence. They give us only evidence of the fact that the divine existence must be affirmed, or of the truth of the attribution of the predicate to the subject in the assertion "God exists".

In short, what we prove when we prove the existence of God is something which infinitely surpasses us – us and our ideas and our proofs. "To demonstrate the existence of God is not to submit Him to our grapplings, nor to define Him, nor to take possession of Him, nor to handle anything else than ideas that are feeble indeed with regard to such an object, nor to judge anything but our own radical dependence. The procedure by which reason demonstrates that God is places reason itself in an attitude of natural adoration and of intelligent admiration." And thus the words "proof" and "demonstration", in reference to the existence of God, must be understood (and in fact are so understood spontaneously) with resonances other than in the current usage – in a sense no less strong as to their rational efficacy but more modest in that which concerns us and more reverential in that which concerns the object. On this condition it remains perfectly legitimate to use them. It is just a matter of marking well the differences in station. This being understood, we shall not hesitate to say "proof" or "demonstration" as well as "way", for all these words are synonymous in the sense we have just specified.

As to the very word *existence*, the existentialist philosophers arbitrarily corrupt its meaning when they say that to exist is "to stand outside oneself". But even in its genuine meaning – to stand "outside its causes" or "outside nothingness" (the etymological sense of the word being *"sistere ex,* that is to say, to stand or to be posited in itself, from an anterior term on which it depends") – the word existence, in order to apply to God, must lose the connotation which thus refers it to created things. It is clear that God does not stand "outside His causes" – as though He were caused; nor "outside nothingness" – as though nothingness preceded God; and that He is not *sistens ex* – as if He depended on some antecedently existing source. Of itself, however, the notion of existence is in no wise restricted to such a connotation, which in fact refers to the analogue that falls first and immediately under our apprehension; from the outset it overflows all pseudo-definitions carried over from this connotation. Just as the notion of being, the notion of existence is of itself, essentially and from the first, an analogous notion, validly applicable to the uncreated as to the created. No doubt, the word being, in contrast to the word existence, does not need to be purified of accidental vestiges due to etymology. Truth to tell, however, the word existence has been spontaneously purified of them, all by itself, and in any event this does not affect at all the meaning itself of the notion. Those who think that one can say "God is", but not "God exists", maintain for being its essential analogicity but refuse it to existence – the strangest of illusions, since being itself is understood only in relation to existence. To say "God is" and "God exists" is to say exactly the same thing. One speaks the language of simple truth in speaking of the ways through which it is shown that God is, or that He *exists*.

PHILOSOPHICAL KNOWLEDGE OF GOD
The Five Ways of St. Thomas

6. What is it, then, that a philosopher ought to know so as to be in condition to grasp on the level of critical reflection the demonstrative value of the philosophical proofs of God's existence?

He ought to know that intellect differs from sense by nature, not just by degree; that what it is looking for in things is Being;

and that Being is, to one degree or another, intelligible or attainable by the intellect (otherwise, only fools would philosophize).

He ought to know that the being of things is not one and the same in all things, but differs in each, while being grasped in the same idea of Being and expressed by the same word (this is what Thomists call the analogy of being and of the transcendentals, i.e., of the objects of thought which overflow every genus and every category); and that, in regions into which the experience of the senses cannot lead us, the being of things which cannot be seen or touched is nevertheless knowable to the human intellect (which, of course, first set out from experience), not, indeed, as if our ideas grasped it immediately, but rather because certain of our ideas, by reason of their very object, pass beyond experience and reach things which are invisible through the relation which unites them to things visible – the relation of likeness which things unseen bear to the world of visible things. (It is this that Thomists call knowledge by analogy.)

He ought to know that the laws of being have as broad an extension as being itself: thus the principle of identity – every being is what it is – is valid over the whole extent of being, absolutely speaking, and the principle of causality holds for the whole extent of being that envelops, in any degree, contingency or mutability. He ought to know that the principle of causality – everything which is contingent has a cause, or again everything which is, without having in itself the whole reason of its intelligibility, is by that token intelligible through another thing – is neither the expression of a simple mental habit acquired as the result of observing empirical sequences and thus bearing on functional connections between phenomena, nor, as Kant would have it, a "synthetic *a priori* judgment" whose necessity follows upon the structure of our mind and whose range is limited to the world of experience. The principle of causality is a principle "known of itself", known by an immediate intellectual intuition that imposes itself upon the mind by virtue of the intrinsic evidence of the objects conceived, and reaches beyond the world of experience, because the "causes" which it asks for are the *raisons d'être* – not necessarily enclosed in the world of experience, any more than being itself is – demanded by things in so far as their *being* is *contingent*.

One sometimes wonders if the five ways of Thomas Aquinas are but different aspects of one and the same proof or if they constitute five specifically distinct proofs. In my opinion, the proper reply to this question is that the nerve of the proof, the formal principle of the demonstration, is the same in each of the five ways, to wit, the necessity of a first cause which is pure Act or Being, itself subsistent in its own right. From this point of view one could say that they form but one proof presented under different modes or aspects. But that which makes a proof is in reality not its formal principle alone, but also its point of departure and the basis on which it rests. And because the proofs of St. Thomas rest on the facts of experience ("philosophic facts"), and because these facts are typically distinct data discerned in the world of experience, it is necessary to say purely and simply that the five ways of Thomas Aquinas constitute specifically distinct proofs.

7. *The First Way: By Motion*. Our world is the world of becoming. There is no fact more indubitable and more universal than motion or change. What is change? This grain of wheat is not yet that which is going to become; it *can* be what it will become, and when the change is accomplished it will *actually* be that. To change is (for a thing already "in act", but also "in potency" in other respects) to pass from being in potency to being in act.

But how could a thing give to itself what it does not have? In respect to what it merely *can* be but at present *is* not, it is impossible that it makes itself become what as yet it is not. It is something belonging to the order of what is already in act, to wit, the physicochemical energies of the environment, which make the grain of wheat pass from that which it is in potency to that which it will be in act. Everything that moves is moved by another. (Everything which passes from indetermination to determination does so under the action of something else.)

And now, what about the thing already in act, the thing whose action causes another thing to change? Is *it*, itself, subject to change? Does it, in acting, become something more than it was as simply existing? If so, then it is because it is moved to act by another thing. And this latter in its turn, is it moved to act by another agent? Imagine all the agents we please! So long as the agent, from whose action the action of the other agents in the series is suspended, itself passes from potency to act, it is necessary to posit another agent which moves it.

But if there were not a First Agent, the reason for the action of all the others would never be posited in existence; nothing would move anything. One cannot regress from agent to agent without end; it is necessary to stop at a First Agent. And because it is first, it is not itself moved; it is exempt from all becoming, separate from every change and from every possibility of change. It is the absolutely immovable Agent who activates or moves all the rest.

8. *The Second Way: By Efficient Causes*. Having considered that *effect* which is everywhere open to our observation, namely change, let us now turn to *causes* and connections between causes. It is a fact and this is also absolutely general, that there are efficient causes at work in the world, and that these causes are linked to each other or form series in which they are subordinated to one another. Examples always convey to philosophical reasoning a touch of dowdiness, as it were. They are nevertheless necessary. At a bindery one binds a book because the printers have first set it – because the editor has prepared the copy to hand over to them – because a typist has copied the manuscript – and because the author has written the manuscript. A plumcot is used in an advertisement by the commercial artist of a publicity firm because Luther Burbank succeeded one day in crossing the plum tree with the apricot tree and because a book of Darwin on plant variations first aroused Burbank to take up his research. This bee would not visit this rose today if the rose bushes were not in bloom in summer – if the rhythm of vegetal life were not controlled by the diversity of the seasons – and if the revolution of the earth around the sun, the inclination of the ecliptic being what it is, did not produce the diversity of the seasons. Carnivorous animals live on flesh because there are other animals that live

on plants – because plants produce carbohydrates – and because chlorophyll fixes the carbon from the air under the action of light.

Thus, while it is impossible for a thing to be the efficient cause of itself (since it would have to precede its own existence), efficient causes are connected by being complementary to each other, or, in however many varied ways, are conditioned and caused by one another. And this interdependence among causes spreads out in all directions.

It is not possible, however, to go on to infinity from cause to cause. Whatever constellations of causes one may consider apart from the rest within the universal interaction of causes, broaden the field as you will – if there were not a First Cause over and above them on which all the others depend, then all those other causes simply would not be, since they would never have been caused either to be or to act.

It is necessary then to recognize the existence of an uncaused First Cause which exists immutably of itself, above all the particular causes and all their connections.

8A(a). If it is said that Aristotle's principle, "One cannot go on to infinity in the series of causes", is questionable and does not necessitate the mind's assent, because neither the idea of an infinite multitude nor that of a succession without beginning or end, implies contradiction, this is the answer:

It is perfectly true that neither the idea of an infinite multitude nor that of a succession without beginning or end implies contradiction. But the principle *anankè stênai* neither signifies that no infinite multitude could exist, nor that it is necessary to come to a stop at a first cause in time. The "ways" of St. Thomas do not necessarily conclude to a First Cause in time; rather, they lead to a First Cause in being, in the intelligible conditions of things and in the very exercise of causality.

There is no contradiction or impossibility in supposing a merely successive infinite series of causes and events succeeding one another in time. There is no contradiction, for instance, in supposing a time without beginning or end, in the course of which living beings beget other living beings without beginning or end. In such a case, if one has to stop, it is only because one gets tired counting. This kind of series is what might be called a "horizontal" series of *homogeneous* causes or causes *on the same level*, each of which merely accounts for the positing of the following one in *existence*.

But the causes to which the principle we are discussing refers do not merely succeed one another in time (whether there be succession in time or not is accidental, for after all, intelligible connections are of themselves non-temporal). They are logically superordinated to one another and one completes the other in the order of the very *raison d'être* or intelligible conditioning. While going back from one to the other in the past, we also rise in being or intelligible conditioning. In other words these are *heterogeneous* causes or causes *on different levels*. They follow, so to speak, an oblique line; each one, in a certain measure, acounts for the *nature* – or *determination in being* – of the action of the following one.

Accordingly, in regard to them, the principle *anankè stênai* holds with absolute necessity. This is so not by reason of their succession in time, but by reason of the fact that together they set up a particular line of intelligibility or of reasons for existence to which each contributes something, and which cannot be posited unless it depends upon a term beyond which it is impossible to posit any complement of intelligibility; that is to say, unless beyond all particular lines of intelligibility, it is appendant to the "intelligibility-through-itself" of a First Cause, which exists in its own right.

Finally, it is clear that not only the being, but also the action of all other causes, or the causality itself which they exercise, depend at every moment on that First Cause (since it is the supreme reason for all the rest). If then we consider the relation of any efficient cause whatever to the First Cause, we see that this efficient cause would not act at any moment at all if, at that very moment, it were not activated by the First Cause. Every relation of succession in time in the exercise of causality is here eliminated; the causality of the First Cause embraces and dominates without succession the whole succession of time; it is at each moment the ultimate foundation of the *exercise of the causality* of all the agents which act at the same moment in the world. In other words the line of intelligible conditioning or of reason for existence is, so to speak, "vertical", and leads to a cause which is not only heterogeneous, or on a different level, but transcendent or "separate", infinitely different in Nature.

By proceeding from the fact of change and from the fact that efficient causes are connected to the First Cause by way of superordination, we effect a transition to the infinite. This is quite the opposite of a logical movement passing to the infinite from cause to cause (it is rather a logical movement which passes to an

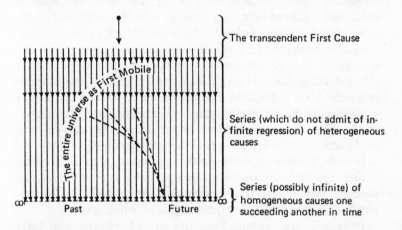

Infinite Cause), and it is possible by reason of the analogical character of being.

Immediately below the First Immobile Mover, Aristotle posited a First Mobile, under which the series of subordinate causes was arranged. But in truth there is no First Mobile, because the First Cause is not first *in* a series, but *beyond* every series. It is the entire universe, with all the natures and clusters of causes dependent upon these natures, which is the "first mobile" in relation to the transcendent First Cause.

9. *The Third Way: By the Contingent and the Necessary.* Although there is chance in the world (that is, events resulting from the meeting of independent causal series), the indeterminism of modern physics, valuable as it may be on the scientific level,

cannot be built up into a philosophical theory. All happenings in
the physical world are determined. This, however, does not prevent their being at the same time contingent to one degree or
another. If the proximate causes which produce them had been
impeded by the intervention of other causal lines in their particular field of action, or if, in the last analysis, the universe were other
than it is, they might not have been produced. In a general way
a thing is contingent when its non-occurrence or its not being
posited in existence is not an impossibility. This definition can be
verified of a thing taken in itself (a star is no more necessary in
itself than a glint of light on a stream), even if it is verified of the
thing considered in relation to the causes which produce it (the
stars have been produced as a *de facto* necessary result of cosmic
evolution). Change implies contingency. A clear sky becomes
clouded; being clear or being clouded are for the sky things whose
non-occurrence is possible. Plants and animals, stars and atoms
are subject to the universal rhythm of destruction and production;
all the forms our eyes perceive are perishable; they can cease to
be. In other words they possess existence in a contingent way.

Is there, however, nothing *but* the contingent, nothing *but* what
is *able not to be*? Can we by thought eliminate *absolutely all
necessity* from things? The hypothesis destroys itself: on the supposition of *pure contingency*, nothing at all would exist.

Imagine a time without beginning or end; imagine that there
was nevertheless absolutely nothing necessary, either in time or
above time: It is then impossible that there *always* was being, for
that for which there is *no necessity* cannot have been *always*. It
is inevitable then that at a certain moment nothing would have
existed. But "if for one moment there be nothing, there will be
nothing eternally", for nothing can come into existence except
through something already existing. And therefore right now
nothing would be existing.

There must be, then, something necessary in things. For example, matter, understood as the common substratum of all
that is subject to destruction and production, must be itself necessary in its permanence through all changes. There must be
necessary laws in Nature. In other words, things cannot be con-

tingent absolutely or in all respects; they must contain intelligible structures or natures necessarily demanding certain effects.

The question now arises regarding whatever may be necessary in the world of things, whether it derives its necessity from no other thing, or, in other terms, whether it is necessary through itself (*per se*) or in essence (*per essentiam*). In the latter case, there would be neither change nor contingency in things. For what is necessary *in essence* excludes every kind of contingency and change, and exists of itself with the infinite plentitude of being, since by definition, it cannot be necessary in one respect only.

But if the necessary in things is not necessary *per se* and in essence, in other words if the necessity of the necessary in things is caused, you can imagine all the causes you wish, each of which, in turn, is itself caused, and it will nevertheless be necessary to stop at a First Cause which accounts for all the necessary there is in things, and whose necessity is not caused, that is to say, a First Cause which is necessary through itself and in essence, in the infinite transcendence of the very act of existence subsisting by itself.

10. *The Fourth Way: By the Degrees Which Are in Things.* It is a fact that there is a qualitative "more or less", that there are degrees of value or perfection in things. There are degrees in the beauty of things (Plato saw this better than anyone); degrees in their goodness; in fine, things *are* to a greater or lesser degree. Knowledge is more highly and more perfectly knowledge in intelligence than in sense; life is more highly and more perfectly life in the free and thinking living thing than in the animal living thing, and in the animal living thing than in the vegetative living thing.

But wherever there exist degrees (wherever there is a *more* and a *less*) it is necessary that there exist, somewhere, a supreme degree or a maximum (a *most*). I am putting this forward as an axiom, the meaning of which is analogical and admits of typically different realizations. This supreme degree may be either (1) the peak *of the totality* of a progressive finite ensemble of values, or (2) the peak of *one* arbitrarily designated *part* in a progressive infinite ensemble of values, or (3) a peak of infinite value beyond and above the totality of a progressive infinite ensemble (take, for example – although there is no question here of qualitative values – a transfinite number of a power higher than such or such an infinite series).

Since goodness, beauty, life, knowledge, love and ultimately Being are in things in divers degrees, it is necessary that there exist somewhere a maximum or a supreme degree of these values.

But the progressive or ascending ensemble of the values in question, inasmuch as they can exist in things, is an infinite ensemble, in which consequently there is no actually supreme degree. One thing is good and another is better, but there can always be another still better. In other words, goodness exceeds or transcends every category of beings, and is not in its fullness in any of them. Each good or beautiful thing is beautiful or good partially or by participation. It is not, then, unto itself the reason for its goodness. For *that* it would be necessary that it be good *by reason of itself* or *in essence* (then it would have goodness in all its plenitude. But such is not the case). Therefore, it derives its goodness from another thing; it is caused in goodness.

But whatever cause be considered, if it is itself caused in goodness, it derives its goodness from something else. Here again it is necessary to come to a stop at a First Cause which is good in essence and by reason of itself.

In other words it is necessary that there exist somewhere a maximum or a supreme degree of goodness (and of the other transcendental values of which we spoke). But this maximum or supreme degree, because it is the First Cause of all that there is of goodness in things, is a peak beyond the infinite series of all possible degrees of goodness in things. It is a supreme degree beyond the whole series. It is a transcendent First Cause which is good by reason of itself, which, therefore, does not *have* goodness but *is* goodness – it is goodness that subsists by reason of itself.

10 A (a). If it be said that the principle "Whenever there are degrees it is necessary that there exist somewhere a maximum or a supreme degree" is but an extrapolation of common experience and possesses neither intrinsic evidence nor universality, we shall reply as follows.

This principle is self-evident inasmuch as it expresses in an entirely general way the logical requirements of the concept of comparative relation. The proposition "Every series composed of a *more* and a *less* connotes a *most*" is a necessary and self-evident proposition. It is verified, as we indicated, in an analogical way and according to typically different modes. It is only if one confuses it with the particular application most familiar to us (the case of a finite progressive ensemble – in a house of many stories there is necessarily a top story) that one can contest its supraempirical and unconditional universality and necessity.

(b) Should it be said that in virtue of this same principle it would be necessary to declare that there is, as ancient physics believed, a supremely hot element (fire), the cause of all the heat there is in Nature; further, that there is something supremely solid, the cause of all there is of solidity in bodies; something supremely red, cause of all there is of red in things; and other equally untenable assertions of the same sort – there is a good answer to that.

The objection rests on the same confusion which we have just pointed out. Without doubt there is as a matter of fact in Nature (this is, however, irrelevant to any scientific explanation) a star whose temperature is the highest, a bird whose plumage is the reddest, a body whose resistance is the hardest. But there would be no point in looking in any such order of things for a being which, presumably, would possess the quality in question *per se* or by virtue of its very essence and would therefore be the cause of that quality in other things, for the reason that these qualities, being generic qualities and not transcendental modes of being, do not exist in things *by participation* (except in regard to the transcendent First Cause, which possesses in a virtual-eminent manner everything there is of being or of perfection in the quality in question). This order of things is the domain of univocity, and of beings, values or perfection confined within genera and categories.

The whole force of the demonstration comes from the fact that it deals with transcendental values or perfections, which surpass every genus and every category, and by their very nature demand existence on ever higher levels of being.

They are analogical, and exist in things by participation, without at any moment being in any subject, however exalted it may be, according to the plenitude of their intelligible content.

Things, as we have seen, hold these values or perfections, which exist in them, from a cause other than themselves, and therefore a cause must ultimately be posited – a cause above the infinite series of all the possible degrees in things – which possesses *through itself* those values or perfections. In that cause these values and perfections exist in perfect unity, in a *formal-eminent* mode, within the infinite transcendence of the Being *per se*.

5

A PROJECTIVE DESCRIPTION

Ludwig Feuerbach

Editor's Introduction

LIKE VAN DER LEEUW and Maritain, Ludwig Feuerbach seeks to find the essence of religion in the religious object – that to which men attend when they behave religiously. Rather than locating this object within the natural order or the supernatural order, however, Feuerbach argues that the object of religion is a projection. God, according to Feuerbach, is man's humanity projected against the sky. This claim that the object of religious thought and devotion is a projection has caused many people to interpret Feuerbach as a hostile, anti-religious sceptic. But to write him off as a fanatic anti-cleric is a mistake. It may be true that Feuerbach attempts to show that God is a projection, but his purpose is not to destroy religion. Rather, Feuerbach is interested in exposing the phony element in much religion, and in discovering the true meaning and significance of religious ideas and practices.

Feuerbach's starting-point is a phenomenological description of consciousness as the unique characteristic of human existence. Consciousness is the ability to abstract. The human mind is not limited to thinking about immediate objects that are presented to it. It can abstract from those objects to their essence and think about them as a genus or type. This ability enables me, for example, to identify the object before me as a typewriter – as one of a class of objects and with which I am familiar through past experiences of other typewriters. I do not meet it, therefore, as a totally new object. Even though I may never have seen this particular typewriter or one of this particular color before, I can relate it to previous experiences of similar typewriters and deal with it on the basis of those experiences, rather than being forced to explore it as if it were a totally new experience for me.

The distinction between the particular object and the abstraction or genus enables men to make judgments about the limitations of an individual object. I can know that my present typewriter has certain limitations and is less than perfect because I can compare it mentally to other typewriters that I have used as well as compare it to an abstract ideal of the perfect typewriter. I can know that the circle I have just drawn on a sheet of paper is less than perfect because I can compare it to a mental image of a perfectly round circle. This kind of abstraction or grouping into types is the precondition of judgment.

In the same way, I can know of my own limitations and shortcomings because I can compare myself with the genus, humanity, as a whole. This comparison is a painful experience, since it calls attention to my own deficiencies. In an effort to escape this painful comparison, Feuerbach argues, we attribute the limitations of which we are conscious in ourselves to humanity as a whole. If it is the nature of man to be gluttonous, I do not have to worry too much about my own gluttony. But when this transfer is made, we have left over the idea of perfected humanity with no place, as it were, to locate it. We project it, therefore, on to the sky, and call it God. Feuerbach points out that the process of projection causes men to be satisfied with their own condition, since they assume it to be natural. Realization of the real location of deficiencies would result, however, in a renewed effort toward improvement of the human condition.

The idea men have of God, Feuerbach continues, is not simply the idea of human perfection. It contains the notion of unlimitedness or infinity. Where does this idea come from? Feuerbach writes that "Consciousness, in the strict or proper sense, is identical with consciousness of the infinite; a limited consciousness is no consciousness; consciousness is essentially infinite in its nature." Obviously he cannot mean that I can know everything. But he does mean that I cannot know of anything I cannot know. I cannot name a single thing I cannot think of. I cannot conceive of anything I cannot conceive of. It is a fallacy to talk about what is beyond comprehension because, if it is beyond comprehension, it is exactly that – beyond comprehension and therefore not anything that can be thought of. An analogy can be drawn to the idea of space. To ask what is beyond space is a non-sense question because "beyond" is a spatial category. Space is unlimited because "limit" is a spatial category. There is nothing spatial "beyond" space.

In many ways, Feuerbach is a forerunner of modern scientific positivism and relativism. That is, he emphasizes the fact that I can only know things from one perspective – my own. I cannot sensibly consider a conceivable object that is not conceivable to me. Moreover, what I know is always a synthesis, a product of the thing in itself and the way I look at it. The only thing I can ever be interested in at all is the thing as it appears to me. It is false and phony to appear to be interested in anything else. This can be put in an even more radical way: what we know when we know something is really another facet of ourselves as we are reflected in the object. "The object of any subject is nothing else than the subject's nature taken objectively." We are condemned to seeing the world from our own point of view. We can never be "objective" in the sense that we can see all sides of an issue or that we are without presuppositions. We are condemned to our individual isolation booth, from which we cannot escape. I can never know you in the same way that another person knows you. And I can never know you as you are in yourself – if the idea of "in-yourself" has any meaning. This does not mean that we can only know what affects us. That is animal existence. We can know the stars, for example, which have no direct effect on us. But we cannot know them except from our own standpoint.

This mutual isolation can be bridged only through the identification of my objective self with the species. The awareness of species, which is a condition of the abstractive ability of the mind, is in some respects similar to the "immediate intuition of being" Maritain describes. But, according to Feuerbach, the notion that this awareness is an awareness of "being" rather than an awareness of "humanness" is attributable to projection.

Feuerbach calls attention to the anthropomorphism contained in all language about God. When we speak of God, we attribute human qualities to him. We describe him in terms of our own highest ideals. Recognizing this, some nineteenth-century religious apologists attempted to argue that God in himself is unknowable and that it is only his attributes that we describe anthropomorphically. They argued that while *what* we know *about* God may be conditioned by our own particular situation, the *knowledge* that there *is* a God is not projectively conditioned. They were willing to admit that what we can know about God, that is, how we conceive of him, is limited by our particular historicity. But they claimed that the *reality* of God is not so conditioned. This was a *tour-de-force* on the part of theologians and philosophers who wanted both to accept the insights of modern positivistic philosophy but also to retain their religious commitments. Feuerbach exposes the paucity of this position. Any object, including God, is the sum of its attributes. Take away the attributes and there is nothing left. I am a particular person, of a particular sex, living at a particular time and in a particular place, and thinking particular things. Take away all of these attributes and there is nothing left. What sense does it make, or what is the content of affirming the existence of some being but denying any particular attributes? Any being is, for us, its attributes. It is nonsense to pretend otherwise.

> But this distinction between what God is in himself, and what he is for me destroys the peace of religion, and is besides in itself an un-founded and untenable distinction. I cannot know whether God is something else in himself or for himself than he is for me; what he is to me is to me all that he is. For me, there lies in these predicates under which he exists for me, what he is in himself, his very nature; he is for me what he can alone ever be for me.

Ludwig Andreas Feuerbach was born in Landshut, Bavaria, in 1804 (the year Kant died). He studied theology at the Universities of Heidelberg and Berlin and then philosophy at the University of Berlin where he came under Hegel's influence. In 1828 he received his doctorate from the University of Erlangen and taught there for the following four years. In 1836 he was dismissed from the University when it was learned that he had published a book critical of Christianity. After his dismissal, he retired to Bruckberg where he lived in semi-seclusion and continued his writing. Feuerbach attracted significant interest early in his career but toward the end of his life was relatively forgotten. He had a profound influence on Karl Marx, who stated that Feuerbach was the pivotal figure in modern philosophy. His thought also has had a great influence on the phenomenological movement. The following selection constitutes most of the introductory chapter from *The Essence of Christianity*, his most popular and important book.

The Essence of Christianity*

1. THE ESSENTIAL NATURE OF MAN

RELIGION HAS ITS basis in the essential difference between man and the brute – the brutes have no religion. It is true that the old uncritical writers on natural history attributed to the elephant, among other laudable qualities, the virtue of religiousness; but the religion of elephants belongs to the realm of fable. Cuvier, one of the greatest authorities on the animal kingdom, assigns, on the strength of his personal observations, no higher grade of intelligence to the elephant than to the dog.

But what is this essential difference between man and the brute? The most simple, general, and also the most popular answer to this question is "consciousness": but consciousness in the strict sense; for the consciousness implied in the feeling of self as an individual, in discrimination by the senses, in the perception and even judgment of outward things according to definite sensible signs, cannot be denied to the brutes. Con-

* Ludwig Feuerbach, part of the introductory chapter to *The Essence of Christianity*, Harper & Row, 1957.

sciousness in the strictest sense is present only in a being to whom his species, his essential nature, is an object of thought. The brute is indeed conscious of himself as an individual – and he has accordingly the feeling of self as the common centre of successive sensations – but not as a species: hence, he is without that consciousness which in its nature, as in its name, is akin to science. Where there is this higher consciousness there is a capability of science. Science is the cognizance of species. In practical life we have to do with individuals; in science, with species. But only a being to whom his own species, his own nature, is an object of thought, can make the essential nature of other things or beings an object of thought.

Hence the brute has only a simple, man a twofold life: in the brute, the inner life is one with the outer; man has both an inner and an outer life. The inner life of man is the life which has relation to his species, to his general, as distinguished from his individual, nature. Man thinks – that is, he converses with himself. The brute can exercise no function which has relation to its species without another individual external to itself; but man can perform the functions of thought and speech, which strictly imply such a relation, apart from another individual. Man is himself at once I and Thou; he can put himself in the place of another, for this reason, that to him his species, his essential nature, and not merely his individuality, is an object of thought.

Religion being identical with the distinctive characteristic of man, is then identical with self-consciousness – with the consciousness which man has of his nature. But religion, expressed generally, is consciousness of the infinite; thus it is and can be nothing else than the consciousness which man has of his own – not finite and limited, but infinite nature. A really finite being has not even the faintest adumbration, still less consciousness, of an infinite being, for the limit of the nature is also the limit of the consciousness. The consciousness of the caterpillar, whose life is confined to a particular species of plant, does not extend itself beyond this narrow domain. It does, indeed, discriminate between this plant and other plants, but more it knows not. A consciousness so limited, but on account of that very limitation so infallible, we do not call consciousness, but instinct. Consciousness, in the strict or proper sense, is identical with consciousness of the infinite; a limited consciousness is no consciousness; consciousness is essentially infinite in its nature. The consciousness of the infinite is nothing else than the consciousness of the infinity of the consciousness; or, in the consciousness of the infinite, the conscious subject has for his object the infinity of his own nature.

What, then, *is* the nature of man, of which he is conscious, or what constitutes the specific distinction, the proper humanity of man? Reason, Will, Affection. To a complete man belong the power of thought, the power of will, the power of affection. The power of thought is the light of the intellect, the power of will is energy of character, the power of affection is love. Reason, love, force of will, are perfections – the perfections of the human being – nay, more, they are absolute perfections of being. To will, to love, to think, are the highest powers, are the absolute nature of man as man, and the basis of his existence. Man exists to think, to love, to will. Now that which is the end, the ultimate aim, is also the true basis and principle of a being. But what is the end of reason? Reason. Of love? Love. Of will? Freedom of the will. We think for the sake of thinking; love for the sake of loving; will for the sake of willing – i.e., that we may be free. True existence is thinking, loving, willing existence. That alone is true, perfect, divine, which exists for its own sake. But such is love, such is reason, such is will. The divine trinity in man, above the individual man, is the unity of reason, love, will. Reason, Will, Love, are not powers which man possesses, for he is nothing without them, he is what he is only by them; they are the constituent elements of his nature, which he neither has nor makes, the animating, determining, governing powers – divine, absolute powers – to which he can oppose no resistance.

How can the feeling man resist feeling, the loving one love, the rational one reason? Who has not experienced the overwhelming power of melody? And what else is the power of melody but the power of feeling? Music is the language of feeling; melody is audible feeling – feeling communicating itself. Who has not experienced the power of love, or at least heard of it? Which is the stronger – love or the individual man? Is it man that possesses love, or is it not much rather love that possesses man? When love impels a man to suffer death even joyfully for the beloved one, is this death-conquering power his own individual power, or is it not rather the power of love? And who that ever truly thought has not experienced that quiet, subtle power – the power of thought? When thou sinkest into deep reflection, forgetting thyself and what is around thee, dost thou govern reason, or is it not reason which governs and absorbs thee? Scientific enthusiasm – is it not the most glorious triumph of intellect over thee? The desire of knowledge – is it not a simply irresistible, and all-conquering power? And when thou suppressest a passion, renouncest a habit, in short, achievest a victory over thyself, is this victorious power thy own personal power, or is it not rather the energy of will, the force of morality, which seizes the mastery of thee, and fills thee with indignation against thyself and thy individual weaknesses?

Man is nothing without an object. The great models of humanity, such men as reveal to us what man is capable of, have attested the truth of this proposition by their lives. They had only one dominant passion – the realization of the aim which was the essential object of their activity. But the object to which a subject essentially necessarily relates, is nothing else than this subject's own, but objective, nature. If it be an object common to several individuals of the same species, but under various conditions, it is still, at least as to the form under which it presents itself to each of them according to their respective modifications, their own, but objective, nature.

Thus the Sun is the common object of the planets, but it is an object to Mercury, to Venus, to Saturn, to Uranus, under other conditions than to the Earth. Each planet has its own sun. The Sun which lights and warms Uranus has no physical (only an astronomical, scientific) existence for the Earth; and not only does the Sun appear different, but it really is *another* sun on Uranus than on the Earth. The relation of the Sun to the Earth is therefore at the same time a relation of the Earth to itself, or to its own nature, for the measure of the size and of the intensity of light which the Sun possesses as the object of the Earth is the measure of the distance which determines the peculiar nature of the Earth. Hence each planet has in its sun the mirror of its own nature.

In the object which he contemplates, therefore, man becomes acquainted with himself; consciousness of the objective is the self-consciousness of man. We know the man by the object, by his conception of what is external to himself; in it his nature becomes evident; this object is his manifested nature, his true objective *ego*. And this is true not merely of spiritual, but also of sensuous objects. Even the objects which are the most remote from man, *because* they are objects to him, and to the extent to which they are so, are revelations of human nature. Even the moon, the sun, the stars, call to man Γνῶθι σεαυτόν. That he sees them, and so sees them, is an evidence of his own nature. The animal is sensible only of the beam which immediately affects life; while man perceives the ray, to him physically indifferent, of the remotest star. Man alone has purely intellectual, disinterested joys and passions; the eye of man alone keeps theoretic festivals. The eye which looks into the starry heavens, which gazes at that light, alike useless and harmless, having nothing in common with the earth and its necessities – this eye sees in that light its own nature, its own origin. The eye is heavenly in its nature. Hence man elevates himself above the earth only with the eye; hence theory begins with the contemplation of the heavens. The first philosophers were astronomers. It is the heavens that admonish man of his destination, and remind him that he is destined not merely to action, but also to contemplation.

The *absolute* to man is his own nature. The power of the object over him is therefore the power of his own nature. Thus the power of the object of feeling is the power of feeling itself; the power of the object of the intellect is the power of the intellect itself; the power of the object of the will is the power of the will itself. The man who is affected by musical sounds is governed by feeling; by the feeling, that is, which finds its corresponding element in musical sounds. But it is not melody as such, it is only melody pregnant with meaning and emotion, which has power over feeling. Feeling is only acted on by that which conveys feeling, i.e., by itself, its own nature. Thus also the will; thus, and infinitely more, the intellect. Whatever kind of object, therefore, we are at any time conscious of, we are always at the same time conscious of our own nature; we can affirm nothing without affirming ourselves. And since to will, to feel, to think, are perfections, essences, realities, it is impossible that intellect, feeling, and will should feel or perceive themselves as limited, finite powers, i.e., as worthless, as nothing. For finiteness and nothingness are identical; finiteness is only a euphemism for nothingness. Finiteness is the metaphysical, the theoretical – nothingness the pathological, practical expression. What is finite to the understanding is nothing to the heart. But it is impossible that we should be conscious of will, feeling, and intellect, as finite powers, because every perfect existence, every original power and essence, is the immediate verification and affirmation of itself. It is impossible to love, will, or think, without perceiving these activities to be perfections – impossible to feel that one is a loving, willing, thinking, being, without experiencing an infinite joy therein. Consciousness consists in a being becoming objective to itself; hence it is nothing apart, nothing distinct from the being which is conscious of itself. How could it otherwise become conscious of itself? It is therefore impossible to the conscious of a perfection as an imperfection, impossible to feel feeling limited, to think thought limited.

Consciousness is self-verification, self-affirmation, self-love, joy in one's own perfection. Consciousness is the characteristic mark of a perfect nature; it exists only in a self-sufficing, complete being. Even human vanity attests this truth. A man looks in the glass; he has complacency in his appearance. This complacency is a necessary, involuntary consequence of the completeness, the beauty of his form. A beautiful form is satisfied in itself; it has necessarily joy in itself – in self-contemplation. This complacency becomes vanity only when a man piques himself on his form as being his individual form, not when he admires it as a specimen of human beauty in general. It is fitting that he should admire it thus: he can conceive no form more beautiful, more sublime than the human. Assuredly every being loves itself, its existence – and fitly so. To exist is a good. *Quidquid essentia dignum est, scientia dignum est.* Everything that exists has value, is a being of distinction – at least this is true of the species : hence it asserts, maintains itself. But the highest form of self-assertion, the form which is itself a superiority, a perfection, a bliss, a good, is consciousness.

Every limitation of the reason, or in general of the nature of man, rests on a delusion, an error. It is true that the human being, as an individual, can and must – herein consists his distinction from the brute – feel and recognize himself to be limited; but he can become conscious of his limits, his finiteness, only because the perfection, the infinitude of his species, is perceived by him, whether as an object of feeling, of conscience, or of the thinking consciousness. If he makes his own limitations the limitations of the species, this arises from the mistake that he identifies himself immediately with the species – a mistake which is intimately connected with the individual's love of ease, sloth, vanity and egoism. For a limitation which I know to be merely mine humiliates, shames, and perturbs me. Hence to free myself from this feeling of shame, from this state of dissatisfaction, I convert the limits of my individuality into the limits of human nature in general. What is incomprehensible to me is incomprehensible to others; why should I trouble myself further? It is no fault of mine; my understanding is not to blame, but the understanding of the race. But it is a ludicrous and even culpable error to define as finite and limited what constitutes the essence of man, the nature of the species, which is the absolute nature of the individual. Every being is sufficient to itself. No being can deny itself, i.e., its own nature; no being is a limited one to itself. Rather, every being is in and by itself infinite – has its God, its highest conceivable being, in itself. Every limit of a being is cognizable only by another being out of and above him. The life of the ephemera is extraordinarily short in comparison with that of longer-lived creatures; but nevertheless, for the ephemera this short life is as long as a life of years to others. The leaf on which the caterpillar lives is for it a world, an infinite space.

That which makes a being what it is, is its talent, its power, its wealth, its adornment. How can it possibly hold its existence non-existence, its wealth poverty, its talent incapacity? If the plants had eyes, taste, and judgment, each plant would declare its own flower the most beautiful; for its comprehension, its taste, would reach no farther than its natural power of production. What the productive power of its nature has brought forth as the highest, that must also its taste, its judgment, recognize and affirm as the highest. What the nature affirms, the understanding, the taste, the judgment, cannot deny; otherwise the understanding, the judgment, would no longer be the understanding and judgment of this particular being, but of some other. The measure of the nature is also the measure of the understanding. If the nature is limited, so also is the feeling, so also is the understanding. But to a limited being its limited understanding is not felt to be a limitation; on the contrary, it is perfectly happy and contented with this understanding; it regards it, praises and values it, as a glorious, divine power; and the limited understanding on its part, values the limited nature whose understanding it is. Each is exactly adapted to the other; how should they be at issue with each other? A being's understanding is its sphere of vision. As far as thou seest, so far extends thy nature; and conversely. The eye of the brute reaches no farther than its needs, and its nature no farther than its needs. And so far as thy nature reaches, so far reaches thy unlimited self-consciousness, so far art thou God. The discrepancy between the understanding and the nature, between the power of conception and the power of production in the human consciousness, on the one hand, is merely of individual significance and has not a universal application; and, on the other hand, it is only apparent. He who, having written a bad poem, knows it to be bad, is in his intelligence, and therefore in his nature, not so limited as he who, having written a bad poem, admires it and thinks it good.

It follows that if thou thinkest the infinite, thou perceivest and affirmest the infinitude of the power of thought; if thou feelest the infinite, thou feelest and affirmest the infinitude of the power of feeling. The object of the intellect is intellect objective to itself;

the object of feeling is feeling objective to itself. If thou hast no sensibility, no feeling for music, thou perceivest in the finest music nothing more than in the wind that whistles by thy ear, or than in the brook which rushes past thy feet. What, then, is it which acts on thee when thou art affected by melody? What dost thou perceive in it? What else than the voice of thy own heart? Feeling speaks only to feeling; feeling is comprehensible only by feeling, that is, by itself – for this reason, that the object of feeling is nothing else than feeling. Music is a monologue of emotion. But the dialogue of philosophy also is in truth only a monologue of the intellect; thought speaks only to thought. The splendours of the crystal charm the sense, but the intellect is interested only in the laws of crystallization. The intellectual only is the object of the intellect.

All therefore, which, in the point of view of metaphysical, transcendental speculation and religion, has the significance only of the secondary, the subjective, the medium, the organ – has in truth the significance of the primary, of the essence, of the object itself. If, for example, feeling is the essential organ of religion, the nature of God is nothing else than an expression of the nature of feeling. The true but latent sense of the phrase, "Feeling is the organ of the divine", is, feeling is the noblest, the most excellent, i.e., the divine, in man. How couldst thou perceive the divine by feeling, if feeling were not itself divine in its nature? The divine assuredly is known only by means of the divine – God is known only by himself. The divine nature which is discerned by feeling is in truth nothing else than feeling enraptured, in ecstasy with itself – feeling intoxicated with joy, blissful in its own plenitude.

It is already clear from this that where feeling is held to be the organ of the infinite, the subjective essence of religion, the external data of religion lose their objective value. And thus, since feeling has been held the cardinal principle in religion, the doctrines of Christianity, formerly so sacred, have lost their importance. If, from this point of view, some value is still conceded to Christian ideas, it is a value springing entirely from the relation they bear to feeling; if another object would excite the same emotions, it would be just as welcome. But the object of religious feeling is become a matter of indifference, only because when once feeling has been pronounced to be the subjective essence of religion, it in fact is also the objective essence of religion, though it may not be declared, at least directly, to be such. I say directly; for indirectly this is certainly admitted, when it is declared that feeling, as such, is religious, and thus the distinction between specifically religious and irreligious, or at least non-religious, feelings is abolished – a necessary consequence of the point of view in which feeling only is regarded as the organ of the divine. For on what other ground than that of its essence, its nature, dost thou hold feeling to be the organ of the infinite, the divine being? And is not the nature of feeling in general also the nature of every special feeling, be its object what it may? What, then, makes this feeling religious? A given object? Not at all; for this object is itself a religious one only when it is not an object of the cold understanding or memory, but of feeling. What then? The nature of feeling – a nature of which every special feeling, without distinction of objects, partakes. Thus, feeling is pronounced to be religious, simply because it is feeling; the ground of its religiousness is its own nature – lies in itself. But is not feeling thereby declared to be itself the absolute, the divine? If feeling in itself is good, religious, i.e., holy, divine, has not feeling its God in itself?

But if, notwithstanding, thou wilt posit an object of feeling, but at the same time seekest to express thy feeling truly, without introducing by thy reflection any foreign element, what remains to thee but to distinguish between thy individual feeling and the general nature of feeling; – to separate the universal in feeling from the disturbing, adulterating influences with which feeling is bound up in thee, under thy individual conditions? Hence what thou canst alone contemplate, declare to be the infinite, and define as its essence, is merely the nature of feeling. Thou hast thus no other definition of God than this: God is pure, unlimited, free Feeling. Every other God, whom thou supposest, is a God thrust upon thy feeling from without. Feeling is atheistic in the sense of the orthodox belief, which attaches religion to an external object; it denies an objective God – it is itself God. In this point of view only the negation of feeling is the negation of God. Thou art simply too cowardly or too narrow to confess in words what thy feeling tacitly affirms. Fettered by outward considerations, still in bondage to vulgar empiricism, incapable of comprehending the spiritual grandeur of feeling, thou art terrified before the religious atheism of thy heart. By this fear thou destroyest the unity of thy feeling with itself, in imagining to thyself an objective being distinct from thy feeling, and thus necessarily sinking back into the old questions and doubts – is there a God or not? – questions and doubts which vanish, nay, are impossible, where feeling is defined as the essence of religion. Feeling is thy own inward power, but at the same time a power distinct from thee, and independent of thee; it is in thee, above thee; it is itself that which constitutes the objective in thee – thy own being which impresses thee as another being; in short, thy God. How wilt thou, then, distinguish from this objective being within thee another objective being? how wilt thou get beyond thy feeling?

But feeling has here been adduced only as an example. It is the same with every other power, faculty, potentiality, reality, activity – the name is indifferent – which is defined as the essential organ of any object. Whatever is a subjective expression of a nature is simultaneously also its objective expression. Man cannot get beyond his true nature. He may indeed by means of the imagination conceive individuals of another so-called higher kind, but he can never get loose from his species, his nature; the conditions of being, the positive final predicates which he gives to these other individuals, are always determinations or qualities drawn from his own nature – qualities in which he in truth only images and projects himself. There may certainly be thinking beings besides men on the other planets of our solar system. But by the supposition of such beings we do not change our standing point – we extend our conceptions *quantitatively* not *qualitatively*. For as surely as on the other planets there are the same laws of motion, so surely are there the same laws of perception and thought as here. In fact, we people the other planets, not that we may place there different beings from ourselves, but *more* beings of our own or of a similar nature.

2. THE ESSENCE OF RELIGION CONSIDERED GENERALLY

What we have hitherto been maintaining generally, even with regard to sensational impressions, of the relation between subject and object, applies especially to the relation between the subject and the religious object.

In the perceptions of the senses consciousness of the object is distinguishable from consciousness of self; but in religion, consciousness of the object and self-consciousness coincide. The object of the senses is out of man, the religious object is within him, and therefore as little forsakes him as his self-consciousness or his conscience; it is the intimate, the closest object. "God", says Augustine, for example, "is nearer, more related to us, and therefore more easily known by us, than sensible, corporeal things." The object of the senses is in itself indifferent – independent of the disposition or of the judgment; but the object of religion is a selected object; the most excellent, the first, the supreme being; it essentially presupposes a critical judgment, a discrimination between the divine and the non-divine, between that which is worthy of adoration and that which is not worthy. And here may be applied, without any limitation, the proposition: the object of any subject is nothing else than the subject's own nature taken objectively. Such as are a man's thoughts and dispositions, such is his God; so much worth as a man has, so much and no more has his God. Consciousness of God is self-consciousness, knowledge of God is self-knowledge. By his God thou knowest the man, and by the man his God; the two are identical. Whatever is God to a man, that is his heart and soul; and conversely, God is the manifested inward nature, the expressed self of a man, – religion the solemn unveiling of a man's hidden treasures, the revelation of his intimate thoughts, the open confession of his love-secrets.

But when religion – consciousness of God – is designated as the self-conciousness of man, this is not to be understood as affirming that the religious man is directly aware of this identity; for, on the contrary, ignorance of it is fundamental to the peculiar nature of religion. To preclude this misconception, it is better to say, religion is man's earliest and also indirect form of self-knowledge. Hence, religion everywhere precedes philosophy, as in history of the race, so also in that of the individual. Man first of all sees his nature as if *out of* himself, before he finds it in himself. His own nature is in the first instance contemplated by him as that of another being. Religion is the childlike condition of humanity; but the child sees his nature – man – out of himself; in childhood a man is an object to himself, under the form of another man. Hence the historical progress of religion consists in this: that what by an earlier religion was regarded as objective is now recognized as subjective; that is, what was formerly contemplated and worshipped as God is now perceived to be something *human*. What was at first religion becomes at a later period idolatry; man is seen to have adored his own nature. Man has given objectivity to himself, but has not recognized the object as his own nature: a later religion takes this forward step; every advance in religion is therefore a deeper self-knowledge. But every particular religion, while it pronounces its predecessors idolatrous, excepts itself – and necessarily so, otherwise it would no longer be religion – from the fate, the common nature of all religions: it imputes only to other religions what is the fault, if fault it be, of religion in general. Because it has a different object, a different tenor, because it has transcended the ideas of preceding religions, it erroneously supposes itself exalted above the necessary eternal laws which constitute the essence of religion – it fancies its object, its ideas, to be superhuman. But the essence of religion, thus hidden from the religious, is evident to the thinker, by whom religion is viewed objectively, which it cannot be by its votaries. And it is our task to show that the antithesis of divine and human is altogether illusory, that it is nothing else than the antithesis between the human nature in general and the human individual; that, consequently, the object and contents of the Christian religion are altogether human.

Religion, at least the Christian, is the relation of man to himself, or more correctly to his own nature (i.e., his subjective nature); but a relation to it, viewed as a nature apart from his own. The divine being is nothing else than the human being, or, rather, the human nature purified, freed from the limits of the individual man, made objective – i.e., contemplated and revered as another, a distinct being. All the attributes of the divine nature are, therefore, attributes of the human nature.

In relation to the attributes, the predicates, of the Divine Being, this is admitted without hesitation, but by no means in relation to the subject of these predicates. The negation of the subject is held to be irreligion, nay, atheism; though not so the negation of the predicates. But that which has no predicates or qualities has no effect upon me; that which has no effect upon me has no existence for me. To deny all the qualities of a being is equivalent to denying the being himself. A being without qualities is one which cannot become an object to the mind, and such a being is virtually non-existent. Where man deprives God of all qualities, God is no longer anything more to him than a negative being. To the truly religious man, God is not a being without qualities, because to him he is a positive, real being. The theory that God cannot be defined, and consequently cannot be known by man, is therefore the offspring of recent times, a product of modern unbelief.

As reason is and can be pronounced finite only where man regards sensual enjoyment, or religious emotion, or aesthetic contemplation, or moral sentiment, as the absolute, the true; so the proposition that God is unknowable or undefinable, can only be enunciated and become fixed as a dogma, where this object has no longer any interest for the intellect; where the real, the positive, alone has any hold on man, where the real alone has for him the significance of the essential, of the absolute, divine object, but where at the same time, in contradiction with this purely worldly tendency, there yet exist some old remains of religiousness. On the ground that God is unknowable, man excuses himself to what is yet remaining of his religious conscience for his forgetfulness of God, his absorption in the world: he denies God practically by his conduct, – the world has possession of all his thoughts and inclinations, – but he does not deny him theoretically, he does not attack his existence; he lets that rest. But this existence does not affect or incommode him; it is a merely negative existence, an existence without existence, a self-contradictory existence, – a state of being which, as to its effects, is not distinguishable from non-being. The denial of determinate, positive predicates concerning the divine nature is nothing else than a denial of religion, with, however, an appearance of religion in its favor, so that it is not recognized as a denial; it is simply a subtle, disguised atheism. The alleged religious horror of limiting God by positive predicates is only the irreligious wish to know nothing more of God, to banish God from the mind. Dread of limitation is dread of existence. All real existence, i.e., all existence which is truly such, is qualitative, determinative existence. He who earnestly believes in the Divine existence is not shocked at the attributing even of gross sensuous qualities to God. He who dreads an existence that may give offence, who shrinks from the grossness of a positive predicate, may as well renounce existence altogether. A god who is injured by determinate qualities has not the courage and the strength to exist. Qualities are the fire, the vital breath, the oxygen, the salt of existence. An existence in general, an existence without qualities, is an insipidity, an absurdity. But there can be no more in God than is supplied by religion. Only where man loses his taste for religion, and thus religion itself becomes insipid, does the existence of God become an insipid existence – an existence without qualities.

There is, however, a still milder way of denying the divine predicates than the direct one just described. It is admitted that the predicates of the divine nature are finite, and, more particularly, human qualities, but their rejection is rejected; they are even taken under protection, because it is necessary to man to have a definite conception of God, and since he is man he can form no other than a human conception of him. In relation to God, it is said, these predicates are certainly without any objective validity; but to me, if he is to exist for me, he cannot appear otherwise than as he does appear to me, namely, as a being with attributes analogous to the human. But this distinction between what God is in himself, and what he is for me destroys the peace of religion, and is besides in itself an unfounded and untenable distinction. I cannot know whether God is something else in himself or for himself than he is for me; what he is to me is to me all that he is. For me, there lies in these predicates under which he exists for me, what he is in himself, his very nature; he is for me what he can alone ever be for me. The religious man finds perfect satisfaction in that which God is in relation to himself; of any other relation he knows nothing, for God is to him what he can alone be to man. In the distinction above stated, man takes a point of view above himself, i.e., above his nature, the absolute measure of his being; but this transcendentalism is only an illusion; for I can make the distinction between the object as it is in itself, and the object as it is for me, only where an object can really appear otherwise to me, not where it appears to me such as the absolute measure of my nature determines it to appear – such as it must appear to me. It is true that I may have a merely subjective conception, i.e., one which does not arise out of the general constitution of my species; but if my conception is determined by the constitution of my species, the distinction between what an object is in itself, and what it is for me ceases; for this conception is itself an absolute one. The measure of the species is the absolute measure, law, and criterion of man. And, indeed, religion has the conviction that its conceptions, its predicates of God, are such as every man ought to have, and must have, if he would have the true ones – that they are the conceptions necessary to human nature; nay, further, that they are objectively true, representing God as he is. To every religion the gods of *other* religions are only notions concerning God, but its own conception of God is to it God himself, the true God – God such as he is in himself. Religion is satisfied only with a complete Deity, a God without reservation; it will not have a mere phantasm of God; it demands God himself. Religion gives up its own existence when it gives up the nature of God; it is no longer a truth when it renounces the possession of the true God. Scepticism is the arch-enemy of religion; but the distinction between object and conception – between God as he is in himself, and God as he is for me – is a sceptical distinction, and therefore an irreligious one.

That which is to man the self-existent, the highest being, to which he can conceive nothing higher – that is to him the Divine

Being. How then should he inquire concerning this being, what he is in himself? If God were an object to the bird, he would be a winged being: the bird knows nothing higher, nothing more blissful, than the winged condition. How ludicrous would it be if this bird pronounced: To me God appears as a bird, but what he is in himself I know not. To the bird the highest nature is the bird nature; take away from him the conception of this, and you take from him the conception of the highest being. How, then, could he ask whether God in himself were winged? To ask whether God is in himself what he is for me, is to ask whether God is God, is to lift oneself above one's God, to rise up against him.

Wherever, therefore, this idea, that the religious predicates are only anthropomorphisms, has taken possession of a man, there has doubt, has unbelief, obtained the mastery of faith. And it is only the inconsequence of faint-heartedness and intellectual imbecility which does not proceed from this idea to the formal negation of the predicates, and from thence to the negation of the subject to which they relate. If thou doubtest the objective truth of the predicates, thou must also doubt the objective truth of the subject whose predicates they are. If thy predicates are anthropomorphisms, the subject of them is an anthropomorphism too. If love, goodness, personality, etc., are human attributes, so also is the subject which thou presupposest, the existence of God, the belief that there is a God, an anthropomorphism – a presupposition purely human. Whence knowest thou that the belief in a God at all is not a limitation of man's mode of conception? Higher beings – and thou supposest such – are perhaps so blest in themselves, so at unity with themselves, that they are not hung in suspense between themselves and a yet higher being. To know God and not oneself to be God, to know blessedness and not oneself to enjoy it, is a state of disunity, of unhappiness. Higher beings know nothing of this unhappiness; they have no conception of that which they are not.

Thou believest in love as a divine attribute because thou thyself lovest; thou believest that God is a wise, benevolent being because thou knowest nothing better in thyself than benevolence and wisdom; and thou believest that God exists, that therefore he is a subject – whatever exists is a subject, whether it be defined as substance, person, essence, or otherwise – because thou thyself existest, art thyself a subject. Thou knowest no higher human good than to love, than to be good and wise; and even so thou knowest no higher happiness than to exist, to be a subject; for the consciousness of all reality, of all bliss, is for thee bound up in the consciousness of being a subject, of existing. God is an existence, a subject to thee, for the same reason that he is to thee a wise, a blessed, a personal being. The distinction between the divine predicates and the divine subject is only this, that to thee the subject, the existence, does not appear an anthropomorphism, because the conception of it is necessarily involved in thy own existence as a subject, whereas the predicates do appear anthropomorphisms, because their necessity – the necessity that God should be conscious, wise, good, etc., – is not an immediate necessity, identical with the being of man, but is evolved by his self-consciousness, by the activity of his thought. I am a subject, I exist, whether I be wise or unwise, good or bad. To exist is to man the first datum; it constitutes the very idea of the subject; it is presupposed by the predicates. Hence man relinquishes the predicates, but the existence of God is to him a settled, irrefragable, absolutely certain, objective truth. But, nevertheless, this distinction is merely an apparent one. The necessity of the subject lies only in the necessity of the predicate. Thou art a subject only in so far as thou art a human subject; the certainty and reality of thy existence lie only in the certainty and reality of thy human attributes. What the subject is lies only in the predicate; the predicate is the *truth* of the subject – the subject only the personified, existing predicate, the predicate conceived as existing. Subject and predicate are distinguished only as existence and essence. The negation of the predicates is therefore the negation of the subject. What remains of the human subject when abstracted from the human attributes? Even in the language of common life the divine predicates – Providence, Omniscience, Omnipotence – are put for the divine subject.

The certainty of the existence of God, of which it has been said that it is as certain, nay, more certain to man than his own exist-ence, depends only on the certainty of the qualities of God – it is in itself no immediate certainty. To the Christian the existence of the Christian God only is a certainty; to the heathen that of the heathen God only. The heathen did not doubt the existence of Jupiter, because he took no offence at the nature of Jupiter, be-cause he could conceive of God under no other qualities, because to him these qualities were a certainty, a divine reality. The reality of the predicate is the solo guarantee of existence.

Whatever man conceives to be true, he immediately conceives to be real (that is, to have an objective existence), because, originally, only the real is true to him – true in opposition to what is merely conceived, dreamed, imagined. The idea of being, of existence, is the original idea of truth; or, originally, man makes truth dependent on existence, subsequently, existence dependent on truth. Now God is the nature of man regarded as absolute truth – the truth of man; but God, or, what is the same thing, religion, is as various as are the conditions under which man conceives this his nature, regards it as the highest being. These conditions, then, under which man conceives God, are to him the truth, and for that reason they are also the highest existence, or rather they are existence itself, for only the emphatic, the highest existence, is existence, and deserves this name. Therefore, God is an existent, real being, on the very same ground that he is a particular, definite being; for the qualities of God are nothing else than the essential qualities of man himself, and a particular man is what he is, has his existence, his reality, only in his particular conditions. Take away from the Greek the quality of being Greek, and you take away his existence. On this ground it is true that for a definite positive religion – that is, relatively– the certainty of the existence of God is *immediate*; for just as involuntarily, as neces-sarily, as the Greek was a Greek, so necessarily were his gods Greek beings, so necessarily were they real, existent beings. Reli-gion is that conception of the nature of the world and of man which is essential to, i.e., identical with, a man's nature. But man does not stand above this his necessary conception; on the contrary, it stands above him; it animates, determines, governs him. The necessity of a proof, of a middle term to unite qualities with existence, the possibility of a doubt, is abolished. Only that which is apart from my own being is capable of being doubted by me. How then can I doubt of God, who is my being? To doubt of God is to doubt of myself. Only when God is thought of abstractly, when his predicates are the result of philosophic abstraction, arises the distinction or separation between subject and predicate, existence and nature – arises the fiction that the existence of the subject is something else than the predicate, something immediate, indubitable, in distinction from the predicate, which is held to be doubtful. But this is only a fiction. A God who has abstract predicates has also an abstract existence. Existence, being, varies with varying qualities.

The identity of the subject and predicate is clearly evidenced by the progressive development of religion, which is identical with the progressive development of human culture. So long as man is in a mere state of nature, so long is his god a mere nature-god – a personification of some natural force. Where man inhabits houses, he also encloses his gods in temples. The temple is only a manifestation of the value which man attaches to beautiful buildings. Temples in honor of religion are in truth temples in honor of architecture. With the emerging of man from a state of savagery and wildness to one of culture, with the distinction between what is fitting for man and what is not fitting, arises simultaneously the distinction between that which is fitting and that which is not fitting for God. God is the idea of majesty, of the highest dignity: the religious sentiment is the sentiment of supreme fitness. The later more cultured artists of Greece were the first to embody in the statues of the gods the ideas of dignity, of spiritual grandeur, of imperturbable repose and serenity. But why were these qualities in their view attributes, predicates of God? Because they were in themselves regarded by the Greeks as divinities. Why did those artists exclude all disgusting and low passions? Because they perceived them to be unbecoming, unworthy, unhuman, and consequently ungodlike. The Homeric gods eat and drink; – that implies eating and drinking is a divine pleasure. Physical strength is an attribute of the Homeric gods:

Zeus is the strongest of the gods. Why? Because physical strength, in and by itself, was regarded as something glorious, divine. To the ancient Germans the highest virtues were those of the warrior; therefore their supreme god was the god of war, Odin, – war, "the original or oldest law". Not the attribute of the divinity, but the divineness or deity of the attribute, is the first true Divine Being. Thus what theology and philosophy have held to be God, the Absolute, the Infinite, is not God; but that which they have held not to be God is God: namely, the attribute, the quality, whatever has reality. Hence, he alone is the true atheist to whom the predicates of the Divine Being – for example, love, wisdom, justice – are nothing; not he to whom merely the subject of these predicates is nothing. And in no wise is the negation of the subject necessarily also a negation of the predicates considered in themselves. These have an intrinsic, independent reality; they force their recognition upon man by their very nature; they are self-evident truths to him; they prove, they attest themselves. It does not follow that goodness, justice, wisdom, are chimaeras because the existence of God is a chimaera, nor truths because this is a truth. The idea of God is dependent on the idea of justice, of benevolence; a God who is not benevolent, not just, not wise, is no God; but the converse does not hold. The fact is not that a quality is divine because God has it, but that God has it because it is in itself divine: because without it God would be a defective being. Justice, wisdom, in general every quality which constitutes the divinity of God, is determined and known by itself independently, but the idea of God is determined by the qualities which have thus been previously judged to be worthy of the divine nature; only in the case in which I identify God and justice, in which I think of God immediately as the reality of the idea of justice, is the idea of God self-determined. But if God as a subject is the determined, while the quality, the predicate, is the determining, then in truth the rank of the godhead is due not to the subject, but to the predicate.

Not until several, and those contradictory, attributes are united in one being, and this being is conceived as personal – the personality being thus brought into especial prominence – not until then is the origin of religion lost sight of, is it forgotten that what the activity of the reflective power has converted into a predicate distinguishable or separable from the subject, was originally the true subject. Thus the Greeks and Romans deified accidents as substances; virtues, states of mind, passions, as independent beings. Man, especially the religious man, is to himself the measure of all things, of all reality. Whatever strongly impresses a man, whatever produces an unusual effect on his mind, if it be only a peculiar, inexplicable sound or note, he personifies as a divine being. Religion embraces all the objects of the world: everything existing has been an object of religious reverence; in the nature and consciousness of religion there is nothing else than what lies in the nature of man and in his consciousness of himself and of the world. Religion has no material exclusively its own. In Rome even the passions of fear and terror had their temples. The Christians also made mental phenomena into independent beings, their own feelings into qualities of things, the passions which governed them into powers which governed the world, in short, predicates of their own nature, whether recognized as such or not, into independent subjective existences. Devils, cobolds, witches, ghosts, angels, were sacred truths as long as the religious spirit held undivided sway over mankind....

Man – this is the mystery of religion – projects his being into objectivity, and then again makes himself an object to this projected image of himself thus converted into a subject; he thinks of himself as an object to himself, but as the object of an object, of another being than himself. Thus here. Man is an object to God. That man is good or evil is not indifferent to God; no! He has a lively, profound interest in man's being good; he wills that man should be good, happy – for without goodness there is no happiness. Thus the religious man virtually retracts the nothingness of human activity, by making his dispositions and actions an object to God, by making man the end of God – for that which is an object to the mind is an end in action; by making the divine activity a means of human salvation. God acts, that man may be good and happy. Thus man, while he is apparently humiliated to the lowest degree, is in truth exalted to the highest. Thus, in and through God, man has in view himself alone. It is true that man places the aim of his action in God, but God has no other aim of action than the moral and eternal salvation of man: thus man has in fact no other aim than himself. The divine activity is not distinct from the human....

PART THREE: THE SUBJECT IN RELIGION: PSYCHOLOGICAL DESCRIPTIONS

6

RELIGION AS A FACULTY

Friedrich Schleiermacher

Editor's Introduction

THE PREVIOUS DESCRIPTIONS of religion have focussed on the uniqueness of the object toward which human religiousness is directed. Religion was described as the human response to "power" or to "being" or to the "objectification of the species". In the following selections, Friedrich Schleiermacher describes religion in a radically different way. He identifies the essence of religion, not by a unique object, but by the uniqueness of the human psychic faculties which operate in religious activity.

This shift from the object to the subject of religious activity marked a significant turning-point in the history of theology. It initiated a long tradition which sought to distinguish between superstition or perverted religion and true or legitimate religion by identifying the exact character of the human religious faculties. In *The Varieties of Religious Experience,* William James defines religion as "The feelings, acts, and experiences of individual men in their solitude, so far as they apprehend themselves to stand in relation to whatever they may consider the divine". The important factor for James is not that religion is the human response to "being" or to "power", but that it is a particular religious response to "whatever" one considers divine. The objective is unimportant. What is important is the kind and quality of response.

The distinguishing mark of the subjective descriptions of religion is the identification of religion as a real and vital part of human life. While they may reject any particular religion as a conglomeration of culturally conditioned manifestations, behind the various "positive" forms of religious expression lies a true dimension of human behavior: natural religion.

The faculty-subjective description, which is represented by Schleiermacher, identifies a religious sphere of man's life. Whatever else men may be – physical, moral, mental, social, emotional – they are also religious. Human life is incomplete if the religious side is not developed, and human existence is understood incompletely if its religious facet is not considered.

Schleiermacher attempted to show that the psychic life has three components: knowing, doing, and feeling. He then attempted to demonstrate that just as science is the legitimate expression of human knowing, and ethics the legitimate expression of human doing, religion is the legitimate expression of human feeling.

Schleiermacher's use of the word "feeling" is perhaps unfortunate for it has led to serious misunderstandings. (Although the possibility of misunderstanding is not so great in the original German.) His identification of religion with feeling has led many people to identify religion with a particular emotional attitude or peculiar "inner experience". It should be made very clear that Schleiermacher did not intend to associate religion with an emotional response nor did he seek to ground religion in an inner "religious experience". He uses the word "feeling" to refer to an aspect or component of the psychic life. It refers to a faculty of the mind and not a mental category and is, therefore, a metaphysical or ontological category rather than a psychological one. He uses the synonym, "immediate self-consciousness" for "feeling" and it is useful to substitute that phrase wherever possible. By "immediate self-consciousness" Schleiermacher refers to the self-awareness that accompanies all our mental activity. It is *conscious* as opposed to unconscious; it is a part of our mental awareness; we are in some sense aware of ourselves. But it is also *immediate* as opposed to reflective; it is not a product of a deduction of my own existence, in a quasi-Cartesian sense, but is a direct awareness.

Because Schleiermacher is engaged in a phenomenological description he cannot offer deductive proof for his exposition. He can only describe immediate self-consciousness and offer examples in the hope that he will call attention to a common factor of experience. Immediate self-consciousness has two aspects, or moments. There are times when I am aware of myself as hedged in by others, by commitments, responsibilities, and obligations pulling me one way or the other. This is not a reflective "taking stock" but an immediate awareness of the push of things on me. The accompanying emotion (not to be mistaken for the self-awareness itself) is often one of depression and futility. Schleiermacher calls this the moment or "feeling" of dependence. At other times I am aware of myself as "on top of things", "in control", ordering my world and making strides forward in a number of fronts. Again this is not a reflective evaluation of my position, but an awareness of my own power in controlling things around me. And the accompanying emotion (also not to be mistaken for the self-awareness itself) is often one of elation and confidence. Schleiermacher calls this the moment, or "feeling", of freedom. Most of the time the two are present in varying degrees in our self-awareness. At times, however, either may dominate, almost obscuring the other.

Neither moment, however, can be completely absent from immediate self-awareness. The moment of freedom contains within it the awareness of the object over-against which one feels himself to be free. It is determined and limited, therefore, by the necessity of the object. The moment of dependence requires an awareness of the self which the world is threatening to overwhelm, and this likewise limits it. Immediate self-consciousness contains, therefore, an awareness of the self and of the "other".

Our relation to our environment, to our world, and to everything in it is one of *reciprocity*. We are aware of ourselves as determined by objects in the world and we are aware of ourselves as determining objects in the world. Every relationship to an object in the world or to our world as a whole necessarily contains both elements.

But in addition to this reciprocal relationship to our environment, there is a third moment of self-awareness Schleiermacher calls the "feeling of absolute dependence", or the "absolute feeling of dependence". This moment of self-awareness does not accompany our involvement with any object in the world or with the world as a whole because those relationships are always reciprocal. Rather it is an awareness of the fact that we and the objects of our environment, which are reciprocally related, are both, in their relatedness, dependent and not self-sufficient. The "absolute feeling of dependence" is not merely the "feeling of dependence" carried to the absolute. It is a third type of awareness. We give the name "God" to the correlate of this feeling of absolute dependence.

It is helpful to compare Schleiermacher's description of "immediate self-consciousness" with Maritain's description of the "primordial intuition of being" (Chapter 4). Maritain describes the awareness of being whereas Schleiermacher describes an awareness of the self, but in addition to this important difference, there are important similarities. Both attempt to describe a subtle awareness that accompanies all our dealings with things in our environment. Maritain emphasizes the content of the awareness whereas Schleiermacher emphasizes the subjective awareness itself, but both stress the intentionality of this awareness. That is, in the "primordial intuition of being" or "immediate self-consciousness" the awareness and the content of the awareness are inseparable. Moreover, Maritain's analysis of the primordial intuition of being into the three components of external being, being-with-nothingness, and absolute being corresponds closely to Schleiermacher's description of the feeling of dependence, the feeling of freedom, and the feeling of absolute freedom.

Friedrich Daniel Ernst Schleiermacher was born in Germany in 1768. He studied theology at the University of Halle and was ordained in 1794. In 1796 he was called to a pulpit in Berlin. In 1804 he returned to a teaching position in Halle where he remained for six years. In 1810 he again went to Berlin where he taught at the University and occupied the largest pulpit in the city. During the latter years of his life he was a dominant figure in Berlin, preaching to large congregations, and exerting a profound influence on the life of the city. He died in 1834.

The first of the following selections is from Schleiermacher's first book, *On Religion: Speeches to its Cultured Despisers*. The book was published in Berlin, in 1799, when Schleiermacher was thirty-one years old.

At the turn of the century Berlin was the center of the intellectual and cultural world. Schleiermacher was one of a group of young writers, poets, and artists who, dissatisfied with the established forms in art, music, literature, and philosophy, worked together in a productive effort to chart new directions in all areas of culture. These were the young romantics. Their spiritual godfather was Goethe who did more than anyone else to recall the men of the Enlightenment from their one-sided pursuit of reason and to remind them of the reality and depth of the emotional and non-rational elements of human existence.

Amid the intellectual fervor of the young romantic movement, there was one area of study that was of little interest to them: religion, which was dominated by the rigid and sterile theology of protestant orthodoxy, which had been predominant in Germany for over one hundred years. The orthodox theologians assumed that theology was a discipline which elaborated a system of doctrines based on divinely revealed propositions. For the orthodox, the truly religious man was the man who had "right knowledge" and this right knowledge was gained through the process of rational deduction beginning with certain unquestionable, divinely revealed propositions. It is easy to see why the new romantics, impressed with the depth and mystery of human emotion, had little interest in this kind of religion.

These romantics were the "cultured despisers" to whom Schleiermacher addressed his book. His reinterpretation of religion, showing that religious doctrines were the elaboration of certain basic awareness of the human psyche, was a profound and significant response to the romantics. His description of religion as a vital and necessary part of human life reoriented the discussion of religion away from the concerns of orthodoxy and moved religious speculation into the center of the romantic milieu.

The second selection is taken from the first chapter of Schleiermacher's magnum opus, *The Christian Faith*, published in 1821.

On Religion*

SECOND SPEECH: THE NATURE OF RELIGION

YOU KNOW HOW the aged Simonides, by long and repeated hesitation, put to silence the person who troubled him with the question, What are the gods? Our question, What is religion? is similar and equally extensive, and I would fain begin with a like hesitation. Naturally I would not mean by ultimate silence, as he did, to leave you in perplexity. But you might attempt something for yourselves; you might give steady and continuous attention to the point about which we are enquiring; you might entirely exclude other thoughts. Do not even conjurors of common spirits demand abstinence from earthly things and solemn stillness, as a preparation, and undistracted, close attention to the place where the apparition is to show itself? How much more should I claim? It is a rare spirit that I am to call forth, which can, only when long regarded with fixed attention, be recognized as the object of your desire. You must have that unbiased sobriety of judgment that seizes clearly and accurately every outline. Without being misled by old memories or hindered by preconceptions, you must endeavor to understand the object presented simply by itself. Even then it may not win your love, and otherwise I cannot hope for

* Friedrich Schleiermacher, from *On Religion: Speeches to its Cultured Despisers*, Harper & Row, New York, 1958.

any unanimity about the meaning of religion or any recognition of its worth.

I could wish to exhibit religion in some well-known form, reminding you, by feature, carriage, and deportment, of what here and there at least you have seen in life. Religion, however, as I wish to show it, which is to say, in its original, characteristic form, is not accustomed to appear openly, but is only seen in secret by those who love it. Not that this applies to religion alone. Nothing that is essentially characteristic and peculiar can be quite the same as that which openly exhibits and represents it. Speech, for example, is not the pure work of science nor morals of intention. Among ourselves at the present time this is specially recognized. It belongs to the opposition of the new time to the old that no longer is one person one thing, but everyone is all things. Just as among civilized peoples, by extensive intercourse their characteristic ways of thought no longer appear unalloyed, so in the human mind there is such a complete sociableness founded, that no special faculty or capacity, however much it may be separated for observation, can ever, in separation, produce its work. Speaking broadly, one is, in operation, influenced and permeated by the ready love and support of the others. The predominating power is all you can distinguish. Wherefore every activity of the spirit is only to be understood, in so far as a man can study it in himself. Seeing you maintain that in this way you do not know religion, it is incumbent upon me to warn you against the errors that naturally issue from the present state of things. We shall, therefore, begin by reviewing the main points in your own position to see whether they are right, or whether we may from them reach the right.

Religion is for you at one time a way of thinking, a faith, a peculiar way of contemplating the world, and of combining what meets us in the world: at another, it is a way of acting, a peculiar desire and love, a special kind of conduct and character. Without this distinction of a theoretical and practical you could hardly think at all, and though both sides belong to religion, you are usually acustomed to give heed chiefly to only one at a time. Wherefore, we shall look closely at religion from both sides.

We commence with religion as a kind of activity. Activity is twofold, having to do with life and with art. You would ascribe with the poet earnestness to life and cheerfulness to art; or, in some other way, you would contrast them. Separate them you certainly will. For life, duty is the watchword. The moral law shall order it, and virtue shall show itself the ruling power in it, that the individual may be in harmony with the universal order of the world, and may nowhere encroach in a manner to disturb and confuse. This life, you consider, may appear without any discernible trace of art. Rather is it to be attained by rigid rules that have nothing to do with the free and variable precepts of art. Nay, you look upon it almost as a rule that art should be somewhat in the background, and non-essential for those who are strictest in the ordering of life. On the other hand, imagination shall inspire the artist, and genius shall completely sway him. Now imagination and genius are for you quite different from virtue and morality, being capable of existing in the largest measure along with a much more meager moral endowment. Nay you are inclined, because the prudent power often comes into danger by reason of the fiery power, to relax for the artist somewhat of the strict demands of life.

How now does it stand with piety, in so far as you regard it as a peculiar kind of activity? Has it to do with right living? Is it something good and praiseworthy, yet different from morality, for you will not hold them to be identical? But in that case morality does not exhaust the sphere which it should govern. Another power works alongside of it, and has both right and might to continue working. Or will you perhaps betake yourselves to the position that piety is a virtue, and religion a duty or section of duties? Is religion incorporated into morality and subordinated to it, as a part to the whole? Is it, as some suppose, special duties toward God, and therefore a part of all morality which is the performance of all duties? But, if I have rightly appreciated or accurately reproduced what you say, you do not think so. You rather seem to say that the pious person has something entirely peculiar, both in his doing and leaving undone, and that morality can be quite moral without therefore being pious.

And how are religion and art related? They can hardly be quite alien, because, from of old, what is greatest in art has had a religious character. When, therefore, you speak of an artist as pious, do you still grant him that relaxation of the strict demands of virtue? Rather he is then subjected, like every other person. But then to make the cases parallel, you must secure that those who devote themselves to life do not remain quite without art. Perhaps this combination gives its peculiar form to religion. With your view, there seems no other possible issue.

Religion then, as a kind of activity, is a mixture of elements that oppose and neutralize each other. Pray is not this rather the utterance of your dislike than your conviction? Such an accidental shaking together, leaving both elements unaltered, does not, even though the most accurate equality be attained, make something specific. But suppose it is otherwise, suppose piety is something which truly fuses both, then it cannot be formed simply by bringing the two together, but must be an original unity. Take care, however, I warn you, that you do not make such an admission. Were it the case, morality and genius apart would be only fragments of the ruins of religion, or its corpse when it is dead. Religion were then higher than both, the true divine life itself. But, in return for this warning, if you accept it, and discover no other solution, be so good as tell me how your opinion about religion is to be distinguished from nothing? Till then nothing remains for me but to assume that you have not yet, by examination, satisfied yourselves about this side of religion. Perhaps we shall have better fortune with the other side – what is known as the way of thinking, or faith.

You will, I believe, grant that your knowledge, however many-sided it may appear, falls, as a whole, into two contrasted sciences. How you shall subdivide and name belongs to the controversies of your schools, with which at present I am not concerned. Do not, therefore, be too critical about my terminology, even though it comes from various quarters. Let us call the one division physics or metaphysics, applying both names indifferently, or indicating sections of the same thing. Let the other be ethics or the doctrine of duties or practical philosophy. At least we are agreed about the distinction meant. The former describes the nature of things, or if that seems too much, how man conceives and must conceive of things and of the world as the sum of things. The latter science, on the contrary, teaches what man should be for the world, and what he should do in it. Now, in so far as religion is a way of thinking of something and a knowledge about something, has it not the same object as these sciences? What does faith know about except the relation of man to God and to the world – God's purpose in making him, and the world's power to help or hinder him? Again it distinguishes in its own fashion a good action from a bad. Is then religion identical with natural science and ethics? You would not agree, you would never grant that our faith is as surely founded, or stands on the same level of certainty as your scientific knowledge! Your accusation against it is just that it does not know how to distinguish between the demonstrable and the probable. Similarly, you do not forget to remark diligently that very marvellous injunctions both to do and leave undone have issued from religion. You may be quite right; only do not forget that it has been the same with that which you call science. In both spheres you believe you have made improvements and are better than your fathers.

What, then, are we to say that religion is? As before, that it is a mixture – mingled theoretical and practical knowledge? But this is even less permissible, particularly if, as appears, each of these two branches of knowledge has its own characteristic mode of procedure. Such a mixture of elements that would either counteract or separate, could only be made most arbitrarily. The utmost gain to be looked for would be to furnish us with another method for putting known results into shape for beginners, and for stimulating them to a further study. But if that be so, why do you strive against religion? You might, so long as beginners are to be found, leave it in peace and security. If we presumed to subject you, you might smile at our folly, but knowing for certain that you have left it far behind, and that it is only prepared for us by you wiser people, you would be wrong in losing a serious word on the matter. But it is not so, I think. Unless I am quite mistaken, you have long been laboring to provide the mass of the people with just such an epitome of your knowledge. The name is of no consequence, whether it be "religion" or "enlightenment" or aught else. But there is something different which must first be expelled, or, at least, excluded. This something it is that you call belief, and it is the object of your hostility, and not an article you would desire to extend.

Wherefore, my friends, belief must be something different from a mixture of opinions about God and the world, and of precepts for one life or for two. Piety cannot be an instinct craving for a mess of metaphysical and ethical crumbs. If it were, you would scarcely oppose it. It would not occur to you to speak of religion as different from your knowledge, however much it might be distant. The strife of the cultured and learned with the pious would simply be the strife of depth and thoroughness with superficiality; it would be the strife of the master with pupils who are to emancipate themselves in due time.

Were you, after all, to take this view, I should like to plague you with all sorts of Socratic questions, till I compelled many of you to give a direct answer to the question, whether it is at all possible to be wise and pious at the same time. I should also wish to submit whether in other well-known matters you do not acknowledge the principle that things similar are to be placed together and particulars to be subordinated to generals? Is it that you may joke with the world about a serious subject, that in religion only the principle is not applied? But let us suppose you are serious. How does it come, then, that in religious faith, what, in science, you separate into two spheres, is united and so indissolubly bound together that one cannot be thought of without the other? The pious man does not believe that the right course of action can be determined, except in so far as, at the same time, there is knowledge of the relations of man to God; and again right action, he holds, is necessary for right knowledge. Suppose the binding principle lies in the theoretic side. Why then is a practical philosophy set over against a theoretic, and not rather regarded as a section? Or suppose the principle is in the practical side, the same would apply to a theoretic philosophy. Or both may be united, only in a yet higher, an original knowledge. That this highest, long-lost unity of knowledge should be religion you cannot believe, for you have found it most, and have opposed it most, in those who are furthest from science. I will not hold you to any such conclusion, for I would not take up a position that I cannot maintain. This, however, you may well grant, that, concerning this side of religion, you must take time to consider what is its proper significance.

Let us be honest with one another. As we recently agreed, you have no liking for religion. But, in carrying on an honorable war which is not quite without strain, you would not wish to fight against such a shadow as that with which we have so far been battling. It must be something special that could fashion itself so peculiarly in the human heart, something thinkable, the real nature of which can so be presented as to be spoken of and argued about, and I consider it very wrong that out of things so disparate as modes of knowing and modes of acting, you patch together an untenable something, and call it religion, and then are so needlessly ceremonious with it. But you would deny that you have not gone to work with straightforwardness. Seeing I have rejected systems, commentaries, and apologies, you would demand that I unfold all the original sources of religion from the beautiful fictions of the Greeks to the sacred scriptures of the Christians. Should I not find everywhere the nature of the Gods, and the will of the Gods? Is not that man everywhere accounted holy and blessed who knows the former, and does the latter?

But that is just what I have already said. Religion never appears quite pure. Its outward form is ever determined by something else. Our task first is to exhibit its true nature, and not to assume offhand, as you seem to do, that the outward form and the true nature are the same. Does the material world present you with an element in its original purity as a spontaneous product of Nature? Must you, therefore, as you have done in the intellectual world, take very gross things for simple? It is the one ceaseless aim of all analysis to present something really simple. So also it is in spiritual things. You can only obtain what is original by producing it, as it were, by a second, an artificial creation in yourselves, and even then it is but for the moment of its production. Pray come to an understanding on the point, for you shall be ceaselessly reminded of it....

In order to make quite clear to you what is the original and characteristic possession of religion, it resigns, at once, all claims on anything that belongs either to science or morality. Whether it has been borrowed or bestowed it is now returned. What, then, does your science of being, your natural science, all your theoretical philosophy, in so far as it has to do with the actual world, have for its aim? To know things, I suppose, as they really are; to show the peculiar relations by which each is what it is; to determine for each its place in the Whole, and to distinguish it rightly from all else; to present the whole real world in its mutually conditioned necessity; and to exhibit the oneness of all phenomena with their eternal laws. This is truly beautiful and excellent, and I am not disposed to depreciate it. Rather, if this description of mine, so slightly sketched, does not suffice, I will grant the highest and most exhaustive you are able to give.

And yet, however high you go; though you pass from the laws to the Universal Lawgiver, in whom is the unity of all things, though you allege that Nature cannot be comprehended without God, I would still maintain that religion has nothing to do with this knowledge, and that, quite apart from it, its nature can be known. Quantity of knowledge is not quantity of piety. Piety can gloriously display itself, both with originality and individuality, in those to which this kind of knowledge is not original. They may only know it as everybody does, as isolated results known in connection with other things. The pious man must, in a sense, be a wise man, but he will readily admit, even though you somewhat proudly look down upon him, that, in so far as he is pious, he does not hold his knowledge in the same way as you.

Let me interpret in clear words what most pious persons only guess at and never know how to express. Were you to set God as the apex of your science, as the foundation of all knowing as well as of all knowledge, they would accord praise and honor, but it would not be their way of having and knowing God. From their way, as they would readily grant, and as is easy enough to see, knowledge and science do not proceed.

It is true that religion is essentially contemplative. You would never call anyone pious who went about in impervious stupidity, whose sense is not open for the life of the world. But this contemplation is not turned, as your knowledge of Nature is, to the existence of a finite thing, combined with and opposed to another finite thing. It has not even, like your knowledge of God – if for once I might use an old expression – to do with the nature of the first cause, in itself and in its relation to every other cause and operation. The contemplation of the pious is the immediate consciousness of the universal existence of all finite things, in and through the Infinite, and of all temporal things in and through the Eternal. Religion is to seek this and find it in all that lives and moves, in all growth and change, in all doing and suffering. It is to have life and to know life in immediate feeling, only as such an existence in the Infinite and Eternal. Where this is found religion is satisfied, where it hides itself there is for her unrest and anguish, extremity and death. Wherefore it is a life in the infinite nature of the Whole, in the One and in the All, in God, having and possessing all things in God, and God in all. Yet religion is not knowledge and science, either of the world or of God. Without being knowledge, it recognizes knowledge and science. In itself it is an affection, a revelation of the Infinite in the finite, God being seen in it and it in God.

Similarly, what is the object of your ethics, of your science of action? Does it not seek to distinguish precisely each part of human doing and producing, and at the same time to combine them into a whole, according to actual relations? But the pious man confesses that, as pious, he knows nothing about it. He does, indeed, contemplate human action, but it is not the kind of contemplation from which an ethical system takes its rise. Only one thing he seeks out and detects, action from God, God's activity among men. If your ethics are right, and his piety as well, he will not, it is true, acknowledge any action as excellent which is not embraced in your system. But to know and to construct this system is your business, ye learned, not his. If you will not believe, regard the case of women. You ascribe to them religion, not only as an adornment, but you demand of them the finest feeling for distinguishing the things that excel: do you equally expect them to know your ethics as a science?

It is the same, let me say at once, with action itself. The artist fashions what is given him to fashion, by virtue of his special talent. These talents are so different that the one he possesses another lacks; unless someone, against heaven's will, would possess all. But when anyone is praised to you as pious you are not accustomed to ask which of these gifts dwell in him by virtue of his piety. The citizen – taking the word in the sense of the ancients, not in its present meagre significance – regulates, leads, and influences in virtue of his morality. But this is something different from piety. Piety has also a passive side. While morality always shows itself as manipulating, as self-controlling, piety appears as a surrender, a submission to be moved by the Whole that stands over against man. Morality depends, therefore, entirely on the consciousness of freedom, within the sphere of which all that it produces falls. Piety, on the contrary, is not at all bound to this side of life. In the opposite sphere of necessity, where there is no properly individual action, it is quite as active. Wherefore the two are different. Piety does, indeed, linger with satisfaction on every action that is from God, and every activity that reveals the Infinite in the finite, and yet it is not itself this activity. Only by keeping quite outside the range both of science and of practice can it maintain its proper sphere and character. Only when piety takes its place alongside of science and practice, as a necessary, an indispensable third, as their natural counterpart, not less in worth and splendor than either, will the common field be altogether occupied and human nature on this side complete....

But in order that you may understand what I mean by this unity and difference of religion, science, and art, we shall endeavor to descend into the inmost sanctuary of life. There, perhaps, we may find ourselves agreed. There alone you discover the original relation of intuition and feeling from which alone this identity and difference is to be understood. But I must direct you to your own selves. You must apprehend a living moment. You must know how to listen to yourselves before your own consciousness. At least you must be able to reconstruct from your consciousness your own state. What you are to notice is the rise of your consciousness and not to reflect upon something already there. Your thought can only embrace what is sundered. Wherefore as soon as you have made any given definite activity of your soul, an object of communication or of contemplation, you have already begun to separate. It is impossible, therefore, to adduce any definite example, for, as soon as anything is an example, what I wish to indicate is already past. Only the faintest trace of the original unity could then be shown. Such as it is, however, I will not despise it as a preliminary.

Consider how you delineate an object. Is there not both a stimulation and a determination by the object, at one and the same time, which for one particular moment forms your existence? The more definite your image, the more, in this way, you become the object, and the more you lose yourselves. But just because you can trace the growing preponderance of one side over the other, both must have been one and equal in the first, the original moment that has escaped you. Or sunk in yourselves you find all that you formerly regarded as a disconnected manifold compacted now indivisibly into the one peculiar content of your being. Yet when you give heed, can you not see as it disappears, the image of an object, from whose influence, from whose magical contact this definite consciousness has proceeded? The more your own state sways you the paler and more unrecognizable your image becomes. The greater your emotion, the more you are absorbed in it, the more your whole nature is concerned to retain for the memory an imperishable trace of what is necessarily fleeting, to carry over to what you may engage in, its color and impress, and so unite two moments into a duration, the less you observe the object that caused it. But just because it grows pale and vanishes, it must before have been nearer and clearer. Originally it must have been one and the same with your feeling. But, as was said, these are mere traces. Unless you will go back on the first beginning of this consciousness, you can scarcely understand them.

And suppose you cannot? Then say, weighing it quite generally and originally, what is every act of your life in itself and without distinction from other acts. What is it merely as act, as movement? Is it not the coming into being of something for itself, and at the same time in the Whole? It is an endeavor to return into the Whole, and to exist for oneself at the same time. These are the links from which the whole chain is made. Your whole life is such an existence for self in the Whole. How now are you in the Whole? By your senses. And how are you for yourselves? By the unity of your self-consciousness, which is given chiefly in the possibility of comparing the varying degrees of sensation. How both can only rise together, if both together fashion every act of life, is easy to see. You become sense and the whole becomes object. Sense and object mingle and unite, then each returns to its place, and the object rent from sense is a perception, and you rent from the object are for yourselves, a feeling. It is this earlier moment I mean, which you always experience yet never experience. The phenomenon of your life is just the result of its constant departure and return. It is scarcely in time at all, so swiftly it passes; it can scarcely be described, so little does it properly exist. Would that I could hold it fast and refer to it your commonest as well as your highest activities.

Did I venture to compare it, seeing I cannot describe it, I would say it is fleeting and transparent as the vapor which the dew breathes on blossom and fruit, it is bashful and tender as a maiden's kiss, it is holy and fruitful as a bridal embrace. Nor is it merely like, it is all this. It is the first contact of the universal life with an individual. It fills no time and fashions nothing palpable. It is the holy wedlock of the Universe with the incarnated Reason for a creative, productive embrace. It is immediate, raised above all error and misunderstanding. You lie directly on the bosom of the infinite world. In that moment, you are its soul. Through one part of your nature you feel, as your own, all its powers and its endless life. In that moment it is your body, you pervade, as your own, its muscles and members and your thinking and forecasting set its inmost nerves in motion. In this way every living, original movement in your life is first received. Among the rest it is the source of every religious emotion. But it is not, as I said, even a moment. The incoming of existence to us, by this immediate union, at once stops as soon as it reaches consciousness. Either the intuition displays itself more vividly and clearly, like the figure of the vanishing mistress to the eyes of her lover; or feeling issues from your heart and overspreads your whole being, as the blush of shame and love over the face of the maiden. At length your consciousness is finally determined as one or other, as intuition or feeling. Then, even though you have not quite surrendered to this division and lost consciousness of your life as a unity, there remains nothing but the knowledge that they were originally one, that they issued simultaneously from the fundamental relation of your nature. Wherefore, it is in this sense true what an ancient sage has taught you, that all knowledge is recollection. It is recollection of what is outside of all time, and is therefore justly to be placed at the head of all temporal things.

And, as it is with intuition and feeling on the one hand, so it is with knowledge which includes both and with activity on the other. Through the constant play and mutual influence of these opposites, your life expands and has its place in time. Both knowledge and activity are a desire to be identified with the Universe through an object. If the power of the objects preponderates, if, as intuition or feeling, it enters and seeks to draw you into the circle of their existence, it is always a knowledge. If the preponderating power is on your side, so that you give the impress and reflect yourselves in the objects, it is activity in the narrower sense, external working. Yet it is only as you are stimulated and determined that you can communicate yourselves to things. In founding or establishing anything in the world you are only giving back what that original act of fellowship has wrought in you, and similarly everything the world fashions in you must be by the same act. One must mutually stimulate the other. Only in an interchange of knowing and activity can your life consist. A peaceful existence, wherein one side did not stimulate the other, would not be your life. It would be that from which it first developed, and into which it will again disappear.

There, then, you have the three things about which my Speech has so far turned, – perception, feeling, and activity, and you now understand what I mean when I say they are not identical and yet are inseparable. Take what belongs to each class and consider it by itself. You will find that those moments in which you exercise power over things and impress yourselves upon them, form what you call your practical, or in the narrower sense, your moral life; again the contemplative moments, be they few or many, in which things produce themselves in you as intuition, you will doubtless call your scientific life. Now can either series alone form a human life? Would it not be death? If each activity were not stimulated and renewed by the other, would it not be self-consumed? Yet they are not identical. If you would understand your life and speak comprehensibly of it, they must be distinguished. As it stands with these two in respect of one another, it must stand with the third in respect of both. How then are you to name this third, which is the series of feeling? What life will it form? The religious as I think, and as you will not be able to deny, when you have considered it more closely.

The chief point in my Speech is now uttered. This is the peculiar sphere which I would assign to religion – the whole of it, and nothing more. Unless you grant it, you must either prefer the old confusion to clear analysis, or produce something else, I know not what, new and quite wonderful. Your feeling is piety, in so far as it expresses, in the manner described, the being and life common to you and to the All. Your feeling is piety in so far as it is the result of the operation of God in you by means of the operation of the world upon you. This series is not made up either of perceptions or of objects of perception, either of works or operations or of different spheres of operation, but purely of sensations and the influence of all that lives and moves around, which accompanies them and conditions them. These feelings are exclusively the elements of religion, and none are excluded. There is no sensation that is not pious, except it indicate some diseased and impaired state of the life, the influence of which will not be confined to religion. Wherefore it follows that ideas and principles are all foreign to religion. This truth we here come upon for the second time. If ideas and principles are to be anything, they must belong to knowledge which is a different department of life from religion.

The Christian Faith*

PP. 3. The piety which forms the basis of all ecclesiastical communions is, considered purely in itself, neither a Knowing nor a Doing, but a modification of Feeling, or of immediate self-consciousness....

2. When Feeling and Self-consciousness are here put side by side as equivalent, it is by no means intended to introduce generally a manner of speech in which the two expressions would be simply synonymous. The term "feeling" has in the language of common life been long current in this religious connection; but for scientific usage it needs to be more precisely defined; and it is to do this that the other word is added. So that if anyone takes the word "feeling" in a sense so wide as to include unconscious states, he will by the other word be reminded that such is not the usage we are here maintaining. Again, to the term "self-consciousness" is added the determining epithet "immediate", lest anyone should think of a kind of self-consciousness which is not feeling at all; as, e.g., when the name of self-consciousness is given to that consciousness of self which is more like an objective consciousness, being a representation of oneself, and thus mediated by self-contemplation. Even when such a representation of ourselves, as we exist in a given portion of time, in thinking, e.g., or in willing, moves quite close to, or even interpenetrates, the individual moments of the mental state, this kind of self-consciousness does appear simply as an *accompaniment* of the state itself. But the real immediate self-consciousness, which is not representation but in the proper sense feeling, is by no means always simply an accompaniment. It may rather be

* Friedrich Schleiermacher, from Ch. 1 of *The Christian Faith*, T. & T. Clark, Edinburgh, 1928.

presumed that in this respect everyone has a twofold experience. In the first place, it is everybody's experience that there are moments in which all thinking and willing retreat behind a self-consciousness of one form or another; but, in the second place, that at times this same form of self-consciousness persists unaltered during a series of diverse acts of thinking and willing, taking up no relation to these, and thus not being in the proper sense even an accompaniment of them. Thus joy and sorrow – those mental phases which are always so important in the realm of religion – are genuine states of feeling, in the proper sense explained above; whereas self-approval and self-reproach, apart from their subsequently passing into joy and sorrow, belong in themselves rather to the objective consciousness of self, as results of an analytic contemplation. Nowhere, perhaps, do the two forms stand nearer to each other than here, but just for that reason this comparison puts the difference in the clearest light....

4. But now (these three, Feeling, Knowing, and Doing being granted) while we here set forth once more the oft-asserted view that, of the three, Feeling is one to which piety belongs, it is not in any wise meant, as indeed the above discussion shows, that piety is excluded from all connection with Knowing and Doing. For, indeed, it is the case in general that the immediate self-consciousness is always the mediating link in the transition between moments in which Knowing predominates and those in which Doing predominates, so that a different Doing may proceed from the same Knowing in different people according as a different determination of self-consciousness enters in. And thus it will fall to piety to stimulate Knowing and Doing, and every moment in which piety has a predominant place will contain within itself one or both of these in germ. But just this is the very truth represented by our proposition, and is in no wise an objection to it; for were it otherwise the religious moments could not combine with the others to form a single life, but piety would be something isolated and without any influence upon the other mental functions of our lives. However, in representing this truth, and thus securing to piety its own peculiar province in its

connection with all other provinces, our proposition is opposing the assertions from other quarters that piety is a Knowing, or a Doing, or both, or a state made up of Feeling, Knowing, and Doing; and in this polemical connection our proposition must now be still more closely considered.

If, then, piety did consist in Knowing, it would have to be, above all, that knowledge, in its entirety or in its essence, which is here set up as the content of Dogmatics (*Glaubenslehre*): otherwise it must be a complete mistake for us here to investigate the nature of piety in the interests of our study of Dogmatics. But if piety *is* that knowledge, then the amount of such knowledge in a man must be the measure of his piety. For anything which, in its rise and fall, is not the measure of the perfection of a given object cannot constitute the essence of that object. Accordingly, on the hypothesis in question, the most perfect master of Christian Dogmatics would always be likewise the most pious Christian. And no one will admit this to be the case, even if we premise that the most perfect master is only he who keeps most to what is essential and does not forget it in accessories and side issues; but all will agree rather that the same degree of perfection in that knowledge may be accompanied by very different degrees of piety, and the same degree of piety by very different degrees of knowledge. It may, however, be objected that the assertion that piety is a matter of Knowing refers not so much to the content of that knowledge as to the certainty which characterizes its representations; so that the knowledge of doctrines is piety only in virtue of the certainty attached to them, and thus only in virtue of the strength of the conviction, while a possession of the doctrines without conviction is not piety at all. Then the strength of the conviction would be the measure of the piety; and this is undoubtedly what those people have chiefly in mind who so love to paraphrase the word *Faith* as "fidelity to one's convictions". But in all other more typical fields of knowledge the only measure of conviction is the clearness and completeness of the thinking itself. Now if it is to be the same with *this* conviction, then we should simply be back at our old point, that he who thinks the religious propositions most clearly and completely, individually and in their connections, must likewise be the most pious man. If, then, this conclusion is still to be rejected, but the hypothesis is to be retained (namely, that conviction is the measure of piety), the conviction in this case must be of a different kind and must have a different measure. However closely, then, piety may be connected with this conviction, it does not follow that it is connected in the same way with that knowledge. And if, nevertheless, the knowledge which forms Dogmatics has to relate itself to piety, the explanation of this is that while piety is, of course, the object of this knowledge, the knowledge can only be explicated in virtue of a certainty which inheres in the determinations of self-consciousness.

If, on the other hand, piety consists in Doing, it is manifest that the Doing which constitutes it cannot be defined by its content; for experience teaches that not only the most admirable but also the most abominable, not only the most useful but also the most inane and meaningless things, are done as pious and out of piety. Thus we are thrown back simply upon the form, upon the method and manner in which the thing comes to be done. But this can only be understood from the two *termini*, the underlying motive as the starting-point, and the intended result as the goal. Now no one will pronounce an action more or less pious because of the greater or less degree of completeness with which the intended result is achieved. Suppose we then are thrown back upon the motive. It is manifest that underlying every motive there is a certain determination of self-consciousness, be it pleasure or pain, and that it is by these that one motive can most clearly be distinguished from another. Accordingly an action (a Doing) will be pious in so far as the determination of self-consciousness, the feeling which had become affective and had passed into a motive impulse, is a pious one.

Thus both hypotheses lead to the same point: that there are both a Knowing and a Doing which pertain to piety, but neither of these constitutes the essence of piety: they only pertain to it inasmuch as the stirred-up Feeling sometimes comes to rest in a thinking which fixes it, sometimes discharges itself in an action which expresses it.

Finally, no one will deny that there are states of Feeling, such as penitence, contrition, confidence, and joy in God, which we pronounce pious in themselves, without regard to any Knowing or Doing that proceeds from them, though, of course, we expect both that they will work themselves out in actions which are otherwise obligatory, and that the reflective impulse will turn its attention to them....

Pp. 4. The common element in all howsoever diverse expressions of piety, by which these are conjointly distinguished from all other feelings, or, in other words, the self-identical essence of piety, is this: the consciousness of being absolutely dependent, or, which is the same thing, of being in relation with God.

1. In any actual state of consciousness, no matter whether it merely accompanies a thought or action or occupies a moment for itself, we are never simply conscious of our Selves in their unchanging identity, but are always at the same time conscious of a changing determination of them. The Ego in itself can be represented objectively; but every consciousness of self is at the same time the consciousness of a variable state of being. But in this distinction of the latter from the former, it is implied that the variable does not proceed purely from the self-identical, for in that case it could not be distinguished from it. Thus in every self-consciousness there are two elements, which we might call respectively a self-caused element (*ein Sichselbstsetzen*) and a non-self-caused element (*ein Sichselbstnichtsogesetzthaben*); or a Being and a Having-by-some-means-come-to-be (*ein Sein und ein Irgendwiegewordensein*). The latter of these presupposes for every self-consciousness another factor besides the Ego, a factor which is the source of the particular determination, and without which the self-consciousness would not be precisely what it is. But this Other is not objectively presented in the immediate self-consciousness with which alone we are here concerned. For though, of course, the double constitution of self-consciousness causes us always to look objectively for an Other to which we can trace the origin of our particular state, yet this search is a separate act with which we are not at present concerned. In self-

consciousness there are only two elements: the one expresses the existence of the subject for itself, the other its co-existence with an Other.

Now to these two elements, as they exist together in the temporal self-consciousness, correspond in the subject its *Receptivity* and its (spontaneous) *Activity*. If we could think away the co-existence with an Other, but otherwise think ourselves as we are, then a self-consciousness which predominantly expressed an affective condition of receptivity would be impossible, and any self-consciousness could then express only activity – an activity, however, which, not being directed to any object, would be merely an urge outwards, an indefinite "agility" without form or color. But as we never do exist except along with an Other, so even in every outward-tending self-consciousness the element of receptivity, in some way or other affected, is the primary one; and even the self-consciousness which accompanies an action (acts of knowing included), while it predominantly expresses spontaneous movement and activity, is always related (though the relation is often a quite indefinite one) to a prior moment of affective receptivity, through which the original "agility" received its direction. To these propositions assent can be unconditionally demanded; and no one will deny them who is capable of a little introspection and can find interest in the real subject of our present enquiries.

2. The common element in all those determinations of self-consciousness which predominantly express a receptivity affected from some outside quarter is the *feeling of Dependence*. On the other hand, the common element in all those determinations which predominantly express spontaneous movement and activity is the *feeling of Freedom*. The former is the case not only because it is by an influence from some other quarter that we have come to such a state, but particularly because we *could* not so become except by means of an Other. The latter is the case because in these instances an Other is determined by us, and without our spontaneous activity could not be so determined. These two definitions may, indeed, seem to be still incomplete, inasmuch as there is also a mobility of the subject which is not connected with an Other at all, but which seems to be subject

to the same antithesis as that just explained. But when we become such-and-such from within outwards, for ourselves, without any Other being involved, that is the simple situation of the temporal development of a being which remains essentially self-identical, and it is only very improperly that this can be referred to the concept "Freedom". And when we cannot ourselves, from within outwards, become such-and-such, this only indicates the limits which belong to the nature of the subject itself as regards spontaneous activity, and this could only very improperly be called "Dependence".

Further, this antithesis must on no account be confused with the antithesis between gloomy or depressing and elevating or joyful feelings, of which we shall speak later. For a feeling of dependence may be elevating, if the "having-become-such-and-such" which it expresses is complete; and similarly a feeling of freedom may be dejecting, if the moment of predominating receptivity to which the action can be traced was of a dejecting nature, or again if the manner and method of the activity prove to be a disadvantageous combination.

Let us now think of the feeling of dependence and the feeling of freedom as *one,* in the sense that not only the subject but the corresponding Other is the same for both. Then the total self-consciousness made up of both together is one of *Reciprocity* between the subject and the corresponding Other. Now let us suppose the totality of all moments of feeling, of both kinds, as one whole: then the corresponding Other is also to be supposed as a totality or as one, and then that term "reciprocity" is the right one for our self-consciousness in general, inasmuch as it expresses our connection with everything which either appeals to our receptivity or is subjected to our activity. And this is true not only when we particularize this Other and ascribe to each of its elements a different degree of relation to the twofold consciousness within us, but also when we think of the total "outside" as one, and moreover (since it contains other receptivities and activities to which we have a relation) as one together with ourselves, that is, as a *World.* Accordingly our self-consciousness, as a consciousness of our existence in the world or of our co-existence with the world, is a series in which the feeling of freedom and the feeling of dependence are divided. But neither an absolute feeling of dependence, i.e. without any feeling of freedom in relation to the co-determinant, nor an absolute feeling of freedom, i.e. without any feeling of dependence in relation to the co-determinant, is to be found in this whole realm. If we consider our relations to Nature, or those which exist in human society, there we shall find a large number of objects in regard to which freedom and dependence maintain very much of an equipoise: these constitute the field of equal reciprocity. There are other objects which exercise a far greater influence upon our receptivity than our activity exercises upon them, and also *vice versa*, so that one of two may diminish until it is imperceptible. But neither of the two members will ever completely disappear. The feeling of dependence predominates in the relation of children to their parents, or of citizens to their fatherland; and yet individuals can, without losing their relationship, exercise upon their fatherland not only a directive influence, but even a counter-influence. And the dependence of children on their parents, which very soon comes to be felt as a gradually diminishing and fading quantity, is never from the start free from the admixture of an element of spontaneous activity toward the parents: just as even in the most absolute autocracy the ruler is not without some slight feeling of dependence. It is the same in the case of Nature: toward all the forces of Nature – even, we may say, toward the heavenly bodies – we ourselves do, in the same sense in which they influence us, exercise a counter-influence, however minute. So that our whole self-consciousness in relation to the World or its individual parts remains enclosed within these limits.

3. There can, accordingly, be for us no such thing as a feeling of absolute freedom. He who asserts that he has such a feeling is either deceiving himself or separating things which essentially belong together. For if the feeling of freedom expresses a forthgoing activity, this activity must have an object which has been somehow given to us, and this could not have taken place without an influence of the object upon our receptivity. Therefore in every such case there is involved a feeling of dependence which goes

along with the feeling of freedom, and thus limits it. The contrary could only be possible if the object altogether came into existence through our activity, which is never the case absolutely, but only relatively. But if, on the other hand, the feeling of freedom expresses only an inward movement of activity, not only is every such individual movement bound up with the state of our stimulated receptivity at the moment, but, further, the totality of our free inward movements, considered as a unity, cannot be represented as a feeling of absolute freedom, because our whole existence does not present itself to our consciousness as having proceeded from our own spontaneous activity. Therefore, in any temporal existence a feeling of absolute freedom can have no place. As regards the feeling of absolute dependence which, on the other hand, our proposition does postulate: for just the same reason, this feeling cannot in any wise arise from the influence of an object which has in some way to be *given* to us; for upon such an object there would always be a counter-influence, and even a voluntary renunciation of this would always involve a feeling of freedom. Hence a feeling of absolute dependence, strictly speaking, cannot exist in a single moment as such, because such a moment is always determined, as regards its total content, by what is given, and thus by objects toward which we have a feeling of freedom. But the self-consciousness which accompanies all our activity, and therefore, since that is never zero, accompanies our whole existence, and negatives absolute freedom, is itself precisely a consciousness of absolute dependence; for it is the consciousness that the whole of our spontaneous activity comes from a source outside of us in just the same sense in which anything toward which we should have a feeling of absolute freedom must have proceeded entirely from ourselves. But without any feeling of freedom a feeling of absolute dependence would not be possible.

4. As regards the identification of absolute dependence with "relation to God" in our proposition: this is to be understood in the sense that the *Whence* of our receptive and active existence, as implied in this self-consciousness, is to be designated by the word "God", and that this is for us the really original significa-

tion of that word. In this connection we have first of all to remind ourselves that, as we have seen in the foregoing discussion,
this "Whence" is not the world, in the sense of the totality of
temporal existence, and still less is it any single part of the world.
For we have a feeling of freedom (though, indeed, a limited one)
in relation to the world, since we are complementary parts
of it, and also since we are continually exercising an influence on
its individual parts; and, moreover, there is the possibility of our
exercising influence on all its parts; and while this does permit
a limited feeling of dependence, it excludes the absolute feeling.
In the next place, we have to note that our proposition is intended
to oppose the view that this feeling of dependence is itself conditioned by some previous knowledge about God. And this may
indeed be the more necessary since many people claim to be in
the sure possession of a concept of God, altogether a matter of
conception and original, i.e., independent of any feeling; and in
the strength of this higher self-consciousness, which indeed may
come pretty near to being a feeling of absolute freedom, they put
far from them, as something almost infra-human, that very feeling which for us is the basic type of all piety. Now our proposition is in no wise intended to dispute the existence of such an
original knowledge, but simply to set it aside as something with
which, in a system of Christian doctrine, we could never have any
concern, because plainly enough it has itself nothing to do
directly with piety. If, however, word and idea are always originally one, and the term "God" therefore presupposes an idea, then
we shall simply say that this idea, which is nothing more than
the expression of the feeling of absolute dependence, is the most
direct reflection upon it and the most original idea with which we
are here concerned, and is quite independent of that original
knowledge (properly so called), and conditioned only by our feeling of absolute dependence. So that in the first instance God
signifies for us simply that which is the co-determinant in this
feeling and to which we trace our being in such a state; and any
further content of the idea must be evolved out of this fundamental import assigned to it. Now this is just what is principally
meant by the formula which says that to feel oneself absolutely

dependent and to be conscious of being in relation with God are one and the same thing; and the reason is that absolute dependence is the fundamental relation which must include all others in itself. This last expression includes the God-consciousness in the self-consciousness in such a way that, quite in accordance with the above analysis, the two cannot be separated from each other. The feeling of absolute dependence becomes a clear self-consciousness only as this idea comes simultaneously into being. In this sense it can indeed be said that God is given to us in feeling in an original way; and if we speak of an original revelation of God to man or in man, the meaning will always be just this, that, along with the absolute dependence which characterizes not only man but all temporal existence, there is given to man also the immediate self-consciousness of it, which becomes a consciousness of God. In whatever measure this actually takes place during the course of a personality through time, in just that measure do we ascribe piety to the individual. On the other hand, any possibility of God being in any way *given* is entirely excluded, because anything that is outwardly given must be given as an object exposed to our counter-influence, however slight this may be. The transference of the idea of God to any perceptible object, unless one is all the time conscious that it is a piece of purely arbitrary symbolism, is always a corruption, whether it be a temporary transference, i.e., a theophany, or a constitutive transference, in which God is represented as permanently a particular perceptible existence.

7

RELIGION AS A DIMENSION

Paul Tillich

Editor's Introduction

IN OUR EVERYDAY language we use the word "religion" in two ways. First, we use it to refer to institutionalized and formalized religious groups. Second, we use it to refer to basic attitudes and to the deepest levels of self-understanding. These two uses are evident when we say, for example, "He belongs to the protestant religion, but his real religion is financial success", or "He doesn't subscribe to any religion, but he is a very religious person". This double usuage led John Dewey to distinguish between "religion" and "the religious":

There is a difference between religion, a religion, and the religious; between anything that may be denoted by a noun substantive and the quality of experience that is designated by an adjective.... A religion . . . always signifies a special body of beliefs and practices having some kind of institutional organization, loose or tight. In contrast the adjective "religious" denotes nothing in the way of a specifiable entity, either institutional or as a system of beliefs. It does not denote anything to which one can specifically point as one can point to this and that historic religion or existing church. For it does not denote anything that can exist by itself or that can be organized into a particular and distinctive form of existence. It denotes attitudes that may be taken toward every object and every proposed end or ideal. (John Dewey, *A Common Faith*, pp. 3, 9-10, Yale University Press, 1934 and 1960.)

Dewey is making a distinction between "religion" as an outward expression, codified and institutionalized in the various historical religions and the "religious" element in human nature behind these religions. But he is also making a further distinction. He is distinguishing between "the religious" considered as one aspect or component of human existence and "the religious" as an attitude or disposition manifest in all aspects of life but not localized in any particular component. Dewey would agree with Schleiermacher in locating the essence of religion subjectively, but he would deny that there is a particular human characteristic such as "feeling" or "immediate self-consciousness" that is uniquely religious. People are religious when they exhibit certain "attitudes that lend deep and enduring support to the process of living".

The attempt to describe religion as a separate and independent sphere of individual and human activity did not appear until near the beginning of the nineteenth century, with the rise of the social sciences. Schleiermacher's *On Religion* was one of the first books to regard it as an isolable subject. Prior to that time a religious tradition was identified with the cultural tradition that provided the fundamental means of individual and social identification. It is only within the past century and a half, and only in the West, that religion has been viewed as one component of individual and social life. Traditionally, religion referred to the basic guiding images and principles of an individual or a culture. Religion was identical with style of life.

Among modern theologians, Paul Tillich has done more than any other to recapture the understanding of "religion" as the way in which individuals and societies attempt to understand themselves and articulate this understanding. His well-known cultural theology is an effort to show that religious symbols and myths are the way people understand and express the "depth" dimension of existence. Tillich is like Schleiermacher, therefore, in locating the essence of religion subjectively. But there are two important differences. First, for Tillich, as for Dewey, religion is not a component of human life – even an indispensable one – it is a dimension of existence that influences every segment of human activity. As one moves into the deepest levels of meaning, whether in art, science, ethics, or some other activity, he approaches the religious level. Religion refers to "ultimate concern": one's fundamental values, whatever they may be. Second, the "depth dimension" is not located within an individual's own particular subjectivity. As one moves into the depths of his existence, he moves toward that level of the subconscious mind which is beyond his conscious control. He moves toward the social collective subconscious. In other words, Tillich stresses the social aspect of religion.

When Tillich refers to the "depth dimension" he refers to a level of experience which is common to all men but which is often overlooked. Like Maritain, van der Leeuw, and Schleiermacher, he attempts to identify primary levels of experience as the basis of religion. Tillich's distinction between the "horizontal" and "vertical" has a close parallel in Maritain's notion of the differences between horizontal and vertical regression. Tillich and Maritain differ, however, in their understanding of the relation between the two dimensions and in their interpretation of the way men have access to the "vertical".

For Tillich, the vertical or depth dimension is accessible only through symbols. He points to the way painters, poets, novelists, and dramatists use symbols to open up the deepest levels of human existence. Tillich claims that participation in these levels of existence is possible only through symbols. Symbols are, therefore, an essential part of human life if it is to be lived on the deepest levels. One participates in symbols, and through this participation one is able to see the true dimensions of one's existential situation.

Tillich employs the "method of correlation" as a theological way of relating existential questions and symbolic answers. In correlating these questions and answers, however, Tillich does not suppose that religious symbols supply the answers to an existential situation in which men already find themselves to be, although he sometimes seems to imply that. Both questions and answers arise together when men approach the depths. The method of correlation does not simply connect existential questions and symbolic answers. Rather it is a way of formulating the real questions of existence and understanding the power of religious symbols. The question and the answer emerge together through their correlation.

Moreover, theological correlation cannot supply answers to the existential questions of human existence. These questions are not theoretical but existential, and they cannot be answered theoretically, but only through participation in healing symbols. Theology does not solve existential questions; it poses them in a way that they are open to symbolic resolution.

Paul Johannes Tillich was born in Germany in 1886. After a traditional German education in philosophy and theology, he was ordained in 1912. He served as a Chaplain in World War I and afterward taught philosophy and theology at the Universities of Berlin, Marburg, Dresden, and Frunkfurt. He was dismissed from his position at the University of Frankfurt in 1933 because of his opposition to the Nazi regime. During that same year he came to the United States at the invitation of Reinhold Niebuhr and joined the faculty of Union Theological Seminary in New York. After his retirement from Union in 1954 he was University Professor at Harvard and lectured at the Universities of Chicago and California. Tillich died in 1965. Tillich devoted much of his efforts to clarifying the meaning of traditional theological symbols and words and to showing their close relationship to symbols and ideas employed in other disciplines. Tillich wrote a number of important books and hundreds of articles. His most important books include *Systematic Theology* (1951–1963), *The Shaking of the Foundations* (1948), *The Religious Situation* (1956), *The Dynamics of Faith* (1957), *The Courage to Be* (1952), *The New Being* (1955), and *Love, Power and Justice* (1954). The following selection comprises chapter one in *Theology of Culture* (1959).

Religion as a Dimension in Man's Spiritual Life*

As SOON AS one says anything about religion, one is questioned from two sides. Some Christian theologians will ask whether religion is here considered as a creative element of the human spirit rather than as a gift of divine revelation. If one replies that religion is an aspect of man's spiritual life, they will turn away. Then some secular scientists will ask whether religion is to be considered a lasting quality of the human spirit instead of an effect of changing psychological and sociological conditions. And if one answers that religion is a necessary aspect of man's spiritual life, they turn away like the theologians, but in an opposite direction.

This situation shows an almost schizophrenic split in our collective consciousness, a split which threatens our spiritual freedom by driving the contemporary mind into irrational and compulsive affirmations or negations of religion. And there is as much compulsive reaction to religion on the scientific side as there is on the religious side.

Those theologians who deny that religion is an element of man's spiritual life have a real point. According to them, the meaning of religion is that man received something which does not come *from* him, but which is given *to* him and may stand against him. They insist that the relation to God is not a human possibility and that God must first relate Himself to man. One could summarize the intention of these theologians in the sentence that religion is not a creation of the human spirit (spirit with a small s) but a gift of the divine Spirit (Spirit with a capital S). Man's spirit, they would continue, is creative with respect to itself and its world, but not with respect to God. With respect to God, man is receptive and only receptive. He has no freedom

---

* Paul Tillich, Ch. 1 from *Theology of Culture*, OUP, New York, 1964. The essay was first published in *Man's Right to Knowledge*, copyright by Columbia University Press, 1954.

to relate himself to God. This, they would add, is the meaning of the classical doctrine of the Bondage of the Will as developed by Paul, Augustine, Thomas, Luther, and Calvin. In the face of these witnesses, we certainly ask: Is it then justified to speak of religion as an aspect of the human spirit?

The opposite criticism also has its valid point. It comes from the side of the sciences of man: psychology, sociology, anthropology, and history. They emphasize the infinite diversity of religious ideas and practices, the mythological character of all religious concepts, the existence of many forms of non-religion in individuals and groups. Religion, they say (with the philosopher Comte), is characteristic for a special stage of human development (the mythological stage), but it has no place in the scientific stage in which we are living. Religion, according to this attitude, is a transitory creation of the human spirit but certainly not an essential quality of it.

If we analyze carefully these two groups of arguments, we discover the surprising fact that although they come from opposite directions, they have something definite in common. Both the theological and the scientific critics of the belief that religion is an aspect of the human spirit define religion as man's relation to divine beings, whose existence the theological critics assert and the scientific critics deny. But it is just this idea of religion which makes any understanding of religion impossible. If you start with the question whether God does or does not exist, you can never reach Him; and if you assert that He does exist, you can reach Him even less than if you assert that He does not exist. A God about whose existence or non-existence you can argue is a thing beside others within the universe of existing things. And the question is quite justified whether such a thing does exist, and the answer is equally justified that it does not exist. It is regrettable that scientists believe that they have refuted religion when they rightly have shown that there is no evidence whatsoever for the assumption that such a being exists. Actually, they have not only refuted religion, but they have done it a considerable service. They have forced it to reconsider and to restate the meaning of the tremendous word *God*. Unfortunately, many theologians make the same mistake. They begin their message with the assertion that there is a highest being called God, whose authoritative revelations they have received. They are more dangerous for religion than the so-called atheistic scientists. They take the first step on the road which inescapably leads to what is called atheism. Theologians who make of God a highest being who has given some people information about Himself, provoke inescapably the resistance of those who are told they must subject themselves to the authority of this information.

Against both groups of critics we affirm the validity of our subject: religion as an aspect of the human spirit. But, in doing so, we take into consideration the criticisms from both sides and the elements of truth in each of them.

When we say that religion is an aspect of the human spirit, we are saying that if we look at the human spirit from a special point of view, it presents itself to us as religious. What is this view? It is the point of view from which we can look into the depth of man's spiritual life. Religion is not a special function of man's spiritual life, but it is the dimension of depth in all of its functions. The assertion has far-reaching consequences for the interpretation of religion, and it needs comment on each of the terms used in it.

Religion is not a special function of the human spirit! History tells us the story of how religion goes from one spiritual function to the other to find a home, and is either rejected or swallowed by them. Religion comes to the moral function and knocks at its door, certain that it will be received. Is not the ethical the nearest relative of the religious? How could it be rejected? Indeed, it is not rejected; it is taken in. But it is taken in as a "poor relation" and asked to earn its place in the moral realm by serving morality. It is admitted as long as it helps to create good citizens, good husbands and children, good employees, officials, and soldiers. But the moment in which religion makes claims of its own, it is either silenced or thrown out as superfluous or dangerous for morals.

So religion must look around for another function of man's spiritual life, and it is attracted by the cognitive function. Religion as a special way of knowledge, as mythological imagination or as mystical intuition – this seems to give a home to religion. Again religion is admitted, but as subordinate to pure knowledge, and only for a brief time. Pure knowledge, strengthened by the tremendous success of its scientific work, soon recants its half-hearted acceptance of religion and declares that religion has nothing whatsoever to do with knowledge.

Once more religion is without a home within man's spiritual life. It looks around for another spiritual function to join. And it finds one, namely, the aesthetic function. Why not try to find a place within the artistic creativity of man? religion asks itself, through the mouths of the philosophers of religion. And the artistic realm answers, through the mouths of many artists, past and present, with an enthusiastic affirmative, and invites religion not only to join with it but also to acknowledge that art *is* religion. But now religion hesitates. Does not art express reality, while religion transforms reality? Is there not an element of unreality even in the greatest work of art? Religion remembers that it has old relations to the moral and the cognitive realms, to the good and to the true, and it resists the temptation to dissolve itself into art.

But now where shall religion turn? The whole field of man's spiritual life is taken, and no section of it is ready to give religion an adequate place. So religion turns to something that accompanies every activity of man and every function of man's spiritual life. We call it feeling. Religion is a feeling: this seems to be the end of the wanderings of religion, and this end is strongly acclaimed by all those who want to have the realms of knowledge and morals free from any religious interference. Religion, if banished to the realm of mere feeling, has ceased to be dangerous for any rational and practical human enterprise. But, we must add, it also has lost its seriousness, its truth, and its ultimate meaning. In the atmosphere of mere subjectivity of feeling without a definite object of emotion, without an ultimate content, religion dies. This also is not the answer to the question of religion as an aspect of the human spirit.

In this situation, without a home, without a place in which to dwell, religion suddenly realizes that it does not need such a place, that it does not need to seek for a home. It is at home everywhere, namely, in the depth of all functions of man's spiritual life. Religion is the dimension of depth in all of them. Religion is the aspect of depth in the totality of the human spirit.

What does the metaphor *depth* mean? It means that the religious aspect points to that which is ultimate, infinite, unconditional in man's spiritual life. Religion, in the largest and most basic sense of the word, is ultimate concern. And ultimate concern is manifest in all creative functions of the human spirit. It is manifest in the moral sphere as the unconditional seriousness of the moral demand. Therefore, if someone rejects religion in the name of the moral function of the human spirit, he rejects religion in the name of religion. Ultimate concern is manifest in the realm of knowledge as the passionate longing for ultimate reality. Therefore, if anyone rejects religion in the name of the cognitive function of the human spirit, he rejects religion in the name of religion. Ultimate concern is manifest in the aesthetic function of the human spirit as the infinite desire to express ultimate meaning. Therefore, if anyone rejects religion in the name of the aesthetic function of the human spirit, he rejects religion in the name of religion. You cannot reject religion with ultimate seriousness, because ultimate seriousness, or the state of being ultimately concerned, is itself religion. Religion is the substance, the ground, and the depth of man's spiritual life. This is the religious aspect of the human spirit.

But now the question arises, what about religion in the narrower and customary sense of the word, be it institutional religion or the religion of personal piety? If religion is present in all functions of the spiritual life, why has mankind developed religion as a special sphere among others, in myth, cult, devotion, and ecclesiastical institutions? The answer is, because of the tragic estrangement of man's spiritual life from its own ground and depth. According to the visionary who has written the last book of the Bible, there will be no temple in the heavenly Jerusalem, for God will be all in all. There will be no secular realm, and for this very reason there will be no religious realm. Religion will be again what it is essentially, the all-determining ground and substance of man's spiritual life.

Religion opens up the depth of man's spiritual life which is usually covered by the dust of our daily life and the noise of our secular work. It gives us the experience of the Holy, of something which is untouchable, awe-inspiring, an ultimate meaning, the source of ultimate courage. This is the glory of what we call religion. But beside its glory lies its shame. It makes itself the ultimate and despises the secular realm. It makes its myths and doctrines, its rites and laws into ultimates and persecutes those who do not subject themselves to it. It forgets that its own existence is a result of man's tragic estrangement from his true being. It forgets its own emergency character.

This is the reason for the passionate reaction of the secular world against religion, a reaction which has tragic consequences for the secular realm itself. For the religious and the secular realm are in the same predicament. Neither of them should be in separation from the other, and both should realize that their very existence as separated is an emergency, that both of them are rooted in religion in the larger sense of the word, in the experience of ultimate concern. To the degree in which this is realized the conflicts between the religious and the secular are overcome, and religion has rediscovered its true place in man's spiritual life, namely, in its depth, out of which it gives substance, ultimate meaning, judgment, and creative courage to all functions of the human spirit. . . .

8

RELIGION AS A SOCIAL FUNCTION

Bronislaw Malinowski

Editor's Introduction

THE FOLLOWING SELECTION by Bronislaw Malinowski defines religion as a function of society. It could, therefore, be called a social or a functional description. It is similar to the descriptions of Schleiermacher and Tillich in that attention is directed toward the subject of religious activity rather than toward the object. In this instance, however, the subject is the society rather than an individual. Religion is described as an expression of a social reality, useful and perhaps necessary for preserving the stability of the group.

It is sometimes suggested by proponents of functional descriptions of religion that they do not imply any definition of what religion is, but only a description of how it works. This distinction, they contend, removes any value judgments from their analysis. There is some merit in this distinction. It is possible to examine the way in which religion functions without implying any value judgment regarding any particular religion or religion in general. But this is also true of the other descriptions of religion that have been considered. With possibly one or two exceptions, none directly implies a positive or negative evaluation of religious activity. The contention of the functionalist that his description, because it is functional, is somehow above and removed from confrontation with other descriptions of religion cannot be sustained. He assumes that one can discover the critical element, or at least a critical element, of religion through a description of its function in society. Recognizing this, it is clear that this description, as the others, assumes that the essence of religion can be described by looking in a particular direction or by considering a particular set of data. In this case the direction is toward the social dimension of religion. Finally, it should be noted that as a matter of fact, an implicit evaluation of religious activity is behind many purportedly "objective" or "scientific" functional descriptions of religion. (Obviously this is also true of other kinds of descriptions.) This does not mean that the person in question is a propagandist or dishonest. It means that even when we take the greatest pains to avoid it, hidden and unsuspected motives often influence our thought and activity.

Of course, there is a great variety among sociologists of religion who may broadly be said to be functionalists. Emil Durkheim, one of the first to suggest this approach, attempted to use his description of religion to refute positivists who wanted to attribute all religious activity to superstition. Durkheim contended that religion was not superstition, but was an essential component of social existence. The religious mentality acknowledges some external power to which it owes allegiance. Durkheim argued that there is such a power: the society. Religious ideas and images are the symbolic representation of the dependence of the individual on the society for physical and psychic comfort. Religion is not superstitious nonsense, but a vital and necessary part of social life, impressing on the individual the claims of the group.

Malinowski rejects Durkheim's identification of the object of religion with society. He calls attention to the individual elements in religious behavior and to its power to criticize and judge society. He sees the function of religion to be the enhancement of those social characteristics, sanctioned by tradition, which promote individual and social stability. Malinowski agrees with Durkheim that the essence of religion is to be discovered through an analysis of the way it functions in society – he simply expands Durkheim's identification of that function.

Malinowski employs an anthropological study of primitive

tribes, especially the south-sea Trobriand islanders, as a data-source for his work. He uses the anthropological data to develop and substantiate general theories about human culture. In the following selection, Malinowski is concerned to use his data to defend a particular understanding of religion and to criticize other interpretations. It might be useful to keep in mind two theories he rejects. Malinowski rejects Durkheim's understanding of religion as the way in which society enforces conformity. Religion is not merely the tool of the society, but is an integral element in individual and social existence, working to make the difficult crises of life bearable and to preserve the practical, moral wisdom of the ages through the sanctification of tradition.

Second, Malinowski is concerned to show that religion is not simply superstition grounded on a faulty view of nature and of the forces that control it. Religion has sometimes been understood as a primitive form of science, based on faulty notions of natural processes. For example, it was supposed that myths about dragons in the sky were primitive efforts to explain the natural phenomenon of the phases of the moon. The waning moon resembled a cookie as it was devoured bite by bite and only a dragon could take such big bites. Malinowski's sharp distinction between the sacred and the secular is an effort to refute this notion of religion. Science, he argues, deals with the secular, profane, everyday world of causes and effects. Religion, on the other hand, operates on the fringes, in the sphere of the unknown, the mysterious.

The sacred domain is the domain of religion and magic. But these two forms of human activity are radically different in their function. Magical acts are acts performed with a conscious definite purpose. They are efforts to gain a particular objective through the manipulation of supernatural forces. Religious rites and rituals, on the other hand, appear to have no immediate purpose. A Trobriand islander can tell exactly why he performs a magic ritual but can only say of a religious ritual that it is dictated by tradition. This is not to say that religion has no function. It has the function of promoting the stability of individuals and societies.

But this function is never seen or articulated by the participant. He only knows that tradition demands that he perform the religious act. Magic, because it attempts to control the environment, is a primitive form of science. This element of control is absent, however, from religious activity.

The basic spoken form of religion is myth. And Malinowski's definition of myth could serve as his definition of religion.

Studied alive, myth, as we shall see, is not symbolic, but a direct expression of its subject matter; it is not an explanation in satisfaction of a scientific interest, but a narrative resurrection of primeval reality, told in satisfaction of deep religious wants, moral cravings, social submissions, assertions, even practical requirements. Myth fulfills in primitive culture an indispensable function: It expresses, enhances, and codifies belief; it safeguards and enforces morality; it vouches for the efficiency of ritual and contains practical rules for the guidance of man. Myth is thus a vital ingredient of human civilization; it is not an idle tale, but a hard-worked active force; it is not an intellectual explanation or an artistic imagery, but a pragmatic charter of primitive faith and moral wisdom.

The function of myth, briefly, is to strengthen tradition and endow it with a greater value and prestige by tracing it back to a higher, better, more supernatural reality of initial events.

Bronislaw Kasper Malinowski was born in Poland in 1884. He studied mathematics and physical science at the University of Cracow and later studied anthropology at the Universities of Leipzig and London. He spent a number of years studying primitive tribes at first hand, especially the Trobriand islanders off the coast of New Guinea. He is recognized as one of the major figures in modern anthropology, having established new standards for sympathetic understanding and interpretation of primitive peoples and for exacting methodological concepts.

Malinowski died in 1942. His most important books include *Argonauts of the Western Pacific* (1922), *Crime and Custom in Savage Society* (1926), *The Sexual Life of Savages in Northwestern Melanesia* (1929), and *Coral Gardens and their Magic* (1935). The following selections are taken from a long essay, "Magic, Science and Religion", which first appeared in *Science, Religion, and Reality*, edited by Joseph Needham. In 1948 it appeared in *Magic, Science, and Religion* along with two other essays by Malinowski on primitive religion.

Magic, Science and Religion*

I PRIMITIVE MAN AND HIS RELIGION

THERE ARE NO peoples however primitive without religion and magic. Nor are there, it must be added at once, any savage races lacking either in the scientific attitude or in science, though this lack has been frequently attributed to them. In every primitive community, studied by trustworthy and competent observers, there have been found two clearly distinguishable domains, the Sacred and the Profane; in other words, the domain of Magic and Religion and that of Science.

On the one hand there are the traditional acts and observances, regarded by the natives as sacred, carried out with reverence and awe, hedged around with prohibitions and special rules of behavior. Such acts and observances are always associated with beliefs in supernatural forces, especially those of magic, or with ideas about beings, spirits, ghosts, dead ancestors, or gods. On the other hand, a moment's reflection is sufficient to show that no art or craft however primitive could have been invented or maintained, no organized form of hunting, fishing, tilling, or search for food could be carried out without the careful observation of natural process and a firm belief in its regularity, without the power of reasoning and without confidence in the power of reason; that is, without the rudiments of science.

. . . .

* Bronislaw Malinowski, selections from "Magic, Science, and Religion" in *Science, Religion, and Reality*, ed. Joseph Needham, SPCK, London, 1925.

II   Rational Mastery by Man of His Surroundings

... Magic is undoubtedly regarded by the natives as absolutely indispensable to the welfare of the gardens. What would happen without it no one can exactly tell, for no native garden has ever been made without its ritual, in spite of some thirty years of European rule and missionary influence and well over a century's contact with white traders. But certainly various kinds of disaster, blight, unseasonable droughts, rains, bush-pigs and locusts, would destroy the unhallowed garden made without magic.

Does this mean, however, that the natives attribute all the good results to magic? Certainly not. If you were to suggest to a native that he should make his garden mainly by magic and scamp his work, he would simply smile on your simplicity. He knows as well as you do that there are natural conditions and causes, and by his observations he knows also that he is able to control these natural forces by mental and physical effort. His knowledge is limited, no doubt, but as far as it goes it is sound and proof against mysticism. If the fences are broken down, if the seed is destroyed or has been dried or washed away, he will have recourse not to magic, but to work, guided by knowledge and reason. His experience has taught him also, on the other hand, that in spite of all his forethought and beyond all his efforts there are agencies and forces which one year bestow unwonted and unearned benefits of fertility, making everything run smooth and well, rain and sun appear at the right moment, noxious insects remain in abeyance, the harvest yields a superabundant crop; and another year again the same agencies bring ill luck and bad chance, pursue him from beginning till end and thwart all his most strenuous efforts and his best-founded knowledge. To control these influences and these only he employs magic.

Thus there is a clear-cut division: there is first the well-known set of conditions, the natural course of growth, as well as the ordinary pests and dangers to be warded off by fencing and weeding. On the other hand there is the domain of the unaccountable and adverse influences, as well as the great unearned increment of fortunate coincidence. The first conditions are coped with by knowledge and work, the second by magic.

This line of division can also be traced in the social setting of work and ritual respectively. Though the garden magician is, as a rule, also the leader in practical activities, these two functions are kept strictly apart. Every magical ceremony has its distinctive name, its appropriate time and its place in the scheme of work, and it stands out of the ordinary course of activities completely. Some of them are ceremonial and have to be attended by the whole community, all are public in that it is known when they are going to happen and anyone can attend them. They are performed on selected plots within the gardens and on a special corner of this plot. Work is always tabooed on such occasions, sometimes only while the ceremony lasts, sometimes for a day or two. In his lay character the leader and magician directs the work, fixes the dates for starting, harangues and exhorts slack or careless gardeners. But the two rôles never overlap or interfere : they are always clear, and any native will inform you without hesitation whether the man acts as magician or as leader in garden work.

What has been said about gardens can be paralleled from any one of the many other activities in which work and magic run side by side without ever mixing. Thus in canoe building empirical knowledge of material, of technology, and of certain principles of stability and hydrodynamics, function in company and close association with magic, each yet uncontaminated by the other.

For example, they understand perfectly well that the wider the span of the outrigger the greater the stability yet the smaller the resistance against strain. They can clearly explain why they have to give this span a certain traditional width, measured in fractions of the length of the dugout. They can also explain, in rudimentary but clearly mechanical terms, how they have to behave in a sudden gale, why the outrigger must be always on the weather side, why the one type of canoe can and the other cannot beat. They have, in fact, a whole system of principles of sailing, embodied in a complex and rich terminology, traditionally handed on and obeyed as rationally and consistently as is modern science by modern sailors. How could they sail otherwise under eminently dangerous conditions in their frail primitive craft?

But even with all their systematic knowledge, methodically applied, they are still at the mercy of powerful and incalculable tides, sudden gales during the monsoon season and unknown reefs. And here comes in their magic, performed over the canoe during its construction, carried out at the beginning and in the course of expeditions and resorted to in moments of real danger. If the modern seaman, entrenched in science and reason, provided with all sorts of safety appliances, sailing on steel-built steamers, if even he has a singular tendency to superstition – which does not rob him of his knowledge or reason, nor make him altogether prelogical – can we wonder that his savage colleague, under much more precarious conditions, holds fast to the safety and comfort of magic?

An interesting and crucial test is provided by fishing in the Trobriand Islands and its magic. While in the villages on the inner lagoon fishing is done in an easy and absolutely reliable manner by the method of poisoning, yielding abundant results without danger and uncertainty, there are on the shores of the open sea dangerous modes of fishing and also certain types in which the yield greatly varies according to whether shoals of fish appear beforehand or not. It is most significant that in the lagoon fishing, where man can rely completely upon his knowledge and skill, magic does not exist, while in the open-sea fishing, full of danger and uncertainty, there is extensive magical ritual to secure safety and good results.

Again, in warfare the natives know that strength, courage, and agility play a decisive part. Yet here also they practice magic to master the elements of change and luck.

Nowhere is the duality of natural and supernatural causes divided by a line so thin and intricate, yet, if carefully followed up, so well marked, decisive, and instructive, as in the two most fateful forces of human destiny: health and death. Health to the Melanesians is a natural state of affairs and, unless tampered with, the human body will remain in perfect order. But the natives know perfectly well that there are natural means which can affect health and even destroy the body. Poisons, wounds, burns, falls, are known to cause disablement or death in a natural way. And this is not a matter of private opinion of this or that individual, but it is laid down in traditional lore and even in belief, for there are considered to be different ways to the nether world for those who died by sorcery and those who met "natural" death. Again, it is recognized that cold, heat, overstrain, too much sun, overeating, can all cause minor ailments, which are treated by natural remedies such as massage, steaming, warming at a fire and certain potions. Old age is known to lead to bodily decay and the explanation is given by the natives that very old people grow weak, their oesophagus closes up, and therefore they must die.

But besides these natural causes there is the enormous domain of sorcery and by far the most cases of illness and death are ascribed to this. The line of distinction between sorcery and the other causes is clear in theory and in most cases of practice, but it must be realized that it is subject to what could be called the personal perspective. That is, the more closely a case has to do with the person who considers it, the less will it be "natural", the more "magical". Thus a very old man, whose pending death will be considered natural by the other members of the community, will be afraid only of sorcery and never think of his natural fate. A fairly sick person will diagnose sorcery in his own case, while all the others might speak of too much betel nut or overeating or some other indulgence.

But who of us really believes that his own bodily infirmities and the approaching death is a purely natural occurrence, just an insignificant event in the infinite chain of causes? To the most rational of civilized men health, disease, the threat of death, float in a hazy emotional mist, which seems to become denser and more impenetrable as the fateful forms approach. It is indeed astonishing that "savages" can achieve such a sober, dispassionate outlook in these matters as they actually do.

Thus in his relation to nature and destiny, whether he tries to exploit the first or to dodge the second, primitive man recognizes both the natural and the supernatural forces and agencies, and he tries to use them both for his benefit. Whenever he has been taught by experience that effort guided by knowledge is of some avail, he never spares the one or ignores the other. He knows that a plant cannot grow by magic alone, or a canoe sail or float without being properly constructed and managed, or a fight be won without skill and daring. He never relies on magic alone, while, on the contrary, he sometimes dispenses with it completely, as in fire-making and in a number of crafts and pursuits. But he clings to it, whenever he has to recognize the impotence of his knowledge and of his rational technique.

.   .   .   .

III   LIFE, DEATH, AND DESTINY IN EARLY FAITH AND CULT

We pass now to the domain of the *sacred*, to religious and magical creeds and rites. Our historical survey of theories has left us somewhat bewildered with the chaos of opinions and with the jumble of phenomena. While it was difficult not to admit into the enclosure of religion one after the other, spirits and ghosts, totems and social events, death and life, yet in the process religion seemed to become a thing more and more confused, both an all and a nothing. It certainly cannot be defined by its subject matter in a narrow sense, as "spirit worship", or as "ancestor cult", or as the "cult of nature". It includes animism, animatism, totemism, and fetishism, but it is not any one of them exclusively. The *ism* definition of religion in its origins must be given up, for religion does not cling to any one object or class of objects, though incidentally it can touch and hallow all. Nor, as we have seen, is religion identical with Society or the Social, nor can we remain satisfied by a vague hint that it clings to life only, for death opens perhaps the vastest view on to the other world. As an "appeal to higher powers", religion can only be distinguished from magic and not defined in general, but even this view will have to be slightly modified and supplemented.

The problem before us is, then, to try to put some order into the facts. This will allow us to determine somewhat more precisely the character of the domain of the *Sacred* and mark it off from that of the *Profane*. It will also give us an opportunity to state the relation between magic and religion.

The Creative Acts of Religion

It will be best to face the facts first and, in order not to narrow down the scope of the survey, to take as our watchword the vaguest and most general of indices: "Life". As a matter of fact, even a slight acquaintance with ethnological literature is enough to convince anyone that in reality the physiological phases of human life, and, above all, its crises, such as conception, pregnancy, birth, puberty, marriage, and death, form the nuclei of numerous rites and beliefs. Thus beliefs about conception, such as that in reincarnation, spirit-entry, magical impregnation, exist in one form or another in almost every tribe, and they are often associated with rites and observances. During pregnancy the expectant mother has to keep certain taboos and undergo ceremonies, and her husband shares at times in both. At birth, before and after, there are various magical rites to prevent dangers and undo sorcery, ceremonies of purification, communal rejoicings and acts of presentation of the newborn to higher powers or to the community. Later on in life the boys and, much less frequently, the girls have to undergo the often protracted rites of initiation, as a rule shrouded in mystery and marred by cruel and obscene ordeals.

Without going any further, we can see that even the very beginnings of human life are surrounded by an inextricably mixed-up medley of beliefs and rites. They seem to be strongly attracted by any important event in life, to crystallize around it, surround it with a rigid crust of formalism and ritualism – but to what purpose? Since we cannot define cult and creed by their objects, perhaps it will be possible to perceive their function.

A closer scrutiny of the facts allows us to make from the outset a preliminary classification into two main groups. Compare a rite carried out to prevent death in childbed with another typical custom, a ceremony in celebration of a birth. The first rite is carried out as a means to an end, it has a definite practical purpose which is known to all who practice it and can be easily elicited from any native informant. The post-natal ceremony, say a presentation of a newborn or a feast of rejoicing in the event, has no purpose: it is not a means to an end but an end in itself. It expresses the feelings of the mother, the father, the relatives, the whole community, but there is no future event which this ceremony foreshadows, which it is meant to bring about or to prevent. This difference will serve us as a *prima facie* distinction between magic and religion. While in the magical act the underlying idea and aim is always clear, straightforward, and definite, in the religious ceremony there is no purpose directed toward a subsequent event. It is only possible for the sociologist to establish the function, the sociological *raison d'être* of the act. The native can always state the end of the magical rite, but he will say of a religious ceremony that it is done because such is the usage, or because it has been ordained, or he will narrate an explanatory myth.

In order to grasp better the nature of primitive religious ceremonies and their function, let us analyze the ceremonies of initiation. They present right through the vast range of their occurrence certain striking similarities. Thus the novices have to undergo a more or less protracted period of seclusion and preparation. Then comes initiation proper, in which the youth, passing through a series of ordeals, is finally submitted to an act of bodily mutilation: at the mildest, a slight incision or the knocking out of a tooth; or, more severe, circumcision; or, really cruel and dangerous, an operation such as the subincision practiced in some Australian tribes. The ordeal is usually associated with the idea of the death and rebirth of the initiated one, which is sometimes enacted in a mimetic performance. But besides the ordeal, less conspicuous and dramatic, but in reality more important, is the second main aspect of initiation: the systematic instruction of the youth in sacred myth and tradition, the gradual unveiling of tribal mysteries and the exhibition of sacred objects.

The ordeal and the unveiling of tribal mysteries are usually believed to have been instituted by one or more legendary ancestors or culture heroes, or by a Superior Being of superhuman character. Sometimes he is said to swallow the youths, or to kill them, and then to restore them again as fully initiated men. His voice is imitated by the hum of the bull-roarer to inspire awe in the uninitiated women and children. Through these ideas initiation brings the novice into relationship with higher powers and personalities, such as the Guardian Spirits and Tutelary Divinities of the North American Indians, the Tribal All-Father of some Australian Aborigines, the Mythological Heroes of Melanesia and other parts of the world. This is the third fundamental element, besides ordeal and the teaching of tradition, in the rites of passing into manhood.

Now what is the sociological function of these customs, what part do they play in the maintenance and development of civilization? As we have seen, the youth is taught in them the sacred traditions under most impressive conditions of preparation and ordeal and under the sanction of Supernatural Beings – the light of tribal revelation bursts upon him from out of the shadows of fear, privation, and bodily pain.

Let us realize that in primitive conditions tradition is of supreme value for the community and nothing matters as much as the conformity and conservatism of its members. Order and civilization can be maintained only by strict adhesion to the lore and knowledge received from previous generations. Any laxity in this weakens the cohesion of the group and imperils its cultural outfit to the point of threatening its very existence. Man has not yet devised the extremely complex apparatus of modern science which enables him nowadays to fix the results of experience into imperishable moulds, to test it ever anew, gradually to shape it into more adequate forms and enrich it constantly by new additions. The primitive man's share of knowledge, his social fabric, his customs and beliefs, are the invaluable yield of the devious experience of his forefathers, bought at an extravagant price and to be maintained at any cost. Thus, of all his qualities, truth to tradition is the most important, and a society which makes its tradition sacred has gained by it an inestimable advantage of power and permanence. Such beliefs and practices, therefore, which put a halo of sanctity round tradition and a supernatural stamp upon it, will have a "survival value" for the type of civilization in which they have been evolved.

We may, therefore, lay down the main function of initiation ceremonies: they are a ritual and dramatic expression of the supreme power and value of tradition in primitive societies; they also serve to impress this power and value upon the minds of each generation, and they are at the same time an extremely efficient means of transmitting tribal lore, of insuring continuity in tradition and of maintaining tribal cohesion.

We still have to ask: What is the relation between the purely physiological fact of bodily maturity which these ceremonies mark, and their social and religious aspect? We see at once that religion does something more, infinitely more, than the mere "sacralizing of a crisis of life". From a natural event it makes a social transition, to the fact of bodily maturity it adds the vast conception of entry into manhood with its duties, privileges, responsibilities, above all with its knowledge of tradition and the communion with sacred things and beings. There is thus a creative element in the rites of religious nature. The act establishes not only a social event in the life of the individual but also a spiritual metamorphosis, both associated with the biological event but transcending it in importance and significance.

Initiation is a typically religious act, and we can see clearly here how the ceremony and its purpose are one, how the end is realized in the very consummation of the act. At the same time we can see the function of such acts in society in that they create mental habits and social usages of inestimable value to the group and its civilization.

Another type of religious ceremony, the rite of marriage, is also an end in itself in that it creates a supernaturally sanctioned bond, superadded to the primarily biological fact: the union of man and woman for lifelong partnership in affection, economic community, the procreation and rearing of children. This union, monogamous marriage, has always existed in human societies – so modern anthropology teaches in the face of the older fantastic hypotheses of "promiscuity" and "group marriage". By giving monogamous marriage an imprint of value and sanctity, religion offers another gift to human culture.

. . . .

Magic and Science

We have had to make a digression on mythology since we found that myth is engendered by the real or imaginary success of witchcraft. But what about its failures? With all the strength which magic draws from the spontaneous belief and spontaneous ritual of intense desire or thwarted emotion, with all the force given it by the personal prestige, the social power and success common in the magician and practitioner – still there are failures and breakdowns, and we should vastly underrate the savage's intelligence, logic, and grasp of experience if we assumed that he is not aware of it and that he fails to account for it.

First of all, magic is surrounded by strict conditions: exact remembrance of a spell, unimpeachable performance of the rite, unswerving adhesion to the taboos and observances which shackle the magician. If any one of these is neglected, failure of magic follows. And then, even if magic be done in the most perfect manner, its effects can be equally well undone: for against every magic there can be also counter-magic. If magic, as we have shown, is begotten by the union of man's steadfast desire with the wayward whim of chance, then every desire, positive or negative, may – nay, must – have its magic. Now in all his social and worldly ambitions, in all his strivings to catch good fortune and trap propitious luck, man moves in an atmosphere of rivalry, of envy, and of spite. For luck, possessions, even health, are matters of degree and of comparison, and if your neighbor owns more cattle, more wives, more health, and more power than yourself, you feel dwarfed in all you own and all you are. And such is human nature that a man's desire is as much satisfied by the thwarting of others as by the advancement of himself. To this sociological play of desire and counter-desire, of ambition and spite, of success and envy, there corresponds the play of magic and counter-magic, or of magic, white and black.

In Melanesia, where I have studied this problem at first-hand, there is not one single magical act which is not firmly believed to possess a counter-act which, when stronger, can completely annihilate its effects. In certain types of magic, as for instance, that of health and disease, the formulas actually go in couples. A sorcerer who learns a performance by which to cause a definite disease will at the same time learn the formula and the rite which can annul completely the effects of his evil magic. In love, again, not only does there exist a belief that, when two formulas are performed to win the same heart, the stronger will override the weaker one, but there are spells uttered directly to alienate the affections of the sweetheart or wife of another. Whether this duality of magic is as consistently carried out all the world over as in the Trobriands it is difficult to say, but that the twin forces of white and black, of positive and negative, exist everywhere is beyond doubt. Thus the failures of magic can always be accounted for by the slip of memory, by slovenliness in performance or in observance of a taboo, and, last but not least, by the fact that someone else has performed some counter-magic.

We are now in a position to state more fully the relation between magic and science already outlined above. Magic is akin to science in that it always has a definite aim intimately associated with human instincts, needs, and pursuits. The magic art is directed toward the attainment of practical aims. Like the other arts and crafts, it is also governed by a theory, by a system of principles which dictate the manner in which the act has to be performed in order to be effective. In analyzing magical spells, rites, and substances we have found that there are a number of general principles which govern them. Both science and magic develop a special technique. In magic, as in the other arts, man can undo what he has done or mend the damage which he has wrought. In fact, in magic, the quantitative equivalents of black and white seem to be much more exact and the effects of witchcraft much more completely eradicated by counter-witchcraft than is possible in any practical art or craft. Thus both magic and science show certain similarities, and, with Sir James Frazer, we can appropriately call magic a pseudo-science.

And the spurious character of this pseudo-science is not hard to detect. Science, even as represented by the primitive knowledge of savage man, is based on the normal universal experience of everyday life, experience won in man's struggle with Nature for his subsistence and safety, founded on observation, fixed by reason. Magic is based on specific experience of emotional states in which man observes not Nature but himself, in which the truth is revealed not by reason but by the play of emotions upon the human organism. Science is founded on the conviction that experience, effort, and reason are valid; magic on the belief that hope cannot fail nor desire deceive. The theories of knowledge are dictated by logic, those of magic by the association of ideas under the influence of desire. As a matter of empirical fact the body of rational knowledge and the body of magical lore are incorporated each in a different tradition, in a different social setting and in a different type of activity, and all these differences are clearly recognized by the savages. The one constitutes the domain of the profane; the other, hedged round by observances, mysteries, and taboos, makes up half of the domain of the sacred.

Magic and Religion

Both magic and religion arise and function in situations of emotional stress: crises of life, lacunae in important pursuits, death and initiation into tribal mysteries, unhappy love and unsatisfied hate. Both magic and religion open up escapes from such situations and such impasses as offer no empirical way out except by ritual and belief into the domain of the supernatural. This domain embraces, in religion, beliefs in ghosts, spirits, the primitive forebodings of providence, the guardians of tribal mysteries; in magic, the primeval force and virtue of magic. Both magic and religion are based strictly on mythological tradition, and they also both exist in the atmosphere of the miraculous, in a constant revelation of their wonder-working power. They both are surrounded by taboos and observances which mark off their acts from those of the profane world.

Now what distinguishes magic from religion? We have taken for our starting-point a most definite and tangible distinction: we have defined, within the domain of the sacred, magic as a practical art consisting of acts which are only means to a definite end expected to follow later on; religion as a body of self-contained acts being themselves the fulfillment of their purpose. We can now follow up this difference into its deeper layers. The practical art of magic has its limited, circumscribed technique: spell, rite, and the condition of the performer form always its trite trinity. Religion, with its complex aspects and purposes, has no such simple technique, and its unity can be seen neither in the form of its acts nor even in the uniformity of its subject matter, but rather in the function which it fulfills and in the value of its belief and ritual. Again, the belief in magic, corresponding to its plain practical nature, is extremely simple. It is always the affirmation of man's power to cause certain definite effects by a definite spell and rite. In religion, on the other hand, we have a whole supernatural world of faith: the pantheon of spirits and demons, the benevolent powers of totem, guardian spirit, tribal all-father, the vision of the future life, create a second supernatural reality for primitive man. The mythology of religion is also more varied and complex as well as more creative. It usually centers round the various tenets of belief, and it develops them into cosmogonies, tales of culture heroes, accounts of the doings of gods and demigods. In magic, important as it is, mythology is an ever-recurrent boasting about man's primeval achievements.

Magic, the specific art for specific ends, has in every one of its forms come once into the possession of man, and it had to be handed over in direct filiation from generation to generation. Hence it remains from the earliest times in the hands of specialists, and the first profession of mankind is that of a wizard or witch. Religion, on the other hand, in primitive conditions is an affair of all, in which everyone takes an active and equivalent part. Every member of the tribe has to go through initiation, and then himself initiates others. Everyone wails, mourns, digs the grave and commemorates, and in due time everyone has his turn in being mourned and commemorated. Spirits are for all, and everyone becomes a spirit. The only specialization in religion – that is, early spiritualistic mediumism – is not a profession but a personal gift. One more difference between magic and religion is the play of black and white in witchcraft, while religion in its primitive stages has but little of the contrast between good and evil, between the beneficent and malevolent powers. This is due also to the practical character of magic, which aims at direct quantitative results, while early religion, though essentially moral, has to deal with fateful, irremediable happenings and supernatural forces and beings, so that the undoing of things done by man does not enter into it. The maxim that fear first made gods in the universe is certainly not true in the light of anthropology.

In order to grasp the difference between religion and magic and to gain a clear vision of the three-cornered constellation of magic, religion, and science, let us briefly realize the cultural function of each. The function of primitive knowledge and its value have been assessed already and indeed are not difficult to grasp. By acquainting man with his surroundings, by allowing him to use the forces of Nature, science, primitive knowledge, bestows on man an immense biological advantage, setting him far above all the rest of creation. The function of religion and its value we have learned to understand in the survey of savage creeds and cults given above. We have shown there that religious faith establishes, fixes, and enhances all valuable mental attitudes, such as reverence for tradition, harmony with environment, courage and confidence in the struggle with difficulties and at the prospect of death. This belief, embodied and maintained by cult and ceremonial, has an immense biological value, and so reveals to primitive man truth in the wider, pragmatic sense of the word.

What is the cultural function of magic? We have seen that all the instincts and emotions, all practical activities, lead man into impasses where gaps in his knowledge and the limitations of his early power of observation and reason betray him at a crucial moment. Human organism reacts to this in spontaneous outbursts, in which rudimentary modes of behavior and rudimentary beliefs in their efficiency are engendered. Magic fixes upon these beliefs and rudimentary rites and standardizes them into permanent traditional forms. Thus magic supplies primitive man with a number of ready-made ritual acts and beliefs, with a definite mental and practical technique which serves to bridge over the dangerous gaps in every important pursuit or critical situation. It enables man to carry out with confidence his important tasks, to maintain his poise and his mental integrity in fits of anger, in the throes of hate, of unrequited love, of despair and anxiety. The function of magic is to ritualize man's optimism, to enhance his faith in the victory of hope over fear. Magic expresses the greater value for man of confidence over doubt, of steadfastness over vacillation, of optimism over pessimism.

Looking from far and above, from our high places of safety in developed civilization, it is easy to see all the crudity and irrelevance of magic. But without its power and guidance early man could not have mastered his practical difficulties as he has done, nor could man have advanced to the higher stages of culture. Hence the universal occurrence of magic in primitive societies and its enormous sway. Hence do we find magic an invariable adjunct of all important activities. I think we must see in it the embodiment of the sublime folly of hope, which has yet been the best school of man's character.

9

RELIGION AS STRUCTURE AND
ARCHETYPE

Mircea Eliade

Editor's Introduction

THE FOLLOWING SELECTIONS by Eliade and Buber illustrate dialectical or relational definitions of religion. These definitions hold that religion can best be defined neither in terms of what a man attends to in religious behavior (power, being, or the projection of humanity, for example) nor in terms of the human capabilities and facilities with which people behave religiously (immediate self-awareness, the depth dimension, or the need for social stability), but in terms of the *way* in which men relate to the object of their attention. This means that there must be more than one way of attending to the world. What makes a situation "religious" is neither the subjective element nor the objective element, but the way in which these elements come into contact.

The previous selection by Bronislaw Malinowski identifies two ways in which men relate to their environment – the sacred (religious) and profane (non-religious). The difference between these two "spheres" was defined neither by the object of attention (the natives relate in both a sacred and a profane way toward a corpse) nor by the subjective mentality (both sacred and profane spheres involve emotion, intellect, tradition, society as a whole, etc.). Rather "sacred" and "profane" point to two relationships: two different ways in which the islanders experience their environment or a particular situation.

The following selection by Mircea Eliade builds on the recognition of the fact that we can experience our environment in different ways. The idea that there can be two ways of attending to the world is a difficult proposition to comprehend because the basic presupposition of the modern world is that there is only one way of attending to our environment. Modern man's environment is the empirical world of sense data which he discovers through experience. Eliade calls this modern world a "desacralized universe". Modern man lives in a one-dimensional, profane world.

Eliade does not attempt to argue for the relative merits of the traditional world view which separates experience into sacred and profane, and the modern one-dimensional world view. He simply points out that all societies with the exception of modern western civilization have recognized these two dimensions and that the premise of the modern mentality makes it difficult for us to understand what is meant by these two realms.

According to Eliade, purely secular man is a recent phenomenon. Men have traditionally lived in two spheres: sacred and profane. In the profane sphere men were involved in give and take with objects in the world. Objects in their environment offered some resistance to them as, for example, when rocks littered the agricultural site, but these objects were also susceptible to influence; the rocks could be moved. In the sacred dimension men were confronted with objects over which they had no control, such as the forces of nature. Their only response could be one of awe and wonder. They were faced with something "out there" beyond control.

It would be a mistake, however, to think that the distinction between sacred and profane lies in a difference between kinds of objects. For modern man there are almost no·events or objects which he cannot control to some extent. And understanding the distinction in this way has led to his inability to understand the sacred. As men gained increasing control over their environment, the sphere of the sacred seemed to shrink into nothing. The distinction lies in the way men relate to things and events in their environment and not in the objects. But it would also be a mistake to think that this distinction lies between different faculties that are brought into play when we see the world as sacred and as profane. The same mental operations are involved. The distinction is a factor of the framework in which men view their world.

Some insight into the way in which we can experience our environment in different ways may be gained from examining the way in which trans-experimental factors limit, modify, distort, and clarify our experience. We all know that experience can be deceiving. For example, I see a girl across the street and recognize her as my friend. As she comes closer, I realize that she is not my friend at all but a total stranger. But, earlier, I really "experienced" seeing my friend. In this case certain conditioned reflexes functioned as perceptive factors which determined my experience to such a degree that the immediate perception was distorted. The mental expectations that I brought to the experience determined its content. These expectations can be called trans-experiential in the sense that they are not part of the content of the present experience but are factors which condition and shape that experience.

These trans-experiential factors are also operative in organizing experience into manageable pieces. Our sense organs are constantly bombarded by a flood of random sense data. Colors, sounds, shapes, noises, objects all flood in upon our sense organs constantly. Why is it that we do not experience the world as a "buzzing, booming confusion"? The reason is obvious. We consciously and unconsciously select certain sense data and exclude others. Without this principle of selectivity we would be flooded with random and unconnected sensa. Here again trans-experiential factors operate to shape and structure the contents of our experience.

A major problem throughout the history of western philosophical thought has been the ontological status of these trans-experiential factors. Plato called them the ideal forms and thought they existed in an ideal world of forms. Aristotle agreed about the importance of forms as the organizing principles of experience and knowledge, but rejected the notion that they existed "out there" apart from the world of empirical data. For him the forms were abstractions from empirical objects. The medieval scholastic philosophers called the forms universals, and a major philosophical battle of the Middle Ages was whether the universals had any independent reality or whether they were merely approximations based on similar individual experiences. Kant revolutionized modern philosophical thought when he suggested that the forms exist as categories of judgment within the mind so that what we experience is a product of the way in which sense data are received and shaped by the mind itself. But, while there has been a great variety of opinion on the ontological status of these trans-experiential factors, no one has doubted their importance. It may be the case that they are simply the conglomeration of past experiences which accompanies us into each new experience. This does not alter the fact that they are not themselves a part of the new experience, but are trans-experiential factors which shape and condition it.

What we experience is a product of the data in our environment and the images, models, ideas, and expectations we bring to it. These trans-experiential factors may come from a number of places and function in a variety of ways, but they have a significant influence in shaping our experienced world. When these images and models constitute our fundamental world-view or life style, they become religious. Religious symbols and images provide the fundamental archetypes or paradigmatic models for organizing and shaping the religious man's environment.

Modern men have lost the dimension of the sacred because they have lost sight of the way in which their experienced environment is a product of the images and symbols they bring to it. They are convinced that the empirical world of objects they experience is the "real" world. Primitive men, on the other hand, were more immediately aware of the deceptiveness of the experienced world. They sought to establish those models and paradigms that discriminated between real events and mere appearances. Of course, modern men still recognize that experience can be deceiving. That is why we use various experimental methods of checking our experience. We sometimes remark that something or someone is "not real", meaning that it or he is phony or not related to the dynamics of actuality that determine the course of events.

The sacred is not, therefore, another world alongside the "real world" of experience. The sacred world is the world of real events and things residing within the experienced world. Religious symbols and images provide the framework for uncovering this real world. The desire of the religious man to live "in the sacred" is, as Eliade says, his desire to live in tune with "real events" and not according to phony or deceiving experiences.

The profane world is composed of things and objects shaped by our own "mental efforts", aspirations, fears, and expectations. It is organized according to the trans-experiential factors that come from our own individual or social background. The sacred world, on the other hand, is composed of things and objects shaped by the images and symbols contained in a religious tradition. The profane world is a world of objects which we can control and manipulate. The sacred world, however, cannot be so controlled. Whereas the purpose of man in relation to the profane world is to shape it according to his needs, his purpose in relation to the sacred world is to bring himself into conformity with it. This way of experiencing elements within our environment is similar to the "feeling of dependence" described by Schleiermacher. Religious myths and rituals, according to Eliade, are not efforts to gain control over new dimensions of our environment. This would be to conceive of religion as a primitive form of science or as magic – a notion which Malinowski also rejects. Rather, religious rites and myths are efforts on the part of religious man to bring himself and his world into harmony with the objectively real world which he cannot control. The desire of the religious man is to bring himself and his world into correlation with reality.

The subjective and changing world meets the real world at

various intersections. These intersections become for the religious man holy places. Each of us can look back to those times and places in his own life when the subjectively oriented existence he was leading was suddenly expanded and transformed by confrontation with someone or something. We suddenly saw ourselves in a new light, or saw our projects and dreams in a new light. We gained a new insight into what the world is really like. In these times and places our profane world has been impinged on by another reality. These are the intersections that form the holy places and events for religious man.

Religious man, according to Eliade, ignores the profane world in favor of the sacred world. This is not to say, however, that he escapes from the existential world into some sort of fantastic reality. On the contrary, he raises the question of exactly what is the real world? What is its shape? How does it work? What forces are active in it? He is convinced that reality is not to be identified with what can be empirically experienced. Rather, it is identified by the myths, images, and symbols of his religious traditions.

Mircea Eliade is a popular and well-known authority on the history of religions and the phenomenology of religion. He was born in Bucharest, Rumania, in 1907 and studied at the University of Bucharest and at the University of Calcutta. Following his years as a student, he taught at the University of Bucharest and at the Sorbonne. Since 1958 he has been a professor at the University of Chicago. Among his many publications are *The Myth of the Eternal Return* (1954), *Patterns in Comparative Religions* (1958), *Birth and Rebirth* (1958), *The Forge and the Crucible* (1962), and *Shamanism* (1964). The following selections are taken from his most popular book, *The Sacred and the Profane* (1961).

The Sacred and the Profane*

SACRED SPACE AND MAKING THE WORLD SACRED

... Some Conclusions

If we should attempt to summarize the result of the descriptions that have been presented in this chapter, we could say that the experience of sacred space makes possible the "founding of the world": where the sacred manifests itself in space, *the real unveils itself*, the world comes into existence. But the irruption of the sacred does not only project a fixed point into the formless fluidity of profane space, a center into chaos; it also effects a break in plane, that is, it opens communication between the cosmic planes (between earth and heaven) and makes possible ontological passages from one mode of being to another. It is such a break in the heterogeneity of profane space that creates the center through which communication with the transmundane is established, that, consequently, founds the world, for the center renders *orientation* possible. Hence the manifestation of the sacred in space has a cosmological valence; every spatial hierophany or consecration of a space is equivalent to a cosmogony. The first conclusion we might draw would be: *the world becomes apprehensible as world, as cosmos, in the measure in which it reveals itself as a sacred world*.

Every world is the work of the gods, for it was either created directly by the gods or was consecrated, hence cosmicized, by men ritually reactualizing the paradigmatic act of Creation. This is as much as to say that religious man can live only in a sacred world, because it is only in such a world that he participates in being, that he has a *real existence*. This religious need expresses an unquenchable ontological thirst. Religious man thirsts for *being*. His terror of the chaos that surrounds his inhabited world corresponds to his terror of nothingness. The unknown space that extends beyond his world – an uncosmicized because

* Mircea Eliade, selections from *The Sacred and the Profane*, tr. William R. Trask, Harcourt, Brace & World, New York, 1959.

unconsecrated space, a mere amorphous extent into which no orientation has yet been projected, and hence in which no structure has yet arisen – for religious man, this profane space represents absolute non-being. If, by some evil chance, he strays into it, he feels emptied of his ontic substance, as if he were dissolving in Chaos, and he finally dies.

This ontological thirst is manifested in many ways. In the realm of sacred space which we are now considering, its most striking manifestation is religious man's will to take his stand at the very heart of the real, at the Center of the World – that is, exactly where the cosmos came into existence and began to spread out toward the four horizons, and where, too, there is the possibility of communication with the gods; in short, precisely where he is *closest to the gods*. We have seen that the symbolism of the center is the formative principle not only of countries, cities, temples, and palaces but also of the humblest human dwelling, be it the tent of a nomad hunter, the shepherd's yurt, or the house of the sedentary cultivator. This is as much as to say that every religious man places himself at the Center of the World and by the same token at the very source of absolute reality, as close as possible to the opening that ensures him communication with the gods.

But since to settle somewhere, to inhabit a space, is equivalent to repeating the cosmogony and hence to imitating the work of the gods, it follows that, for religious man, every existential decision to situate himself in space in fact constitutes a religious decision. By assuming the responsibility of creating the world that he has chosen to inhabit, he not only cosmicizes chaos but also sanctifies his little cosmos by making it like the world of the gods. Religious man's profound nostalgia is to inhabit a "divine world", is his desire that his house shall be like the house of the gods, as it was later represented in temples and sanctuaries. In short, this religious nostalgia expresses *the desire to live in a pure and holy cosmos, as it was in the beginning, when it came fresh from the Creator's hands.*

The experience of sacred time will make it possible for religious man periodically to experience the cosmos as it was *in principio*, that is, at the mythical moment of Creation.

Periodically Becoming Contemporary with the Gods

In the preceding chapter, when we studied the cosmological symbolism of cities, temples, and houses, we showed that it is bound up with the idea of a Center of the World. The religious symbolism implicit in the symbolism of the center appears to be this: man desires to have his abode in a space opening upward, that is, communicating with the divine world. To live near to a Center of the World is, in short, equivalent to living as close as possible to the gods.

We find the same desire for a close approach to the gods if we analyze the meaning of religious festivals. To reintegrate the sacred time of origin is equivalent to becoming contemporary with the gods, hence to living in their presence – even if their presence is mysterious in the sense that it is not always visible. The intention that can be read in the experience of sacred space and sacred time reveals a desire to reintegrate a primordial situation – that in which the gods and the mythical ancestors were *present*, that is, were engaged in creating the world, or in organizing it, or in revealing the foundations of civilization to man. This primordial situation is not historical, it is not calculable chronologically; what is involved is a mythical anteriority, the time of origin, what took place "in the beginning", *in principio*.

Now, what took place "in the beginning" was this: the divine or semidivine beings were active on earth. Hence the nostalgia for origins is equivalent to a *religious* nostalgia. Man desires to recover the active presence of the gods; he also desires to live in the world as it came from the Creator's hands, fresh, pure, and strong. It is the nostalgia for the *perfection of beginnings* that chiefly explains the periodical return *in illo tempore*. In Christian terms, it could be called a nostalgia for paradise, although on the level of primitive cultures the religious and ideological context is entirely different from that of Judaeo-Christianity. But the mythical time whose reactualization is periodically attempted is a time sanctified by the divine presence, and we may say that the desire to live in *the divine presence* and in *a perfect world* (perfect because newly born) corresponds to the nostalgia for a paradisal situation.

As we noted above, this desire on the part of religious man to travel *back* periodically, his effort to reintegrate a mythological situation (the situation as it was in the *beginning*) may appear intolerable and humiliating to modern eyes. Such a nostalgia inevitably leads to the continual repetition of a limited number of gestures and patterns of behavior. From one point of view it may even be said that religious man – especially the religious man of primitive societies – is above all a man paralyzed by the myth of the eternal return. A modern psychologist would be tempted to interpret such an attitude as anxiety before the danger of the new, refusal to assume responsibility for a genuine historical existence, nostalgia for a situation that is paradisal precisely because it is embryonic, insufficiently detached from Nature.

That problem is too complex to be discussed here. In any case, it lies outside the field of our investigation, for, in the last analysis, it implies the problem of the opposition between pre-modern and modern man. Let us rather say that it would be wrong to believe that the religious man of primitive and archaic societies refuses to assume the responsibility for a genuine existence. On the contrary, as we have seen and shall see again, he courageously assumes immense responsibilities – for example, that of collaborating in the creation of the cosmos, or of creating his own world, or of ensuring the life of plants and animals, and so on. But it is a different kind of responsibility from those that, to us moderns, appear to be the only genuine and valid responsibilities. It is *a responsibility on the cosmic plane*, in contradistinction to the moral, social, or historical responsibilities that are alone regarded as valid in modern civilizations. From the point of view of profane existence, man feels no responsibility except to himself and to society. For him, the universe does not properly constitute a cosmos – that is, a living and articulated unity; it is simply the sum of the material reserves and physical energies of the planet, and the great concern of modern man is to avoid stupidly exhausting the economic resources of the globe. But, existentially, the primitive always puts himself in a cosmic context. His personal experience lacks neither genuineness nor depth; but the fact that it is expressed in a language unfamiliar to us makes it appear spurious or infantile to modern eyes.

To revert to our immediate subject: we have no warrant for interpreting periodic return to the sacred time of origin as a rejection of the real world and an escape into dream and imagination. On the contrary, it seems to us that, here again, we can discern the *ontological obsession* to which we have referred and which, moreover, can be considered an essential characteristic of the man of the primitive and archaic societies. For to wish to reintegrate the *time of origin* is also to wish to return to the *presence of the gods*, to recover the *strong, fresh, pure world* that existed *in illo tempore*. It is at once thirst for the *sacred* and nostalgia for *being*. On the existential plane this experience finds expression in the certainty that life can be periodically begun over again with a maximum of good fortune. Indeed, it is not only an optimistic vision of existence, but a total cleaving to being. By all his behavior, religious man proclaims that he believes only in being, and that his participation in being is assured him by the primordial revelation of which he is the guardian. The sum total of primordial revelations is constituted by his myths.

MYTH = PARADIGMATIC MODEL

The myth relates a sacred history, that is, a primordial event that took place at the beginning of time, *ab initio*. But to relate a sacred history is equivalent to revealing a mystery. For the persons of the myth are not human beings; they are gods or culture heroes, and for this reason their *gesta* constitute mysteries; man could not know their acts if they were not revealed to him. The myth, then, is the history of what took place *in illo tempore*, the recital of what the gods or the semidivine beings did at the beginning of time. To tell a myth is to proclaim what happened *ab origine*. Once told, that is, revealed, the myth becomes apodictic truth; it establishes a truth that is absolute. "It is so because it is said that it is so", the Netsilik Eskimos declare to justify the validity of their sacred history and religious traditions. The myth proclaims the appearance of a new cosmic situation or of a primordial event. Hence it is always the recital of a creation; it tells how something was accomplished, began to *be*. It is for this reason that myth is bound up with ontology; it speaks only of *realities*, of what *really* happened, of what was fully manifested.

Obviously these realities are sacred realities, for it is the *sacred* that is pre-eminently the *real*. Whatever belongs to the sphere of the profane does not participate in being, for the profane was not ontologically established by myth, has no perfect model. As we shall soon see, agricultural work is a ritual revealed by the gods or culture heroes. This is why it constitutes an act that is at once *real* and *significant*. Let us think, by comparison, of agricultural work in a desacralized society. Here, it has become a profane act, justified by the economic profit that it brings. The ground is tilled to be exploited; the end pursued is profit and food. Emptied of religious symbolism, agricultural work becomes at once opaque and exhausting; it reveals no meaning, it makes possible no opening toward the universal, toward the world of spirit. No god, no culture hero ever revealed a profane act. Everything that the gods or the ancestors did, hence everything that the myths have to tell about their creative activity, belongs to the sphere of the sacred and therefore participates in *being*. In contrast, what men do on their own initiative, what they do without a mythical model, belongs to the sphere of the profane; hence it is a vain and illusory activity, and, in the last analysis, unreal. The more religious man is, the more paradigmatic models does he possess to guide his attitudes and actions. In other words, the more religious he is, the more does he enter into the *real* and the less is he in danger of becoming lost in actions that, being non-paradigmatic, "subjective", are, finally, aberrant.

This is the aspect of myth that demands particular emphasis here. The myth reveals absolute sacrality, because it relates the creative activity of the gods, unveils the sacredness of their work. In other words, the myth describes the various and sometimes dramatic irruptions of the sacred into the world. This is why, among many primitives, myths cannot be recited without regard for time or place, but only during the seasons that are ritually richest (autumn, winter) or in the course of religious ceremonies – in short, during *a sacred period of time*. It is the irruption of the sacred into the world, an irruption narrated in the myths, that *establishes* the world as a reality. Every myth shows how a reality came into existence, whether it be the total reality, cosmos, or only a fragment – an island, a species of plant, a human institution. To tell how things came into existence is to explain them and at the same time indirectly to answer another question: *Why* did they come into existence? The why is always implied in the how – for the simple reason that to tell *how* a thing was born is to reveal an irruption of the sacred into the world, and the sacred is the ultimate cause of all real existence.

Moreover, since every creation is a divine work and hence an irruption of the sacred, it at the same time represents an irruption of creative energy into the world. Every creation springs from an abundance. The gods create out of an excess of power, an overflow of energy. Creation is accomplished by a surplus of ontological substance. This is why the myth, which narrates this sacred ontophany, this victorious manifestation of a plentitude of being, becomes the paradigmatic model for all human activities. For it alone reveals the *real*, the superabundant, the effectual. "We must do what the Gods did in the beginning", says an Indian text (*Shatapatha Brāhmana,* VII, 2, 1, 4). "Thus the Gods did; thus men do", the *Taittirīya Brahmana* adds (1, 5, 9, 4). Hence the supreme function of the myth is to "fix" the paradigmatic models for all rites and all significant human activities – eating, sexuality, work, education, and so on. Acting as a fully responsible human being, man imitates the paradigmatic gestures of the gods, repeats their actions, whether in the case of a simple physiological function such as eating or of a social, economic, cultural, military, or other activity.

In New Guinea a great many myths tell of long sea voyages, thus providing "exemplars for the modern voyagers", as well as for all other activities, "whether of love, or war, or rain-making, or fishing, or whatever else.... The narrative gives precedents

for the stages of construction, the tabu on sexual intercourse, etc."
When a captain goes to sea he personifies the mythical hero Aori.
"He wears the costume which Aori is supposed to have worn,
with blackened face ... [and] the same kind of *love* in his hair
which Aori plucked from Iviri's head. He dances on the platform
and extends his arms like Aori's wings .... A man told me that
when he went fish shooting (with bow and arrow) he pretended
to be Kivavia himself." He did not pray to the mythical hero for
aid and favor; he identified himself with him.

This symbolism of mythical precedents is also found in other
primitive cultures. Writing on the Karuk Indians of California,
J. P. Harrington says: "Everything that the Karuk did was enacted because the Ikxareyavs were believed to have set the example in story times. The Ikxareyavs were the people who were
in America before the Indians came. Modern Karuks, in a quand-
ary how to render the word, volunteer such translations as 'the
princes', 'the chiefs', 'the angels'.... [The Ikxareyavs]
remain[ed] with the Karuk only long enough to state and start
all customs, telling them in every instance, 'Humans will do the
same.' These doings and sayings are still related and quoted in the
medicine formulas of the Karuk."

This faithful repetition of divine models has a twofold result:
(1) by imitating the gods, man remains in the sacred, hence in
reality; (2) by the continuous reactualization of paradigmatic
divine gestures, the world is sanctified. Men's religious behavior
contributes to maintaining the sanctity of the world.

REACTUALIZING MYTHS

It is not without interest to note that religious man assumes a
humanity that has a trans-human, transcendent model. He does not
consider himself to be *truly man* except in so far as he imitates
the gods, the culture heroes, or the mythical ancestors. This is as
much as to say that religious man wishes to be *other* than he is
on the plane of his profane experience. Religious man is not *given*;
he *makes* himself, by approaching the divine models. These
models, as we said, are preserved in myths, in the history of the

divine *gesta*. Hence religious man, too, regards himself as *made* by history, just as profane man does; but the only history that concerns him is the *sacred history* revealed by the myths – that is, the history of the gods; whereas profane man insists that he is constituted only by human history, hence by the sum of the very acts that, for religious man, are of no importance because they have no divine models. The point to be emphasized is that, from the beginning, religious man sets the model he is to attain on the trans-human plane, the plane revealed by his myths. *One becomes truly a man only by conforming to the teaching of the myths, that is, by imitating the gods* ....

SACRED HISTORY, HISTORY, HISTORICISM

Let us recapitulate: Religious man experiences two kinds of time – profane and sacred. The one is an evanescent duration, the other a "succession of eternities", periodically recoverable during the festivals that made up the sacred calendar. The liturgical time of the calendar flows in a closed circle; it is the cosmic time of the year, sanctified by the works of the gods. And since the most stupendous divine work was the creation of the world, commemoration of the cosmogony plays an important part in many religions. The New Year coincides with the first day of Creation. The year is the temporal dimension of the cosmos. "The world has passed" expresses that a year has run its course.

At each New Year the cosmogony is reiterated, the world re-created, and to do this is also to create time – that is, to regenerate it by beginning it anew. This is why the cosmogonic myth serves as paradigmatic model for every creation or construction; it is even used as a ritual means of healing. By symbolically becoming contemporary with the Creation, one reintegrates the primordial plenitude. The sick man becomes well because he begins his life again with its sum of energy intact.

The religious festival is the reactualization of a primordial event, of a sacred history in which the actors are the gods or semidivine beings. But sacred history is recounted in the myths. Hence the participants in the festivals become contemporaries of the gods and the semidivine beings. They live in the primordial time that is sanctified by the presence and activity of the gods. The sacred calendar periodically regenerates time, because it makes it coincide with the *time of origin*, the strong, pure time. The religious experience of the festival – that is, participation in the sacred – enables man periodically to live in the presence of the gods. This is the reason for the fundamental importance of myths in all pre-Mosaic religions, for the myths narrate the *gesta* of the gods and these *gesta* constitute paradigmatic models for all human activities. In so far as he imitates his gods, religious man lives in the *time of origin*, the time of myths. In other words, he emerges from profane duration to recover an unmoving time, eternity.

Since, for religious man of the primitive societies, myths constitute his sacred history, he must not forget them; by reactualizing the myths, he approaches his gods and participates in sanctity. But there are also tragic divine histories, and man assumes a great responsibility toward himself and toward nature by periodically reactualizing them. Ritual cannibalism, for example, is the consequence of a tragic religious conception.

In short, through the reactualization of his myths, religious man attempts to approach the gods and to participate in *being*; the imitation of paradigmatic divine models expresses at once his desire for sanctity and his ontological nostalgia.

In the primitive and archaic religions the eternal repetition of the divine exploits is justified as an *imitatio dei*. The sacred calendar annually repeats the same festivals, that is, the commemoration of the same mythical events. Strictly speaking, the sacred calendar proves to be the "eternal return" of a limited number of divine *gesta* – and this is true not only for primitive religions but for all others. The festal calendar everywhere constitutes a periodical return of the same primordial situations and hence a reactualization of the same sacred time. For religious man, reactualization of the same mythical events constitutes his greatest hope; for with each reactualization he again has the opportunity to transfigure his existence, to make it like its divine model. In short, for religious man of the primitive and archaic societies, the

eternal repetition of paradigmatic gestures and the eternal re-
covery of the same mythical time of origin, sanctified by the gods,
in no sense implies a pessimistic vision of life. On the contrary,
for him it is by virtue of this eternal return to the sources of the
sacred and the real that human existence appears to be saved from
nothingness and death.

The perspective changes completely when the sense of *the
religiousness of the cosmos becomes lost.* This is what occurs
when, in certain more highly evolved societies, the intellectual
élites progressively detach themselves from the patterns of the
traditional religion. The periodical sanctification of cosmic time
then proves useless and without meaning. The gods are no longer
accessible through the cosmic rhythms. The religious meaning
of the repetition of paradigmatic gestures is forgotten. But
repetition emptied of its religious content necessarily leads to a
pessimistic vision of existence. When it is no longer a vehicle for
reintegrating a primordial situation, and hence for recovering
the mysterious presence of the gods, that is, *when it is desacralized,* cyclic time becomes terrifying; it is seen as a circle forever
turning on itself, repeating itself to infinity.

This is what happened in India, where the doctrine of cosmic
cycles (*yugas*) was elaborately developed. A complete cycle, a
mahāyuga, comprises 12,000 years. It ends with a dissolution, a
pralaya, which is repeated more drastically (*mahāpralaya,* the
Great Dissolution) at the end of the thousandth cycle. For the
paradigmatic schema "creation-destruction-creation-etc." is reproduced *ad infinitum.* The 12,000 years of a *mahāyuga* were regarded as divine years, each with a duration of 360 years, which
gives a total of 4,320,000 years for a single cosmic cycle. A
thousand such *mahāyugas* make up a *kalpa* (form); 14 *kalpas*
make up a *manvantāra* (so named because each *manvantāra* is
supposed to be ruled by Manu, the mythical Ancestor-King). A
kalpa is equivalent to a day in the life of Brahma; a second
kalpa to a night. One hundred of these "years" of Brahma, in
other words 311,000 milliards of human years, constitute the life
of Brahma. But even this duration of the god's life does not exhaust time, for the gods are not eternal and the cosmic creations

and destructions succeed one another forever.

This is the true eternal return, the eternal repetition of the fundamental rhythm of the cosmos – its periodical destruction and re-creation. In short, *it is the primitive conception of the Year-Cosmos, but emptied of its religious content.* Obviously, the doctrine of *yugas* was elaborated by intellectual élites, and if it became a pan-Indian doctrine, we must not suppose that it revealed its terrifying aspect to all the peoples of India. It was chiefly the religious and philosophical élites who felt despair in the presence of cyclic time repeating itself *ad infinitum*. For to Indian thought, this eternal return implied eternal return to existence by force of *karma*, the law of universal causality. Then, too, time was homologized to the cosmic illusion (*māyā*), and the eternal return to existence signified indefinite prolongation of suffering and slavery. In the view of these religious and philosophical élites, the only hope was non-return-to-existence, the abolition of karma; in other words, final deliverance (*moksha*), implying a transcendence of the cosmos.

Greece, too, knew the myth of the eternal return, and the Greek philosophers of the late period carried the conception of circular time to its furthest limits. To quote the perceptive words of H. C. Puech: "According to the celebrated Platonic definition, time, which is determined and measured by the revolution of the celestial spheres, is the moving image of unmoving eternity, which it imitates by revolving in a circle. Consequently all cosmic becoming, and, in the same manner, the duration of this world of generation and corruption in which we live, will progress in a circle or in accordance with an indefinite succession of cycles in the course of which the same reality is made, unmade, and remade in conformity with an immutable law and immutable alternatives. Not only is the same sum of existence preserved in it, with nothing being lost and nothing created, but in addition certain thinkers of declining antiquity – Pythagoreans, Stoics, Platonists – reached the point of admitting that within each of these cycles of duration, of these *aiones*, these *aeva*, the same situations are reproduced that have already been produced in previous cycles and will be reproduced in subsequent cycles – *ad infinitum*. No event is unique, occurs once and for all (for example, the condemnation and death of Socrates), but it has occurred, occurs, and will occur, perpetually; the same individuals have appeared, appear, and will appear again at every return of the cycle upon itself. Cosmic duration is repetition and *anakuklosis*, eternal return."

Compared with the archaic and palaeo-oriental religions, as well as with the mythic-philosophical conceptions of the eternal return, as they were elaborated in India and Greece, Judaism presents an innovation of the first importance. For Judaism, time has a beginning and will have an end. The idea of cyclic time is left behind. Yahweh no longer manifests himself in *cosmic time* (like the gods of other religions) but in a historical time, which is irreversible. Each new manifestation of Yahweh in history is no longer reducible to an earlier manifestation. The fall of Jerusalem expresses Yahweh's wrath against his people, but it is no longer the same wrath that Yahweh expressed by the fall of Samaria. His gestures are *personal* interventions in history and reveal their deep meaning *only for his people*, the people that Yahweh had *chosen*. Hence the historical event acquires a new dimension; it becomes a *theophany*.

Christianity goes even further in valorizing *historical time*. Since God was *incarnated*, that is, since he took on a *historically conditioned human existence*, history acquires the possibility of being sanctified. The *illud tempus* evoked by the Gospels is a clearly defined historical time – the time in which Pontius Pilate was Governor of Judaea – but it was *sanctified by the presence of Christ*. When a Christian of our day participates in liturgical time, he recovers the *illud tempus* in which Christ lived, suffered, and rose again – but it is no longer a mythical time, it is the time when Pontius Pilate governed Judaea. For the Christian, too, the sacred calendar indefinitely rehearses the same events of the existence of Christ – but these events took place in history; they are no longer facts that happened at the *origin of time*, "in the beginning". (But we should add that, for the Christian, time begins anew with the birth of Christ, for the Incarnation establishes a new situation of man in the cosmos.) This is as much as to say that history reveals itself to be a new dimension of the presence of God in the world.

History becomes *sacred history* once more – as it was conceived, but in a mythical perspective, in primitive and archaic religions.

Christianity arrives not at a *philosophy* but at a *theology* of history. For God's interventions in history, and above all his Incarnation in the historical person of Jesus Christ, have a trans-historical purpose – the *salvation* of man.

Hegel takes over the Judaeo-Christian ideology and applies it to universal history in its totality: the universal spirit *continually* manifests itself in historical events and manifests itself *only* in historical events. Thus *the whole* of history becomes a theophany; everything that has happened in history *had to happen as it did*, because the universal spirit so willed it. The road is thus opened to the various forms of twentieth-century historicistic philoso-phies. Here our present investigation ends, for all these new valor-izations of time and history belong to the history of philosophy. Yet we must add that historicism arises as a decomposition pro-duct of Christianity; it accords decisive importance to the his-torical event (which is an idea whose origin is Christian) but to the *historical event as such*, that is, by denying it any possibility of revealing a trans-historical, soteriological intent.

As for the conceptions of time on which certain historicistic and existentialist philosophies have insisted, the following obser-vation is not without interest: although no longer conceived as a circle, time in these modern philosophies once again wears the terrifying aspect that it wore in the Indian and Greek philosophies of the eternal return. Definitively desacralized, time presents itself as a precarious and evanescent duration, leading irremediably to death ....

IO

RELIGION AS ENCOUNTER

Martin Buber

Editor's Introduction

IN THE PRECEDING selection Mircea Eliade developed a dialectical description of religion in which religious images and symbols are seen as archetypes and models of a world structured by the religious mentality. Emphasis is put on the non-homogeneity of the experienced world and on the two basic ways – sacred and profane – men have of relating to their environment. In the following selection Martin Buber also develops a dialectical understanding of religion based on a recognition of two fundamental kinds of experience – two ways men relate to their environment. Buber places his emphasis, however, not on the archetypal structures which shape experience but on the encounter of the old and already experienced world with the transforming presence of the new. At the intersection where the sacred impinges on the profane, reality is encountered. It is this encounter that Buber seeks to describe.

In Chapter 5 of this book Ludwig Feuerbach described the way in which what we experience in our environment is not things as they are in themselves but things as they appear to us. All the objects of our experience – things, other people, God – can be known only from our own perspective. What we see in them is not really the other one existing as an object, but a reflection of ourselves. We are really in a self-constructed isolation booth with no door to the outside. We live in a hall of mirrors and where we see only various reflections of ourselves. It is impossible for us to experience reality as it exists in itself and apart from the way our minds structure it. We are condemned to spend our entire lives "out of touch".

Buber's writing should be seen against this Feuerbachian backdrop. He describes occasions when, contrary to what we can expect on the basis of Feuerbach's essentially correct analysis, some one or some thing breaks through the mirrors and encounters us. There are times when the "other" breaks through our worlds and confronts us as a being which exists in itself and apart from our interaction with it. In these encounters there is no longer any question of our controlling and shaping the being which confronts us: it presents itself to us as something real in itself. This confrontation Buber calls the "I-Thou relationship".

The "I-Thou" encounter is not some kind of supernatural numinous experience. It is a kind of experience that is common to all men, although modern men have tended to ignore it. Buber attempts to call attention to this kind of experience through a phenomenological description, just as Maritain, van der Leeuw, and Schleiermacher, for example, attempted to call attention to a kind of experience we sometimes overlook.

If we have lost the ability to understand what Buber is talking about, it is because we have lost the ability to experience our world in any way other than as a collection of objects for us to control and predict. We have lost the immediate experience of our environment as prior to our theoretical modeling of it. We meet nothing in our world other than objects with which we interact. The question is whether we have gained a clearer picture of our environment or whether we have lost sight of significant existential parameters.

There is one aspect of experience over which we have no control and cannot be said to interact: the future. We do not know and cannot control what will happen to us in the next moment. Each conscious moment confronts us with the new, defined not by our own conscious organizing principles, but by the external situation over which we exercise no control. As soon as the contents of the moment become present for us, we can begin to gain mastery over them, manipulate them, and interact with them, but in the moment that the new meets us, we are completely under its power.

This confrontation with the new – with what does not make up a part of the already recognized and organized world, is a frightening experience and it is easy to understand why we often seek to avoid it. We try to avoid the future through prediction. We seek to control our environment so that nothing new will threaten us. This effort is really a destruction of the future by turning it into the past-perfect. When the future does meet us, however, we are faced with something like what the primitive man faced when he confronted the uncontrolable aspects of his environment that he called sacred. And it is in this open encounter that the "I-Thou" relationship is established.

We cannot move out to encounter the other. Our efforts always are directed toward projected objects – mirrors. Rather we find ourselves encountered. Moreover, to a philosophical analysis of human possibilities this encounter appears improbable and perhaps even impossible. The objects of our attention are always projections. In spite of this improbability, we have all had the experience of being confronted by some one or some thing in such a new and profound way that it could not be experienced as an object of our own making. In this encounter, the other is a new reality which meets us and shatters the pigeon-holes in which we had put our previous experience. Of course, we immediately converted the other into an object for us. But in the initial encounter, we faced the other as it is in itself.

This encounter with the "other" or the "Thou" is man's encounter with God. The divine-human encounter, therefore, is not a form of mysticism in which man somehow is removed from his everyday world. This encounter is a normal part of our worldly existence. It is unique, however, in that in this relationship we encounter objects in our environment in a fundamentally different way. In the "I-Thou" encounter they are not objects in our environment with which we interact, but subjects which we meet.

It is a mistake to read a sort of humanistic personalism into Buber's description of the "I-Thou" encounter. For one thing we meet the "Thou" not only in other people but also in things around us. In the second place, when we meet the "Thou" it is not the other person as such that we meet but the eternal Thou as it manifests itself in him. The sort of personalism which attempts to "accept the other person as a person" can be the severest form of the "I-It" relationship when it masks a refusal to risk one's own self in an open meeting. The distinction Buber seeks to draw between "I-Thou" and "I-It" relationships is not a distinction between how we relate the objects and how we relate the persons but a distinction between two ways of relating to anything within our environment.

It should also be pointed out that the "I-It" relationship is not necessarily an evil relationship according to Buber. The "I-It" relationship is the relationship we establish toward things in our world in terms of usefulness. It is only in terms of this relationship that we are able to manipulate and control our environment and therefore get anything at all done. The danger arises only when this "I-It" relationship threatens to obscure the "I-Thou" dimension.

Religious activity for Buber is activity which takes place on the basis of an "I-Thou" relationship. In this encounter or dialogue there can be no formulas. It is really an open conversation in which both parties are probed. It is a conversation in which I am not concerned to acquire knowledge or convince the other person of the value of my own position. It is a conversation in which I am not conscious of myself conversing. I am completely involved with the other person. This is why Buber can say that in the "I-Thou" dialogue the "larger Thou" leads and the two conversants follow.

Martin Buber was born in Vienna in 1878 and had a traditional Jewish education. He was influenced by Jewish Hasidism, a form of humanistic, prophetic Judaism that stressed the mercy of God, joyous religious expression in music and dance, and purity of heart rather than moralism or legalism. Under the influence of Hasidism, Buber at first developed a kind of mystic theology but turned from "the religious" to "the everyday" – away from mysticism toward existentialism and then toward a dialogical theology. He wrote his most famous book, *I and Thou*, from which the following selection is taken, in 1923 while he taught at the University of Frankfurt. When Hitler came to power in 1933, Buber lost his teaching position and began to devote his attention to the care for German Jews. In 1938 he fled to Palestine. He retired in 1951 at the age of seventy-three but continued to travel and lecture widely. He died in 1965.

*I and Thou**

To MAN THE world is twofold, in accordance with his twofold attitude.

The attitude of man is twofold, in accordance with the twofold nature of the primary words which he speaks.

The primary words are not isolated words, but combined words.

The one primary word is the combination *I-Thou.*

The other primary word is the combination *I-It*; wherein, without a change in the primary word, one of the words *He* and *She* can replace *It.*

Hence the *I* of man is also twofold.

For the *I* of the primary word I-Thou is a different I from that of the primary word *I-It.*

Primary words do not signify things, but they intimate relations.

Primary words do not describe something that might exist independently of them, but being spoken they bring about existence.

Primary words are spoken from the being.

If *Thou* is said, the *I* of the combination *I-Thou* is said along with it.

If *It* is said, the *I* of the combination *I-It* is said along with it.

* Martin Buber, selections from Parts I–III of *I and Thou*, tr. R. Gregor Smith, Charles Scribners' Sons, New York, 2nd ed. 1958, and T. & T. Clark, Edinburgh, 1937.

The primary word *I-Thou* can only be spoken with the whole being.

The primary word *I-It* can never be spoken with the whole being.

There is no *I* taken in itself, but only the *I* of the primary word *I-Thou* and the *I* of the primary word *I-It*.

When a man says *I* he refers to one or other of these. The *I* to which he refers is present when he says *I*. Further, when he says *Thou*, or *It*, the *I* of one of the two primary words is present.

The existence of *I* and the speaking of *I* are one and the same thing.

When a primary word is spoken the speaker enters the word and takes his stand in it.

The life of human beings is not passed in the sphere of transitive verbs alone. It does not exist in virtue of activities alone which have some *thing* for their object.

I perceive something. I am sensible of something. I imagine something. I will something. I feel something. I think something. The life of human beings does not consist of all this and the like alone.

This and the like together establish the realm of *It*.

But the realm of *Thou* has a different basis.

When *Thou* is spoken, the speaker has no thing for his object. For where there is a thing there is another thing. Every *It* is bounded by others; *It* exists only through being bounded by others. But when *Thou* is spoken, there is no thing. *Thou* has no bounds.

When *Thou* is spoken, the speaker has no *thing*; he has indeed nothing. But he takes his stand in relation.

It is said that man experiences his world. What does that mean?

Man travels over the surface of things and experiences them. He extracts knowledge about their constitution from them: he wins an experience from them. He experiences what belongs to the things.

But the world is not presented to man by experiences alone. These present him only with a world composed of *It* and *He* and *She* and *It* again.

I experience something – If we add "inner" to "outer" experiences, nothing in the situation is changed. We are merely following the uneternal division that springs from the lust of the human race to whittle away the secret of death. Inner things or outer things, what are they but things and things!

I experience something. – If we add "secret" to "open" experiences, nothing in the situation is changed. How self-confident is that wisdom which perceives a closed compartment in things, reserved for the initiate and manipulated only with the key. O secrecy without a secret! O accumulation of information! It, always It!

The man who experiences has not part in the world. For it is "in him" and not between him and the world that the experience arises.

The world has no part in the experience. It permits itself to be experienced, but has no concern in the matter. For it does nothing to the experience, and the experience does nothing to it.

As experience, the world belongs to the primary word *I-It*.
The primary word *I-Thou* establishes the world of relation.

The spheres in which the world of relation arises are three.

First, our life with Nature. There the relation sways in gloom, beneath the level of speech. Creatures live and move over against us, but cannot come to us, and when we address them as *Thou*, our words cling to the threshold of speech.

Second, our life with men. There the relation is open and in the form of speech. We can give and accept the *Thou*.

Third, our life with spiritual beings. There the relation is clouded, yet it discloses itself; it does not use speech, yet begets it. We perceive no *Thou*, but none the less we feel we are addressed and we answer – forming, thinking, acting. We speak the primary word with our being, though we cannot utter *Thou* with our lips.

But with what right do we draw what lies outside speech into relation with the world of the primary word?

In every sphere in its own way, through each process of becoming that is present to us we look out toward the fringe of the eternal *Thou*; in each we are aware of a breath from the eternal *Thou*; in each *Thou* we address the eternal *Thou*.

I consider a tree.

I can look on it as a picture: stiff column in a shock of light, or splash of green shot with the delicate blue and silver of the background.

I can perceive it as movement: flowing veins on clinging, pressing pith, suck of the roots, breathing of the leaves, ceaseless commerce with earth and air – and the obscure growth itself.

I can classify it in a species and study it as a type in its structure and mode of life.

I can subdue its actual presence and form so sternly that I recognize it only as an expression of law – of the laws in accordance with which a constant opposition of forces is continually adjusted, or of those in accordance with which the component substances mingle and separate.

I can dissipate it and perpetuate it in number, in pure numerical relation.

In all this the tree remains my object, occupies space and time, and has its nature and constitution.

It can, however, also come about, if I have both will and grace, that in considering the tree I become bound up in relation to it. The tree is now no longer *It*. I have been seized by the power of exclusiveness.

To effect this it is not necessary for me to give up any of the ways in which I consider the tree. There is nothing from which I would have to turn my eyes away in order to see, and no knowledge that I would have to forget. Rather is everything, picture and movement, species and type, law and number, indivisibly united in this event.

Everything belonging to the tree is in this: its form and structure, its colours and chemical composition, its intercourse with the elements and with the stars, are all present in a single whole.

The tree is no impression, no play of my imagination, no value depending on my mood; but it is bodied over against me and has to do with me, as I with it – only in a different way.

Let no attempt be made to sap the strength from the meaning of the relation: relation is mutual. The tree will have a consciousness, then, similar to our own? Of that I have no experience. But do you wish, through seeming to succeed in it with yourself, once again to disintegrate that which cannot be disintegrated? I encounter no soul or dryad of the tree, but the tree itself.

If I face a human being as my *Thou*, and say the primary word *I-Thou* to him, he is not a thing among things, and does not consist of things.

Thus a human being is not *He* or *She*, bounded from every other *He* and *She*, a specific point in space and time within the net of the world; nor is he a nature able to be experienced and described, a loose bundle of named qualities. But with no neighbor, and whole in himself, he is *Thou* and fills the heavens. This does not mean that nothing exists except himself. But all else lives in *his* light.

Just as the melody is not made up of notes nor the verse of words nor the statue of lines, but they must be tugged and dragged till their unity has been scattered into these many pieces, so with the man to whom I say *Thou*. I can take out from him the color of his hair, or of his speech, or of his goodness. I must continually do this. But each time I do it he ceases to be *Thou*.

And just as prayer is not in time but time in prayer, sacrifice not in space but space in sacrifice, and to reverse the relation is to abolish the reality, so with the man to whom I say *Thou*. I do not meet with him at some time and place or other. I can set him in a particular time and place; I must continually do it: but I set only a *He* or a *She*, that is an *It*, no longer my *Thou*.

So long as the heaven of *Thou* is spread out over me the winds of causality cower at my heels, and the whirlpool of fate stays its course.

I do not experience the man to whom I say *Thou*. But I take my stand in relation to him, in the sanctity of the primary word.

Only when I step out of it do I experience him once more. In the act of experience *Thou* is far away.

Even if the man to whom I say *Thou* is not aware of it in the midst of his experience, yet relation may exist. For *Thou* is more than *It* realizes. No deception penetrates here; here is the cradle of the Real Life.

This is the eternal source of art: a man is faced by a form which desires to be made through him into a work. This form is no offspring of his soul, but is an appearance which steps up to it and demands of it the effective power. The man is concerned with an act of his being. If he carries it through, if he speaks the primary word out of his being to the form which appears, then the effective power streams out, and the work arises.

The act includes a sacrifice and a risk. This is the sacrifice: the endless possibility that is offered up on the altar of the form. For everything which just this moment in play ran through the perspective must be obliterated; nothing of that may penetrate the work. The exclusiveness of what is facing it demands that it be so. This is the risk: the primary word can only be spoken with the whole being. He who gives himself to it may withhold nothing of himself. The work does not suffer me, as do the tree and the man, to turn aside and relax in the world of *It*; but it commands. If I do not serve it aright it is broken, or it breaks me.

I can neither experience nor describe the form which meets me, but only body it forth. And yet I behold it, splendid in the radiance of what confronts me, clearer than all the clearness of the world which is experienced. I do not behold it as a thing among the *"inner"* things nor as an image of my "fancy", but as that which exists in the present. If test is made of its objectivity the form is certainly not "there". Yet what is actually so much present as it is? And the relation in which I stand to it is real, for it affects me, as I affect it.

To produce is too draw forth, to invent is to find, to shape is to discover. In bodying forth I disclose. I lead the form across – into the world of *It*. The work produced is a thing among things, able to be experienced and described as a sum of qualities. But from time to time it can face the receptive beholder in its whole embodied form.

– What, then, do we experience of *Thou*?

– Just nothing. For we do not experience it.

– What, then, do we know of *Thou*?

– Just everything. For we know nothing isolated about it any more.

The *Thou* meets me through grace – it is not found by seeking. But my speaking of the primary word to it is an act of my being, is indeed *the* act of my being.

The *Thou* meets me. But I step into direct relation with it. Hence the relation means being chosen and choosing, suffering and action in one; just as any action of the whole being, which means the suspension of all partial actions and consequently of all sensations of actions grounded only in their particular limitation, is bound to resemble suffering.

The primary word *I-Thou* can be spoken only with the whole being. Concentration and fusion into the whole being can never take place through my agency, nor can it ever take place without me. I become through my relation to the *Thou*; as I become *I*, I say *Thou*.

All real living is meeting.

The relation to the *Thou* is direct. No system of ideas, no foreknowledge, and no fancy intervene between *I* and *Thou*. The memory itself is transformed, as it plunges out of its isolation into the unity of the whole. No aim, no lust, and no anticipation intervene between *I* and *Thou*. Desire itself is transformed as it plunges out of its dream into the appearance. Every means is an obstacle. Only when every means has collapsed does the meeting come about.

In the face of the directness of the relation everything indirect becomes irrelevant. It is also irrelevant if my *Thou* is already the *It* for the other *I's* ("an object of general experience"), or can become so through the very accomplishment of this act of my being. For the real, though certainly swaying and swinging, boundary runs neither between experience and non-experience, nor between what is given and what is not given, nor yet between the world of being and the world of value; but cutting indifferently across all these provinces it lies between *Thou* and *I*, between the present and the object.

The present, and by that is meant not the point which indicates from time to time in our thought merely the conclusion of "finished" time, the mere appearance of a termination which is fixed and held, but the real, filled present, exists only in so far as actual presentness, meeting, and relation exist. The present arises only in virtue of the fact that the *Thou* becomes present.

The *I* of the primary word *I-It*, that is, the *I* faced by no *Thou*, but surrounded by a multitude of "contents", has no present, only the past. Put in another way, in so far as man rests satisfied with the things that he experiences and uses, he lives in the past, and his moment has no present content. He has nothing but objects. But objects subsist in time that has been.

The present is not fugitive and transient, but continually present and enduring. The object is not duration, but cessation, suspension, a breaking off and cutting clear and hardening, absence of relation and of present being.

True beings are lived in the present, the life of objects is in the past.

In the Beginning is Relation

Consider the speech of "primitive" peoples, that is, of those that have a meager stock of objects, and whose life is built up within a narrow circle of acts highly charged with presentness. The nuclei of this speech, words in the form of sentences and original pregrammatical structures (which later, splitting asunder, give rise to the many various kinds of words), mostly indicate the wholeness of a relation. We say "far away"; the Zulu has for that a word which means, in our sentence form. "There where someone cries out: 'O mother, I am lost.'" The Fuegian soars above our analytic wisdom with a seven-syllabled word whose precise meaning is, "They stare at one another, each waiting for the other to volunteer to do what both wish, but are not able to do." In this total situation the persons, as expressed both in nouns and pronouns, are embedded, still only in relief and without finished independence. The chief concern is not with these products of analysis and reflection but with the true original unity, the lived relation.

We greet the man we meet, wishing him well or assuring him of our devotion or commending him to God. But how indirect these worn-out formulas are! What do we discern even dimly in "Hail!" of the original conferring of power? Compare these with the ever fresh Kaffir greeting, with its direct bodily relation, "I see you!" or with its ridiculous and sublime American variant, "Smell me!"

It may be supposed that characterizations and ideas, but also representations of persons and things, have been taken out from representations of incidents and situations that are specifically relational. The elementary impressions and emotional stirrings that waken the spirit of the "natural man" proceed from incidents – experience of a being confronting him – and from situations – life with a being confronting him – that are relational in character. He is not disquieted by the moon that he sees every night, till it comes bodily to him, sleeping or waking, draws near and charms him with silent movements, or fascinates him with the evil or sweetness of its touch. He does not retain from this the visual representation, say, of the wandering orb of light, or of a demonic being that somehow belongs to it, but at first he has in him only the dynamic, stirring image of the moon's effect, streaming through his body. Out of this the image of the moon personally achieving the effect only gradually emerges. Only now, that is to say, does the memory of the unknown that is nightly taken into his being begin to kindle and take shape as the doer and bringer of the effect. Thus it makes possible the transformation of the unknown into an object, a *He* or a *She* out of a *Thou* that could not originally be experienced, but simply suffered.

This initial and long-continuing relational character of every essential phenomenon makes it also easier to understand a certain spiritual element of primitive life that is much discussed and observed, but not yet properly grasped, in present-day study. I mean that mysterious power the idea of which has been traced, through many variations, in the form of the beliefs or in the knowledge (both being still one) of many nature peoples. Known as Mana or Orenda, it opens a way to the Brahman in its primal meaning, and further to the Dynamis and Charis of the Magical Papyri and of the Apostolic Epistles. It has been characterized as a supersensuous or supernatural power – descriptions which depend on our categories and do not correspond to those of the primitive man. The limits of his world are set by his bodily experience, to which visits from the dead, say, quite "naturally" belong. To accept what has no sensuous qualities at all as actually existing must strike him as absurd. The appearances to which he ascribes the "mystical power" are all elementary incidents that are relational in character, that is, all incidents that disturb him by stirring his body and leaving behind in him a stirring image. The moon and the dead, visiting him by night with pain or pleasure, have that power. But so, too, have the burning sun and the howling beast and the chief whose glance constrains him and the sorcerer whose singing loads him with power for the hunt. Mana is simply the effective force, that which has made the person of the moon, up there in the heavens, into a blood-stirring *Thou*. The memory of it left its track when the image of the object was separated out from the total stirring image; although it itself, indeed, never appears other than in the doer and bringer of an effect. It is that with which man himself, if he possesses it – perhaps in a wonderful stone – can be effective in this way. The "world-image" of primitive man is magical not because human magical power is set in the midst of it but because this human power is only a particular variety of the general magic power from which all effective action is derived. Causality in his world-image is no unbroken sequence but an ever new flashing forth of power and moving out toward its production; it is a volcanic movement without continuity. Mana is a primitive abstraction, probably more primitive than, say, number, but not any more supernatural than it. The memory as it is being trained ranges the grand relational events, the elemental emotional shocks. The most important for the instinct of preservation and the most noteworthy for the instinct to understand – that is, "that which effects", stands out most forcibly of all, and becomes independent. The less important, the non-communal, the changing *Thou* of experiences, retires and remains isolated in the memory, and is gradually transformed into an object and very slowly drawn into groups and classes. As third in the arrangement, terrible when thus separated, at times more ghostly than the dead and the moon, but always more and more irrefutably clear, there arises up the other, "unchanging" partner, "I".

Consciousnessness of the "I" is not connected with the primitive sway of the instinct for self-preservation any more than with that of the other instincts. It is not the "I" that wishes to propagate itself, but the body, that knows as yet of no "I". It is not the "I" but the body that wishes to make things, a tool or a toy, that wishes to be a "creator". Further, a *cognosco ergo sum*, in however naïve a form and however childlike a conception of an experiencing subject, cannot be found in the primitive function of knowledge. The "I" emerges as a single element out of the primal experiences, out of the vital primal words *I-affecting-Thou* and *Thou-affecting-I*, only after they have been split asunder and the participle has been given eminence as an object.

And in all the seriousness of truth, hear this: without *It* man cannot live. But he who lives with *It* alone is not a man.

... The primary word *I-It* is not of evil – as matter is not of evil. It is of evil – as matter is, which presumes to have the quality of present being. If a man lets it have the mastery, the continually growing world of *It* overruns him and robs him of the reality of his own *I*, till the incubus over him and the ghost within him whisper to one another the confession of their non-salvation.

... The extended lines of relations meet in the eternal *Thou*. Every particular *Thou* is a glimpse through to the eternal *Thou*;

by means of every particular *Thou* the primary word addresses the eternal *Thou*. Through this mediation of the *Thou* of all beings fulfillment, and non-fulfillment, of relation comes to them: the inborn *Thou* is realized in each relation and consummated in none. It is consummated only in the direct relation with the *Thou* that by its nature cannot become *It*.

Men have addressed their eternal *Thou* with many names. In singing of Him who was thus named they always had the *Thou* in mind: the first myths were hymns of praise. Then the names took refuge in the language of *It*; men were more and more strongly moved to think of and to address their eternal *Thou* as an *It*. But all God's names are hallowed, for in them He is not merely spoken about, but also spoken to.

Many men wish to reject the word God as a legitimate usage, because it is so misused. It is indeed the most heavily laden of all the words used by men. For that very reason it is the most imperishable and most indispensable. What does all mistaken talk about God's being and works (though there has been, and can be, no other talk about these) matter in comparison with the one truth that all men who have addressed God had God Himself in mind? For he who speaks the word God and really has *Thou* in mind (whatever the illusion by which he is held), addresses the true *Thou* of his life, which cannot be limited by another Thou, and to which he stands in a relation that gathers up and includes all others.

But when he, too, who abhors the name, and believes himself to be godless, gives his whole being to addressing the *Thou* of his life, as a *Thou* that cannot be limited by another, he addresses God.

If we go on our way and meet a man who has advanced toward us and has also gone on *his* way, we know only our part of the way, not his – his we experience only in the meeting.

Of the complete relational event we know, with the knowledge of life lived, our going out to the relation, our part of the way. The other part only comes upon us, we do not know it; it comes upon us in the meeting. But we strain ourselves on it if we speak of it as though it were some thing beyond the meeting.

We have to be concerned, to be troubled, not about the other side but about our own side, not about grace but about will. Grace concerns us in so far as we go out to it and persist in its presence; but it is not our object.

The *Thou* confronts me. But I step into direct relation with it. Hence the relation means being chosen and choosing, suffering and action in one; just as any action of the whole being which means the suspension of all partial actions, and consequently of all sensations of actions grounded only in their particular limitation, is bound to resemble suffering.

This is the activity of the man who has become a whole being, an activity that has been termed doing nothing: nothing separate or partial stirs in the man any more, thus he makes no intervention in the world; it is the whole man, enclosed and at rest in his wholeness, that is effective – he has become an effective whole. To have won stability in this state is to be able to go out to the supreme meeting.

To this end the world of sense does not need to be laid aside as though it were illusory. There is no illusory world, there is only the world – which appears to us as twofold in accordance with our twofold attitude. Only the barrier of separation has to be destroyed. Further, no "going beyond sense-experience" is necessary; for every experience, even the most spiritual, could yield us only an *It*. Nor is any recourse necessary to a world of ideas and values; for they cannot become presentness for us. None of these things is necessary. Can it be said what really is necessary? – Not in the sense of a precept. For everything that has ever been devised and contrived in the time of the human spirit as precept, alleged preparation, practice, or meditation, has nothing to do with the primal, simple fact of the meeting. Whatever the advantages in knowledge or the wielding of power for which we have to thank this or that practice, none of this affects the meeting of which we are speaking; it all has its place in the world of *It* and does not lead one step, does not take *the* step, out of it. Going out to the relation cannot be taught in the sense of precepts being given. It can only be indicated by the drawing of a circle which excludes everything that is not this going out. Then the one thing that matters is visible, full acceptance of the present.

To be sure, this acceptance presupposes that the further a man has wandered in separated being the more difficult is the venture and the more elemental the turning. This does not mean a giving up of, say, the *I*, as mystical writings usually suppose: the *I* is as indispensable to this, the supreme, as to every relation, since relation is only possible between *I* and *Thou*. It is not the *I*, then, that is given up, but that false self-asserting instinct that makes a man flee to the possessing of things before the unreliable, perilous world of relation which has neither density nor duration and cannot be surveyed.

Every real relation with a being or life in the world is exclusive. Its *Thou* is freed, steps forth, is single, and confronts you. It fills the heavens. This does not mean that nothing else exists; but all else lives in *its* light. As long as the presence of the relation continues, this its cosmic range is inviolable. But as soon as a *Thou* become *It*, the cosmic range of the relation appears as an offence to the world, its exclusiveness as an exclusion of the universe.

In the relation with God unconditional exclusiveness and unconditional inclusiveness are one. He who enters on the absolute relation is concerned with nothing isolated any more, neither things nor beings, neither earth nor heaven; but everything is gathered up in the relation. For to step into pure relation is not to disregard everything but to see everything in the *Thou*, not to renounce the world but to establish it on its true basis. To look away from the world, or to stare at it, does not help a man to reach God; but he who sees the world in Him stands in His presence. "Here world, there God" is the language of *It*; "God in the world" is another language of *It*; but to eliminate or leave behind nothing at all, to include the whole world in the *Thou*, to give the world its due and its truth, to include nothing beside God but everything in him – this is full and complete relation.

Men do not find God if they stay in the world. They do not find Him if they leave the world. He who goes out with his whole being to meet his *Thou* and carries to it all being that is in the world, finds Him who cannot be sought.

Of course God is the "wholly Other"; but He is also the wholly Same, the wholly Present. Of course He is the *Mysterium Tremendum* that appears and overthrows; but He is also the mystery of the self-evident, nearer to me than my *I*.

If you explore the life of things and of conditioned being you come to the unfathomable, if you deny the life of things and of conditioned being you stand before nothingness, if you hallow this life you meet the living God.

Man's sense of *Thou*, which experiences in the relations with every particular *Thou* the disappointment of the change to *It*, strives out but not away from them all to its eternal *Thou*; but not as something is sought: actually there is no such thing as seeking God, for there is nothing in which He could not be found. How foolish and hopeless would be the man who turned aside from the course of his life in order to seek God; even though he won all the wisdom of solitude and all the power of concentrated being he would miss God. Rather is it as when a man goes his way and simply wishes that it might be the way: in the strength of his wish his striving is expressed. Every relational event is a stage that affords him a glimpse into the consummating event. So in each event he does not partake, but also (for he is waiting) does partake, of the one event. Waiting, not seeking, he goes his way; hence he is composed before all things, and makes contact with them which helps them. But when he has *found*, his heart is not turned from them, though everything now meets him in the one event. He blesses every cell that sheltered him, and every cell into which he will yet turn. For this finding is not the end, but only the eternal middle, of the way.

It is a finding without seeking, a discovering of the primal, of origin. His sense of Thou, which cannot be satiated till he finds the endless *Thou*, had the *Thou* present to it from the beginning; the presence had only to become wholly real to him in the reality of the hallowed life of the world.

God cannot be inferred in anything – in nature, say, as its author, or in history as its master, or in the subject as the self that is thought in it. Something else is not "given" and God then elicited from it; but God is the Being that is directly, most nearly, and lastingly, over against us, that may properly only be addressed, not expressed.

Men wish to regard a feeling (called feeling of dependence, and recently, more precisely, creaturely feeling) as the real element in the relation with God. In proportion as the isolation and definition of this element is accurate, its unbalanced emphasis only makes the character of complete relation the more misunderstood.

What has already been said of love is even more unshakably valid here. Feelings are a mere accompaniment to the metaphysical and metaphysical fact of the relation, which is fulfilled not in the soul but between *I* and *Thou*. A feeling may be considered ever so essential, it remains nevertheless subject to the dynamic of the soul, where one feeling is outstripped, outdone, and abolished by another. In distinction from relation a feeling has its place in a scale. But above all, every feeling has its place within a polar tension, obtaining its color and significance not from itself alone, but also from the opposite pole: every feeling is conditioned by its opposite. Thus the absolute relation (which gathers up into reality all those that are relative, and is no more a part, as these are, but is the whole that completes and unifies them all), in being reduced to the status of an isolated and limited feeling, is made into a relative psychological matter.

If the soul is the starting-point of our consideration, complete relation can be understood only in a bipolar way, only as the *coincidentia oppositorum*, as the coincidence of oppositions of feeling. Of course, the one pole – suppressed by the person's basic religious attitude – often disappears from the reflective consciousness, and can only be recalled in the purest and most ingenuous consideration of the depths of the being.

Yes; in pure relation you have felt yourself to be simply dependent, as you are able to feel in no other relation – and simply free, too, as in no other time or place: you have felt yourself to be both creaturely and creative. You had the one feeling then no longer limited by the other, but you had both of them limitlessly and together.

You know always in your heart that you need God more than everything; but do you not know too that God needs you – in the fullness of His eternity needs you? How would man be, how would you be, if God did not need him, did not need you? You need God, in order to be – and God needs you, for the very meaning of your life. In instruction and in poems men are at pains to say more, and they say too much – what turgid and presumptuous talk that is about the "God who becomes"; but we know unshakably in our hearts that there is a becoming of the God that is. The world is not divine sport, it is divine destiny. There is divine meaning in the life of the world, of man, of human persons, of you and of me.

Creation happens to us, burns itself into us, recasts us in burning – we tremble and are faint, we submit. We take part in creation, meet the Creator, reach out to Him, helpers and companions.

Two great servants pace through the ages, prayer and sacrifice. The man who prays pours himself out in unrestrained dependence, and knows that he has – in an incomprehensible way – an effect upon God, even though he obtains nothing from God; for when he no longer desires anything for himself he sees the flame of his effect burning at its highest. – And the man who makes sacrifice? – I cannot despise him, this upright servant of former times, who believed that God yearned for the scent of his burnt-offering. In a foolish but powerful way he knew that we can and ought to give to God. This is known by him, too, who offers up his little will to God and meets Him in the grand will. "Thy will be done", he says, and says no more; but truth adds for him, "through me whom Thou needest".

What distinguishes sacrifice and prayer from all magic?– Magic desires to obtain its effects without entering into relation, and practices its tricks in the void. But sacrifice and prayer are set "before the Face", in the consummation of the holy primary word that means mutual action: they speak the *Thou*, and then they hear.

To wish to understand pure relations as dependence is to wish to empty one of the bearers of the relation, and hence the relation itself, of reality....

... A modern philosopher supposes that every man necessarily believes either in God or in "idols", that is, in some sort of finite good – his nation, his art, power, knowledge, the amassing of money, "the ever new subjugation of woman" – which has become for him an absolute value and has set itself up between him and God; it is only necessary to demonstrate to him the conditioned nature of this good, in order to "shatter" the idol, and the diverted religious act will automatically return to the fitting object.

This conception presupposes that man's relation to the finite goods he has "idolized" is of the same nature as his relation to God, and differs only in its object; for only with this presupposition could the mere substitution of the true for the false object save the erring man. But a man's relation to the "special something" that usurps the throne of the supreme value of his life, and supplants eternity, rests always on experiencing and using an *It*, a thing, an object of enjoyment. For this relation alone is able to obstruct the prospect which opens toward God – it is the impenetrable world of *It*; but the relation which involves the saying of the *Thou* opens up this prospect ever anew. He who is dominated by the idol that he wishes to win, to hold, and to keep – possessed by a desire for possession – has no way to God but that of turning, which is a change not only of goal but also of the nature of his movement. The man who is possessed is saved by being wakened and educated to solidarity of relation, not by being led in his state of possession toward God. If a man remains in this state what does it mean when he calls no longer on the name of a demon or of a being demonically distorted for him, but on the name of God? It means that from now on he blasphemes. It is blasphemy when a man wishes, after the idol has crashed behind the altar, to pile up an unholy sacrifice to God on the desecrated place.

He who loves a woman, and brings her life to present realization in his, is able to look in the *Thou* of her eyes into a beam of the eternal *Thou*. But he who eagerly desires "ever new subjugation" – do you wish to hold out to his desire a phantom of the Eternal? He who serves his people in the boundlessness of destiny, and is willing to give himself to them, is really thinking of God. But do you suppose that the man to whom the nation is a god, in whose service he would like to enlist everything (for in the nation's he exalts his own image), need only be given a feeling of disgust – and he would see the truth? And what does it mean that a man is said to treat money, embodied non-being, "as if it were God"? What has the lust of grabbing and of laying up treasure in common with the joy in the presence of the Present One? Can the servant of Mammon say *Thou* to his money? And how is he to behave toward God when he does not understand how to say *Thou*? He cannot serve two masters – not even one after the other: he must first learn to serve *in a different way*.

He who has been converted by this substitution of object now "holds" a phantom that he calls God. But God, the eternal Presence, does not permit Himself to be held. Woe to the man so possessed that he thinks he possesses God!

The "religious" man is spoken of as one who does not need to take his stand in any relation to the world and to living beings, since the status of social life, that is defined from outside, is in him surpassed by means of a strength that works only from within. But in this idea of the social life two basically different things are combined – first, the community that is built up out of relation, and second, the collection of human units that do not know relation – modern man's palpable condition of lack of relation. But the bright building of community, to which there is an escape even from the dungeon of "social life", is the achievement of the same power that works in the relation between man and God. This does not mean that this one relation is set beside the others; for it is the universal relation, into which all streams pour, yet without exhausting their waters. Who wishes to make division and define boundaries between sea and streams? There we find only the one flow from *I* to *Thou*, unending, the one boundless flow of the real life. Life cannot be divided between a real relation with God and an unreal relation of *I* and *It* with the world – you cannot both truly pray to God and profit by the world. He who knows the world as something by which he is to profit knows God also in the same way. His prayer is a procedure of exoneration heard by the ear of the void. He – not the "atheist", who addresses the Nameless out of the night and yearning of his garret-window – is the godless man.

It is further said that the "religious" man stands as a single, isolated, separated being before God, since he has also gone beyond the status of the "moral" man, who is still involved in duty and obligation to the world. The latter, it is said, is still burdened with responsibility for the action of those who act, since he is wholly defined by the tension between being and "ought to be", and in grotesque and hopeless sacrificial courage casts his heart piece by piece into the insatiable gulf that lies between them. The "religious" man, on the other hand, has emerged from that tension into the tension between the world and God; there the command reigns that the unrest of responsibility and of demands on oneself be removed; there is no willing of one's own, but only the being joined into what is ordained; every "ought" vanishes in unconditioned being, and the world, though still existing, no longer counts. For in it the "religious" man has to perform his particular duties, but as it were without obligation – beneath the aspect of the nothingness of all action. But that is to suppose that God has created His world as an illusion and man for frenzied being. He who approaches the Face has indeed surpassed duty and obligation – but not because he is now remote from the world; rather because he has truly drawn closer to it. Duty and obligation are rendered only to the stranger; we are drawn to and full of love for the intimate person. The world, lit by eternity, becomes fully present to him who approaches the Face, and to the Being of beings he can in a single response say *Thou*. Then there is no more tension between the world and God, but only the one reality. The man is not freed from responsibility; he has exchanged the torment of the finite, pursuit of effects, for the motive power of the infinite, he has got the mighty responsibility of love for the whole untraceable world-event, for the profound belonging to the world before the Face of God. He has, to be sure, abolished moral judgments for ever; the "evil" man is simply one who is commended to him for greater responsibility, one more needy of love; but he will have to practice, till death itself, decision in the depths of spontaneity, unruffled decision, made ever anew, to right action. Then action is not empty, but purposive, enjoined, needed, part of creation; but this action is no longer imposed upon the world, it grows on it as if it were non-action.

What is the eternal, primal phenomenon, present here and now, of that which we term revelation? It is the phenomenon that a man does not pass, from the moment of the supreme meeting, the same being as he entered into it. The moment of meeting is not an "experience" that stirs in the receptive soul and grows to perfect blessedness; rather, in that moment something happens to the man. At times it is like a light breath, at times like a wrestling-bout, but always – it *happens*. The man who emerges from the act of pure relation that so involves his being has now in his being something more that has grown in him, of which he did not know before and whose origin he is not rightly able to indicate. However the source of this new thing is classified in scientific orientation of the world, with its authorized efforts to establish an unbroken causality, we, whose concern is real consideration of the real, cannot have our purpose served with subconsciousness or any other apparatus of the soul. The reality is that we receive what we did not hitherto have, and receive it in such a way that we know it has been given to us. In the language of the Bible, "Those who wait upon the Lord shall renew their strength." In the language of Nietzsche, who in his account remains loyal to reality, "We take and do not ask who it is there that gives."

Man receives, and he receives not a specific "content" but a Presence, a Presence as power. This Presence and this power include three things, undivided, yet in such a way that we may consider them separately. First, there is the whole fullness of real mutual action, of the being raised and bound up in relation: the man can give no account at all of how the binding in relation is brought about, nor does it in any way lighten his life – it makes life heavier, but heavy with meaning. Secondly, there is the inexpressible confirmation of meaning. Meaning is assured. Nothing can any longer be meaningless. The question about the meaning of life is no longer there. But were it there, it would not have to be answered. You do not know how to exhibit and define the meaning of life, you have no formula or picture for it, and yet it has more certitude for you than the perceptions of your senses. What does the revealed and concealed meaning purpose with us, desire from us? It does not wish to be explained (nor are we able to do that) but only to be done by us. Thirdly, this meaning is not that of "another life", but that of this life of ours, not one of a world "yonder", but that of this world of ours, and it desires its confirmation in this life and in relation with this world. This meaning can be received, but not experienced; it cannot be experienced but it can be done, and this is its purpose with us. The assurance I have of it does not wish to be sealed within me, but it wishes to be born by me into the world. But just as the meaning itself does not permit itself to be transmitted and made into knowledge generally current and admissible, so confirmation of it cannot be transmitted as a valid Ought; it is not prescribed, it is not specified on any tablet, to be raised above all men's heads. The meaning that has been received can be proved true by each man only in the singleness of his being and the singleness of his life. As no prescription can lead us to the meeting, so none leads from it. As only acceptance of the Presence is necessary for the approach to the meeting, so in a new sense is it so when we emerge from it. As we reach the meeting with the simple *Thou* on our lips, so with the *Thou* on our lips we leave it and return to the world.

That before which, in which, out of which, and into which we live, even the mystery, has remained what it was. It has become present to us and in its presentness has proclaimed itself to us as salvation; we have "known" it, but we acquire no knowledge from it which might lessen or moderate its mysteriousness. We have come near to God, but not nearer to unveiling being or solving its riddle. We have felt release, but not discovered a "solution". We cannot approach others with what we have received, and say "You must know this, you must do this." We can only go, and confirm its truth. And this, too, is no "ought", but we can, we *must*.

This is the eternal revelation that is present here and now. I know of no revelation and believe in none whose primal pheno-menon is not precisely this. I do not believe in a self-naming of God, a self-definition of God before men. The Word of revelation is *I am that I am*. That which reveals is that which reveals. That which is *is*, and nothing more. The eternal source of strength streams, the eternal contact persists, the eternal voice sounds forth, and nothing more.